Through the
with Warren

Other Titles by Warren W. Wiersbe (selected)

Being a Child of God
Be Myself
The Bible Exposition Commentary (2 vols.)
The Bumps Are What You Climb On
Developing a Christian Imagination
Elements of Preaching
God Isn't in a Hurry: Learning to Slow Down and Live
Living with the Giants: The Lives of Great Men of the Faith
Meet Yourself in the Psalms
On Being a Servant of God
Prayer, Praise, and Promises: A Daily Walk through the Psalms
Run with the Winners
So That's What a Christian Is! 12 Pictures of the Dynamic
   Christian Life
The Strategy of Satan
Turning Mountains into Molehills: And Other Devotional Talks
Victorious Christians You Should Know
Wiersbe's Expository Outlines on the New Testament
Wiersbe's Expository Outlines on the Old Testament
Windows on the Parables

Through the Year with Warren W. Wiersbe

366 Daily Devotionals

Second Edition

Edited by
James R. Adair

BakerBooks

A Division of Baker Book House Co.
Grand Rapids, Michigan 49516

Published by Baker Books
a division of Baker Book House Company
P.O. Box 6287, Grand Rapids, MI 49516-6287

Printed in the United States of America

Library of Congress Cataloging-in-Publication Data

Wiersbe, Warren W.
    Through the year with Warren W. Wiersbe : 366 Daily Devotionals / edited by James R. Adair.–2nd ed.
      p.   cm.
    Rev. ed. of : A time to be renewed. c1986.
    ISBN 0-8010-5702-7 (pbk.)
    1. Devotional calendars–Baptists. I. Adair, James R., 1923– . II. Wiersbe, Warren W. Time to be renewed. III. Title.
BV4811.W59   1999
242'.2–dc21
                              99-28027

For information about academic books, resources for Christian leaders, and all new releases available from Baker Book House, visit our web site:
http://www.bakerbooks.com

*Dedicated to Mary O. George, who,
though small of stature, has stood tall
as a faithful servant of God for many
years, helping others in the Philadelphia
area to be renewed through Bible
teaching, witness, and prayer.*

CONTENTS

———

PREFACE

This book is a revised and expanded edition of *A Time to Be Renewed*, which was first published in 1986. My good friend and former Victor Books editor Jim Adair made the original selections from my New Testament BE series, which since then has been completed. This volume also includes fifty-seven selections from the Old Testament BE series that I hope to complete within the next few years, God willing.

I want to thank Jim for his excellent editorial work. He "shepherded" me through a number of the original BE books and knows this material very well.

This is your book, so use it in the way that helps you most in your own personal walk with the Lord. Even though it contains biblical exposition, it's not a substitute for your Bible; but if it helps you better understand and apply God's Word, it will have served its purpose. And keep in mind that the blessing comes not when we read or study the Word but when we obey it and do what the Lord commands us to do (James 1:25).

Warren W. Wiersbe

ACKNOWLEDGMENTS

Warren W. Wiersbe and I wish to express our gratitude to the team at Victor Books who worked with us on the original book, *A Time to Be Renewed,* and to the staff at Baker Book House, particularly Jim Weaver, who worked with us on this revised edition. And thanks to my wife, Ginnie, her late sister, Mary George, and Data May Woodruff, who helped select readings from the "Be" books. Mary and Data May also helped with "Action Assignments."

January

Be Renewed:

"Be not conformed to this world: but be ye transformed by the renewing of your mind, that ye may prove what is that good, and acceptable, and perfect, will of God."

Romans 12:2

1

CHANGE NEED NOT BE COMPROMISE

It's unfortunate when the unity of God's people is shattered because generations are looking in opposite directions. The older men in Ezra 3 were weeping as they looked back with longing; they had seen the original temple before it was destroyed, and the new edifice was nothing in comparison. The younger men were looking around at the new temple with joy. Both the older and younger men should have been looking up and praising the Lord for what He had accomplished.

We have similar generational disagreements in the church today, especially when it comes to styles of worship. Older saints enjoy singing the traditional hymns with their doctrinal substance; younger members of the church want worship that has a more contemporary approach. But it isn't a question of accepting one and rejecting the other, unless you want to divide families and split the church. It's a matter of balance: the old must learn from the young and the young from the old, in a spirit of love and submission (1 Peter 5:1–11).

The church is a family; and as a family grows and matures, some things have to fall away so other things can take their place. This happens in our homes and it must happen in the house of God. To some people, "change" is a synonym for "compromise," but where there's love, "change" becomes a synonym for "cooperation with one another and concern for one another."

Paul admonishes: "Teach the older men to be temperate, worthy of respect, self-controlled, and sound in faith, in love and in endurance. . . . Encourage the young men to be self-controlled. In everything set them an example by doing what is good. In your teaching show integrity, seriousness and soundness of speech that cannot be condemned" (Titus 2:2, 6–8, NIV).

Read: Ezra 3

Action assignment: Pray for churches—perhaps your own church—that have conflicts relating to views of younger and older people.

HAVING A POSITIVE RELATIONSHIP
WITH OTHERS

A positive relationship with others (Prov. 3:27–35) is a blessing the
believer enjoys when he or she walks in the wisdom of God. Wise
Christians will be generous to their neighbors and live peaceably
with them (vv. 27–30), doing their best to avoid unnecessary disagreements (Rom. 12:18). After all, if we truly love God, we will
love our neighbors as we would want them to love us.

On the other hand, if our neighbors are perverse persons who
scoff at our faith (Prov. 3:31–35), the Lord will guide us in letting
our light shine and His love show so that we will influence them
but they won't lead us astray. Sometimes it takes a great deal of
patience, prayer, and wisdom to rightly relate to people who don't
want Christians in the neighborhood, but perhaps that's why God
put us there.

It's possible to have a godly home in the midst of an ungodly
neighborhood, for God "blesses the home of the righteous" (v. 33,
NIV). We are the salt of the earth and the light of the world, and
one dedicated Christian in a neighborhood can make a great deal
of difference and be a powerful witness for the Lord.

It's true: "The LORD's curse is on the house of the wicked, but
he blesses the home of the righteous" (Prov. 3:33, NIV).

Read: Proverbs 3

Action assignment: Are you on the outs with anyone? If so,
ask the Lord to give you the courage to know how to establish a
positive relationship with that person. If you have no such problem, simply reread today's reading and pray that you can be salt
and light in your neighborhood, among your family and friends.

BEHOLD HIS GLORY

You and I are not going to heaven until we die or until our Lord returns. In the meantime, we have a marvelous encouragement because *today* we are seated with Christ in the heavenly places in a position of authority and victory. While we have not seen God's glory as Paul did, we do share God's glory now; one day we will enter into heaven and behold the glory of Christ (John 17:22, 24).

Such an honor as Paul's would have made most people very proud. Instead of keeping quiet for fourteen years, they would have immediately told the world and become famous. But Paul did not become proud. He simply told the truth—it was not empty boasting—and let the facts speak for themselves. His great concern was that nobody rob God of the glory.

Verse for today: "Father, I want those You have given Me to be with Me where I am, and to see My glory, the glory You have given Me because You loved Me before the creation of the world" (John 17:24, NIV).

More from God's Word: Jeremiah 9:23-24; John 17:4-5; 1 Corinthians 1:26-31; Galatians 5:26; 6:14; Ephesians 2:6-7.

Action assignment: What will it be like when we truly behold God's glory in heaven? Spend several minutes meditating on the prospect. If Christ were physically present with you now, what would your reaction be? Thank God that He is with you even when you do not see glimpses of His glory. Praise Him for His presence through the Holy Spirit, who is able to fine-tune you to appreciate God's goodness, grace, and glory!

WHO IS NO. 1 IN YOUR LIFE?

Jesus made it clear that *the Son* is to be worshiped as well as the Father, "that all may honor the Son just as they honor the Father. He who does not honor the Son does not honor the Father, who sent Him" (John 5:23-24, NIV).

The late Dr. M.R. DeHaan, noted radio Bible teacher, told about a preacher who was confronted by a cultist who rejected the deity of Jesus Christ.

"Jesus cannot be the eternal Son of God, for a father is always older than his son," the man argued. "If the Father is not eternal, then He is not God. If Jesus is His Son, then He is not eternal."

The preacher was ready with an answer. "The thing that makes a person a father is having a son. But if God is the *eternal* Father, then He must have an *eternal* son! This means that Jesus Christ is eternal—and that He is God!"

Jesus Christ is the Saviour, the Creator, the Head of the church, and the beloved of the Father. He is eternal God . . . and in our lives He deserves to have the preeminence.

Is Jesus Christ preeminent in your life?

Verse to remember: "And He [Christ] is the head of the body, the church: who is the beginning, the firstborn from the dead; that in all things He might have the preeminence" (Colossians 1:18).

Other Scripture: Proverbs 8:22-25; Isaiah 9:6; Micah 5:2; John 1:1; Revelation 1:8.

Action assignment: Think about what it really means to give Jesus preeminence in your life. How will it affect your life in the next few hours if Christ is preeminent? Talk it over with God.

5

LIVING THE TRUTH

The next time you sing "Come, Thou Fount of Every Blessing," recall the following story. The hymn's composer, Robert Robinson, was converted under the mighty preaching of George Whitefield, but later drifted from the Lord. Greatly used as a pastor, Robinson nevertheless neglected spiritual things. In an attempt to find peace, he began to travel. During one of his journeys, he met a young woman who handed him a hymnbook and asked, "What do you think of this hymn I have been reading?"

It was his own hymn! He tried to avoid her question, but knew the Lord was speaking to him. Finally, he broke down and confessed who he was and how he had been living away from the Lord.

"But these 'streams of mercy' are still flowing," the spiritually sensitive woman assured him. Through her encouragement, Robinson was restored to fellowship with the Lord.

Do *you* need to be restored to fellowship with the Lord?

Verse for today: "Watch your life and doctrine closely. Persevere in them, because if you do, you will save both yourself and your hearers" (1 Timothy 4:16, NIV).

Consider: Matthew 21:28-32; 2 Chronicles 29:8-11; 1 Corinthians 11:29-32.

Action assignment: Write down three bits of advice that you have given or thought about giving in the last week. Have you followed your own advice? Ask God to help you obey the wisdom He has already given you.

THE GOODNESS OF GOD

Greatness without goodness would make God a selfish tyrant; goodness without greatness would make Him willing to help us but incapable of acting. Whatever God thinks, says, does, plans, and accomplishes is good. He can never will anything evil for us because He is the giver of everything good. In spite of the fact that there is evil in the world, and evil seems to be winning, "the earth is full of the goodness of the Lord" (Psalm 33:5). If this were not true, we could never quote Romans 8:28 and really believe it!

The goodness of God enables us to face life without fear. We sing "This is my Father's world," and it is true. The world is not a prison, built to make us miserable; it is a school in which the Father is training us for glory. Because He is good, all things are working together for good for those who love and obey Him. God goes before us "with the blessings of goodness." When we look back, we see only "goodness and mercy." Why should we fret and be afraid when God's goodness goes before us and follows behind us?

Verse for today: "Every good gift and every perfect gift is from above, and cometh down from the Father of lights, with whom is no variableness, neither shadow of turning" (James 1:17).

Also read: Exodus 33:19; Psalms 33:5; 23:6; 86:5; 100:5; 106:1; Jeremiah 31:14; John 10:11.

Action assignment: A good formula for eliminating fear from our lives is to make a study of God's goodness and then believe His promises. After reading today's verses, make a list of the good and perfect things in your life. Also make a list of the bad things. Ask God to give you patience, understanding, love, and obedience. Then thank Him for the knowledge that He is good and that He is working for your good in all aspects of the school of life.

7

IN PURSUIT OF WISDOM

Ask God for wisdom (James 1:5) and make diligent use of the means He gives us for securing His wisdom, especially knowing and doing the Word of God (Matt. 7:21–29). It is not enough merely to study; we must also obey what God tells us to do (John 7:17). As we walk by faith, we discover the wisdom of God in the everyday things of life. Spiritual wisdom is not abstract: it is very personal and very practical.

As we fellowship with other believers in the church and share with one another, we can learn wisdom. Reading the best books can also help us grow in wisdom and understanding. The important thing is that we focus on Christ, for He is our wisdom (1 Cor. 1:24) and in Him is hidden "all the treasures of wisdom and knowledge" (Col. 2:3). The better we know Christ and the more we become like Him, the more we will walk in wisdom and understand the will of the Lord. We must allow the Holy Spirit to open the eyes of our hearts so we can see God in His Word and understand more of the riches we have in Christ (Eph. 1:15–23).

Verse for today: "Let the wise listen and add to their learning, and let the discerning get guidance" (Prov. 1:5, NIV).

Read: James 1:2–7; Proverbs 3:13–18; 1 Corinthians 1:24; Colossians 2:3

Action assignment: Be alert to some of the ways that you can apply spiritual wisdom to everyday happenings. Meditate on what you think is meant by the above statement: "Allow the Holy Spirit to open the eyes of our hearts so we can see God in His Word and understand the more of the riches we have in Christ." Share your thoughts with a family member or a friend. Miracles of grace occur daily! Be on the lookout for one as you read or converse or labor! God is real, remember!

PLAYING FAVORITES

The religious experts in Christ's day judged Him by their human standards—and rejected Him. He came from the wrong city, Nazareth of Galilee. He was not a graduate of their accepted schools. He did not have the official approval of the people in power. He had no wealth. His followers were a nondescript mob and included publicans and sinners. Yet He was the very glory of God! No wonder Jesus warned the religious leaders, "Stop judging by mere appearances, and make a right judgment" (John 7:24, NIV).

Sad to say, we often make the same mistakes. When visitors come into our churches, we tend to judge them by dress, color of skin, fashion, and other superficial standards. We cater to the rich and we avoid the poor. Jesus did not do this, and He cannot approve of it.

How do we practice the deity of Christ in our human relationships? It is really quite simple: Look at everyone through the eyes of Christ. If the visitor is a Christian, accept him because Christ lives in him. If he is not a Christian, receive him because Christ died for him. It is Christ who is the link between us and others, and He is a link of love.

Remember: "My brothers, as believers in our glorious Lord Jesus Christ, don't show favoritism" (James 2:1, NIV).

Related Scripture: James 2:1-12; 1 Corinthians 16:19-20; Ephesians 2:21-22.

Action assignment: Think about what it would mean if you looked at everyone through the eyes of Christ. Talk to God about helping you do it.

9

WHY WORRY?

Jesus said that worry is sinful. We may dignify worry by calling it by some other name—concern, burden, a cross to bear—but the results are still the same. Instead of helping us live longer, anxiety only makes life shorter.

"Take no thought for your life" (Matthew 6:25). The Greek words translated "take no thought" literally mean "do not be drawn in different directions." Worry pulls us apart. Until man interferes, everything in nature works together, because all of nature trusts God. Man, however, is pulled apart because he tries to live his own life by depending on material wealth.

God feeds the birds and clothes the lilies. He will feed and clothe us. It is our "little faith" that hinders Him from working as He would. He has great blessings for us if only we will yield to Him and live for the riches that last forever.

Worrying about tomorrow does not help either tomorrow or today. If anything, it robs us of our effectiveness today—which means we will be even less effective tomorrow. Someone has said that the average person is crucifying himself between two thieves: the regrets of yesterday and the worries about tomorrow. It is right to plan for the future, but it is a sin to worry about the future and permit tomorrow to rob today of its blessings.

If we have faith in our Father and put Him first, He will meet our needs.

Verse to act on: "Do not be anxious about anything, but in everything, by prayer and petition, with thanksgiving, present your requests to God. And the peace of God, which transcends all understanding, will guard your hearts and your minds in Christ Jesus" (Philippians 4:6-7, NIV).

Other Scripture: Psalm 37:5; 55:22; Matthew 6:25-34; 1 Peter 5:6-7.

Action assignment: Have a dialogue with a friend or a member of your family about worry. Tell what you have learned from this page. Perhaps end the discussion with prayer, with both of you committing your worries to the Lord.

ESTABLISHING VALUES

Food and "covering" (clothing and shelter) are basic needs; if we lose them, we lose the ability to obtain other things. A miser without food would starve to death counting his money. I am reminded of the simple-living Quaker who was watching his new neighbor move in, with all the furnishings and expensive "toys" that "successful" people collect. The Quaker finally went over to his new neighbor and said, "Neighbor, if ever thou dost need anything, come to see me, and I will tell thee how to get along without it." Henry David Thoreau reminded us that a man is wealthy in proportion to the number of things he can afford to do without.

The economic and energy crises that the world faces will probably be used by God to encourage people to simplify their lives. Too many of us know the "price of everything and the value of nothing." We are so glutted with luxuries that we have forgotten how to enjoy our necessities.

Wealth does not bring contentment and is not lasting. Marilyn Monroe once told a friend that hers was a lonely existence. "Did you ever feel lonely in a room by yourself? I have forty rooms, and I'm forty times as lonely."

A mansion does not bring happiness. Only living for Christ does.

From the Word: "For we brought nothing into the world, and we can take nothing out of it. But if we have food and clothing, we will be content with that. People who want to get rich fall into temptation and a trap and into many foolish and harmful desires that plunge men into ruin and destruction" (1 Timothy 6:7-8, NIV).

Also read: Proverbs 10:2, 22; 11:4; 13:7; 23:4-5; Matthew 6:19-21.

Action assignment: List things you have that you feel are necessities. Thank God for them.

OUR HIGH PRIEST

There are two "living sacrifices" in the Bible, and they help us understand what a "living sacrifice" really is. The first is Isaac (Genesis 22); the second is our Lord Jesus Christ. Isaac willingly put himself on the altar and would have died in obedience to God's will, but the Lord sent a ram to take his place. Isaac "died" just the same—he died to self and willingly yielded himself to the will of God. When he got off that altar, Isaac was a "living sacrifice" to the glory of God.

Of course, our Lord Jesus Christ is the perfect illustration of a "living sacrifice." He actually died as a sacrifice, in obedience to His Father's will. But He rose again. And today He is in heaven as a "living sacrifice," bearing in His body the wounds of Calvary. He is our High Priest and our Advocate before the throne of God.

Consider this: "Let us therefore come boldly unto the throne of grace, that we may obtain mercy, and find grace to help in time of need" (Hebrews 4:16).

Other Scripture: Hebrews 4:14-15; 1 John 2:1.

Action assignment: Meditate on this morning hymn, "Awake, My Soul, and with the Sun," written by Francois Barthelemon in the 1780s:

> Awake, my soul, and with the sun
> Thy daily stage of duty run;
> Shake off dull sloth and joyfully rise
> To pay thy morning sacrifice.

> Lord, I my vows to Thee renew;
> Disperse my sins as morning dew;
> Guard my first springs of thought and will
> And with Thyself my spirit fill.

> Direct, control, suggest this day,
> All I design or do or say;
> That all my powers with all their might
> In Thy sole glory may unite.

BE MOTIVATED TO HONOR GOD

When Charles Haddon Spurgeon was a young preacher, his father, the Rev. John Spurgeon, suggested that Charles go to college to gain prominence. It was arranged for him to meet Dr. Joseph Angus, the principal of Stepney College, London. They were to meet at Mr. Macmillan's home in Cambridge, and Spurgeon was there at the appointed hour. He waited for two hours, but the learned doctor never appeared. When Spurgeon finally inquired about the man, he discovered that Dr. Angus had been waiting in another room and, because of another appointment, had already departed. Disappointed, Spurgeon left for a preaching engagement. While he was walking along, he heard a voice clearly say to him, "Seekest thou great things for thyself? Seek them not!" From that moment, Spurgeon determined to do the will of God for the glory of God; and God blessed him in an exceptional way.

Man was *created* to glorify God (Isaiah 43:7), and man is *saved* to glorify God (1 Corinthians 6:19-20). It was the glory of God that motivated the Apostle Paul, and this ought to motivate our lives as well.

Verse to remember: "Should you then seek great things for yourself? Seek them not. For I will bring disaster on all people, declares the Lord, but wherever you go I will let you escape with your life" (Jeremiah 45:5, NIV).

Other Scripture: Isaiah 43:7; 1 Corinthians 6:19-20; Romans 11:36.

Action assignment: Talk with God about honoring Him. Settle in your own mind just how you might glorify God today—and every day.

WALK THE TALK

A congregation was singing the familiar song "For You I Am Praying," as the closing hymn. The preacher turned to a man on the platform and asked quietly, "For whom are you praying?"

The man was stunned. "Why, I guess I'm not praying for anybody. Why do you ask?"

"Well, I just heard you say, 'For you I am praying,' and I thought you meant it," the preacher replied.

"Oh, no," said the man. "I'm just singing."

Pious talk! A religion of words! Is that what you have? To paraphrase James 1:22, "We should be doers of the Word as well as talkers of the Word." We must walk what we talk. It is not enough to know the language; we must also live the life.

Verse for today: "May the God of peace, who through the blood of the eternal covenant brought back from the dead our Lord Jesus, that great Shepherd of the sheep, equip you with everything good for doing His will, and may He work in us what is pleasing to Him, through Jesus Christ, to whom be glory for ever and ever. Amen" (Hebrews 13:20-21, NIV).

Also read: James 1:22, 4:17, 1 John 2:17, 3:21-22; Revelation 22:14.

Action assignment: If you won a diamond ring, would you opt for one with a rhinestone or a genuine diamond? Obviously you would be smart to choose the latter, since you could always sell it and keep the cash. Right?

Now, in the realm of spiritual things, are you opting for the genuine experience of living for Christ—or are you content with just mouthing the jargon that accompanies such an experience? Look at yourself in a mirror and say out loud, "I want to be a genuine doer of God's Word, not a hearer or talker of the Word only." Now ask God to help you live out that desire in tangible ways for the rest of your life—one day at a time.

WE ARE IN CHRIST'S WILL!

One of the funniest cartoons I ever saw showed a pompous lawyer reading a client's last will and testament to a group of greedy relatives. The caption read: "I, John Jones, being of sound mind and body, spent it all!"

When Jesus Christ wrote His last will and testament for His church, He made it possible for all of His true followers to share His spiritual riches. Instead of spending it all, Jesus Christ paid it all. His death on the cross and His resurrection make possible our salvation. He wrote us into His will, then He died so the will would be in force. Then He arose again that He might become the heavenly advocate (lawyer) to make sure the terms of the will were correctly followed!

In Ephesians 1, Paul names just a few of the blessings that make up our spiritual wealth:

He has chosen us.

He has adopted us.

He has accepted us.

He has redeemed us.

He has forgiven us.

He has revealed God's will to us.

He has made us an inheritance.

He has sealed us.

He has given us an earnest (a downpayment to guarantee our redemption).

Rejoice! "God . . . has blessed us in the heavenly realms with every spiritual blessing in Christ. For He chose us in Him before the creation of the world to be holy and blameless in His sight" (Ephesians 1:3-4, NIV).

Read: Ephesians 1:1-14 and find each of the above listed riches that you, as a Christian, have in Jesus Christ.

Action assignment: Match the list of spiritual blessings mentioned in today's reading with verses in Ephesians 1:1-14. After you have done that, see if you can from memory write out the list of spiritual blessings. Thank God for making these blessings yours.

15

CONCERN FOR THE LOST

If God sends a "fiery trial" to His own children, and they are saved "with difficulty," what will happen to lost sinners when God's fiery judgment fails?

When a believer suffers, he experiences glory and knows that there will be greater glory in the future. But a sinner who causes that suffering is only filling up the measure of God's wrath more and more. Instead of being concerned only about ourselves, we need to be concerned about the lost sinners around us. Our present "fiery trail" is nothing compared with the "flaming fire" that will punish the lost when Jesus returns in judgment. The idea is expressed in Proverbs 11:31: "If the righteous receive their due on earth, how much more the ungodly and the sinner!" (NIV)

Times of persecution are times of opportunity for a loving witness to those who persecute us. It was not the earthquake that brought that Philippian jailer to Christ, because that frightened him into almost committing suicide! No, it was Paul's loving concern for him that brought the jailer to faith in Christ. As Christians, we do not seek vengeance on those who have hurt us. Rather, we pray for them and seek to lead them to Jesus Christ.

From the Word: "But I say unto you, Love your enemies, bless them that curse you, do good to them that hate you, and pray for them which despitefully use you, and persecute you" (Matthew 5:44).

Other Scripture: 1 Peter 4:12-18; Matthew 23:29-33; 2 Thessalonians 1:7-10; Matthew 5:10-12, 43-48.

Action assignment: Pray for an unsaved person you know— possibly someone who persecutes you—and ask God to enable you to witness to that person.

THE LAW OF LIBERTY

We shall be judged "by the Law of liberty." Why does James (1:25) use this title for God's Law? When we obey God's Law, it frees us from sin and enables us to walk in liberty (Psalm 119:45).

Liberty does not mean license. License (doing whatever I want to do) is the worst kind of bondage. Liberty means the freedom to be all that I can be in Jesus Christ. License is confinement; liberty is fulfillment.

The Word is also called "the Law of liberty" because God sees our hearts and knows what we would have done had we been free to do so. The Christian student who obeys only because the school has rules is not really maturing. What will he do when he leaves the school? God's Word can change our hearts and give us the desires to do God's will, so that we obey from inward compulsion and not outward constraint.

There is one obvious message here: our beliefs should control our behavior. If we really believe that Jesus is the Son of God, and that God is gracious, His Word is true, and one day He will judge us, then our conduct will reveal our convictions.

Verse for today: "One who looks intently at the perfect Law, the Law of liberty, and abides by it, not having become a forgetful hearer but an effectual doer, this man shall be blessed in what he does" (James 1:25, NASB).

Also read: James 2:12; Galatians 2:4; 6:2; John 8:32; 13:7; Romans 8:2; 1 Peter 2:16.

Action assignment: Patrick Henry cried, "Give me liberty or give me death!" Jot down what you think he meant. Write out your thoughts of how "liberty and death" apply to your Christian life. Ask God to give you a clear understanding of what it means to have liberty in Christ.

THE HARVEST OF GIVING

"Give, and it shall be given unto you" (Luke 6:38) was our Lord's promise. It still holds true. The "good measure" He gives back to us is not always money or material goods, but it is always worth far more than what we gave.

If our giving is to bless us, we must be careful to follow the principles that Paul presents.

1. *The principle of increase: We reap in measure as we sow* (2 Corinthians 9:6). The farmer who sows much seed will have a better chance for a bigger harvest. In both nature and grace, God is a generous giver; and he who would be godly must follow the divine example.

2. *The principle of intent: We reap as we sow with right motives* (2 Corinthians 9:7). Motive makes absolutely no difference to the farmer! If he sows good seed and has good weather, he will reap a harvest whether he is working for profit, pleasure, or price. Not so with the Christian, for whom motive in giving (or in any other activity) is vitally important. Our giving must come from the heart, and the motive in the heart must please God.

After all, giving is not something we *do*, but something we *are*. Giving is a way of life for the Christian who understands the grace of God.

Verse for today: "He who did not spare His own Son, but gave Him up for us all—how will He not also, along with Him, graciously give us all things?" (Romans 8:32, NIV)

Also read: Proverbs 22:9; Ezekiel 36:26; Matthew 13:12; Luke 6:38; 12:48.

Action assignment: Think of times when you have given someone your time, spiritual attention, or material goods. Did you always see the results right away? Did you ever feel you had wasted your time? Were you ever unexpectedly blessed by your giving?

Ask God to help you be a "cheerful giver" who gives as "unto the Lord." In God's own time and way, He will let you reap the harvest of giving.

THE WONDER OF GOD'S POWER

God is omnipotent—all-powerful. The psalmist might have used God's vast creation as an example of God's great power; but instead he used the miracle of birth (Psalm 139:13-18). Conception, development, and birth are perpetual wonders that an understanding of genetics, anatomy, and obstetrics cannot erase. It is tragic that the human fetus is too often considered a nuisance to be removed, like a ruptured appendix, instead of a miracle to be admired and welcomed.

God is personally concerned and has ordained the days of our lives with the conception, development, and birth of each child. This is not the impersonal blueprint of a distant engineer, but the loving plan of a gracious Heavenly Father. First, God makes us as He wants us to be; then He plans for us a life here on earth that will best fulfill all that He put into us. The New Testament parallel is Ephesians 2:10: "For we are His workmanship, created in Christ Jesus for good works, which God prepared beforehand, that we should walk in them" (NASB).

Verse for today: "Thine eyes have seen my unformed substance; and in Thy Book they were all written. The days that were ordained for me, when as yet there was not one of them" (Psalm 139:16, NASB).

Also read: Jeremiah 1:5; 29:11; 32:17, 27; Isaiah 49:5; Galatians 1:15-16.

Action assignment: Thank God for the gift of life and that He knew and loved you before you were born. Pray that the world will stop taking life before birth so lightly and that the murder of unborn babies will cease.

19

ON BEING A COMFORTER

The best way to help discouraged and hurting people is to listen with your heart and not just with your ears. It's not *what they say* but *why they say it* that is important. Let them know that you understand their pain by reflecting back to them in different words just what they say to you. Don't argue or try to convince them with logical reasoning. Patiently accept their feelings—even their bitter words against God—and build bridges, not walls.

In his book about his wife's death, *A Grief Observed*, C. S. Lewis wrote from his own painful experience: "Talk to me about the truth of religion, and I'll listen gladly. Talk to me about the duty of religion, and I'll listen submissively. But don't come talking to me about the consolation of religion, or I shall suspect you don't understand" (p. 23).

There is true consolation in our faith, but it is not dispensed in convenient doses like cough medicine. *It can be shared only by those who know what it's like to be so far down in the pit that they feel as though God has abandoned them.* If you want to be a true comforter, there is a price to pay; and not everybody is willing to pay it. Paul wrote about this in 2 Corinthians 1:3–11.

John Henry Jowett said, "God does not comfort us to make us comfortable, but to make us comforters."

Don't forget: "When you pass through the waters, I will be with you; and when you pass through the rivers, they will not sweep over you. When you walk through the fire, you will not be burned; the flames will not set you ablaze" (Isa. 43:2, NIV).

Read: 2 Corinthians 1:3–11

Action assignment: Reread today's passage. List ways you can become a better comforter. If you know someone who needs comforting, reach out to that person.

BECOMING OUR BEST

Beware of "the deceitfulness of sin" (Hebrews 3:13). Sin always promises freedom but in the end brings bondage. It promises life but instead brings death. Sin has a way of gradually binding a person until there is no way of escape, apart from the gracious intervention of the Lord. Even the bondage that sin creates is deceitful, for the people who are bound actually think they are free! Too late they discover that they are prisoners of their own appetites and habits.

Jesus Christ came to bring freedom. In His first sermon in the synagogue at Nazareth, our Lord sounded forth the trumpet call of freedom and the advent of the "Year of Jubilee" (Luke 4:16-44). But Christ's *meaning* of freedom is different from the apostates'— as is His method for achieving it.

In the Bible, freedom does not mean "doing your own thing" or "having it your way." That attitude is the very essence of sin. The freedom that Jesus Christ offers means *enjoying fulfillment in the will of God.* It means achieving your greatest potential to the glory of God. The Quaker leader Rufus Jones, paraphrasing Aristotle, said, "The true nature of a thing is the highest that it can become." Jesus Christ frees us to become our very best in this life, and then to be like Him in the next.

Verse for today: "Ye are a chosen generation, a royal priesthood, an holy nation, a peculiar people; that ye should show forth the praises of Him who hath called you out of darkness into marvelous light ... as free, and not using your liberty for a cloak of maliciousness, but as the servants of God" (1 Peter 2:9, 16).

Also read: 1 Corinthians 6:11; Galatians 1:3-4; 2:20.

Action assignment: Thank God for the marvelous freedom you have in Christ and ask Him to enable you to use your freedom from sin to bring honor to Him today.

UNSPEAKABLE JOY

Because we belong to Jesus Christ by faith and are united to Him, we have access to His fullness. We have within us a "well of living water" that perpetually satisfies. More than that, we have a river of living water that flows from Christ to us, and then through us to bless others.

If happiness is fullness, then you and I should experience the fullness of Christ day by day. We need to be filled with the Spirit and filled with the Word of God. We must be full of faith so that God can use us and answer prayer. If we are yielded, our lives will be filled with the fruits of righteousness, and we will have "joy unspeakable and full of glory" (1 Peter 1:8).

It is not God's will that people have empty lives, or that they live on the sickening substitutes of this world. In Jesus Christ, spiritual fullness is available. God can fill empty lives the way the rains fill dry riverbeds in the desert, but with this difference: while those rivers will one day go dry again, we can go "from blessing to blessing" as we draw on the fullness of Jesus Christ.

Verse for today: "Then was our mouth filled with laughter, and our tongue with singing; then said they among the heathen, 'The Lord hath done great things for them'" (Psalm 126:2).

Also read: Colossians 2:9-10; John 4:10-14; 7:37-39; Ephesians 5:18-21; Colossians 3:16-17; Philippians 1:9-11; 1 Peter 1:8.

Action assignment: Make "Jesus satisfies" your motto. But check to make sure He is filling your life. Under the headings of "Holy Spirit," "Word of God," "Faith," "Fruits of Righteousness," and "Joy," place the Scripture references from the "Also read" list above that apply to each. Ask God to show you if there is any lack, and claim "Christ's fullness." When you are full of His joy, share Christ with someone.

MARVELOUS GRACE!

God's grace involves something more than giving us salvation. We not only are saved by grace, but we are to live by grace. We stand in grace: it is the foundation for the Christian life. Grace gives us the strength we need to be victorious soldiers. Grace enables us to suffer without complaining, and even to use that suffering for God's glory. When a Christian turns away from living by God's grace, he must depend on his own power. This leads to failure and disappointment.

This is what Paul means by "fallen from grace" (Galatians 5:4)—moving out of the sphere of grace into the sphere of law, ceasing to depend on God's resources and depending on our own resources.

No wonder Paul was anxious as he wrote his Epistle to the Galatians. His friends in Christ were deserting the God of grace, perverting the grace of God, and reverting to living by the flesh and their own resources. They had begun their Christian lives in the Spirit, but now they were going to try to continue living in the power of the flesh.

Paul wrote: "By the grace of God I am what I am, and His grace toward me did not prove vain; but I labored even more than all of them, yet not I, but the grace of God with me" (1 Corinthians 15:10, NASB).

Other Scripture: Romans 5:1-2; 2 Corinthians 12:1-10; Galatians 3:3.

Action assignment: Write out your understanding of the term *grace*. Look up a song focusing on God's grace and sing it. Thank God for his marvelous grace.

INSTRUCTIONS FOR PRAYER

Jesus gave four instructions to guide us in our praying (Matthew 6:5-15).

We must pray in secret before we pray in public. If we pray in public, we should be in the habit of praying in private.

We must pray sincerely. The fact that a request is repeated does not make it a "vain repetition," for both Jesus and Paul repeated their petitions. A request becomes a "vain repetition" if it is only a babbling of words without a sincere heart desire to seek and do God's will.

My friend Dr. Robert A. Cook has often said, "All of us have one routine prayer in our systems; and once we get rid of it, then we can really start to pray!"

We must pray in God's will. The purpose of prayer is to glorify God's name, and to ask for help to accomplish His will on earth. The Lord's Prayer begins with God's interests, not ours: God's name, God's kingdom, and God's will.

We must pray, having a forgiving spirit toward others. He was not teaching that believers earned God's forgiveness by forgiving others, for this would be contrary to God's free grace and mercy. However, if we have truly experienced God's forgiveness, then we will have a readiness to forgive others.

For today: "The Spirit helps us in our weakness. We do not know what we ought to pray, but the Spirit Himself intercedes for us with groans that words cannot express" (Romans 8:26, NIV).

Also: read Matthew 6:5-15.

Action assignment: Go back and review the above four instructions concerning prayer. Note them in your Bible as a reminder. Ask God to give you a greater understanding of prayer.

ACTING IN LOVE

Christian love does not mean that I must like a person and agree with him on everything. I may not like his vocabulary or his habits, and I may not want him for an intimate friend. Christian love means treating others the way God has treated me. It is an act of the will, not an emotion that I try to manufacture. The motive is to glorify God. The means is the power of the Spirit within, "for the fruit of the Spirit is love" (Galatians 5:22). As I act in love toward another, I may find myself drawn more and more to him, and I may see in him—through Christ—qualities that before were hidden to me.

Christian love also does not leave a person where it finds him. Love should help the poor man do better; love should help the rich man make better use of his God-given resources. Love always builds up; hatred always tears down.

We only believe as much of the Bible as we practice. If we fail to obey the most important Word—"love thy neighbor as thyself" (Leviticus 19:18)—then we will not do any good with the lesser matters of the Word. It was a glaring fault in the Pharisees that they were careful about the minor matters and careless about the fundamentals. They broke the very Law they thought they were defending!

Christ said: "A new commandment I give you: Love one another. As I have loved you, so you must love one another. All men will know that you are My disciples if you love one another" (John 13:34-35, NIV).

Other references: John 15:12-13; 17:23; Romans 13:10; James 2:8-10; 1 John 4:11-12.

Action assignment: Ask God for opportunities to demonstrate Christian love by treating others the way God has treated us.

ADVERSITY AND PROSPERITY

Wisdom gives us perspective so that we aren't discouraged when times are difficult, or arrogant when things are going well. It takes a good deal of spirituality to be able to accept prosperity as well as adversity, for often prosperity does greater damage (Phil. 4:10–13). Job reminded his wife of this truth when she told him to curse God and die: "What? Shall we receive good at the hand of God, and shall we not receive evil [trouble]?" (Job 2:10, KJV). Earlier, Job had said, "The LORD gave, and the LORD hath taken away; blessed be the name of the LORD" (1:21, KJV).

God balances our lives by giving us enough blessings to keep us happy and enough burdens to keep us humble. If all we had were blessings in our hands, we would fall right over, so the Lord balances the blessings in our hands with burdens on our backs. That helps to keep us steady, and as we yield to Him, He can even turn the burdens into blessings.

Why does God constitute our lives in this way? The answer is simple: to keep us from thinking we know it all and that we can manage our lives by ourselves. "Therefore, a man cannot discover anything about his future" (Eccles. 7:14, NIV). Just about the time we think we have an explanation for things, God changes the situation and we have to throw out our formula. This is where Job's friends went wrong: they tried to use an old road map to guide Job on a brand new journey, and the map didn't fit.

Verse for today: "I know what it is to be in need, and I know what it is to have plenty. I have learned the secret of being content in any and every situation, whether well fed or hungry, whether living in plenty or in want" (Phil. 4:12, NIV).

Read: Ecclesiastes 7

Action assignment: Talk to God and ask Him to enable you to be the right kind of comforter. Resolve not to use familiar clichés and stereotyped Bible verses in conversations with friends and loved ones who are experiencing adversity.

BEWARE OF RICHES

Many people must have more and more material things in order to be happy and feel successful. But riches can be a trap and lead to bondage, not freedom. Instead of giving satisfaction, riches can create additional desires; and these must be satisfied. Instead of providing help and health, an excess of material things hurts and wounds. Paul described the result very vividly: "Harmful desires . . . plunge men into ruin and destruction" (1 Timothy 6:9, NIV). It is the picture of a man drowning! He trusted his wealth and "sailed along," but a storm came and he sank.

It is a dangerous thing to use religion as a cover-up for acquiring wealth. God's laborer is certainly worthy of his hire, but his motive for laboring must not be money. That would make him a "hireling," and not a true shepherd. We should not ask, "How much will I get?" but rather "How much can I give?"

Sad, but true: "People who want to get rich fall into temptation and a trap and into many foolish and harmful desires that plunge men into ruin and destruction. For the love of money is a root of all kinds of evil. Some people, eager for money, have wandered from the faith and pierced themselves with many griefs" (1 Timothy 6:9-10).

Also read: Ecclesiastes 5:10-20; Mark 4:19.

Action assignment: Talk to God about a proper attitude toward money; tell Him you want a real biblical attitude (if that's true!). Consider how you can be a good steward of the money God has given you.

THE LIFE THAT IS REAL

"I would like to become a Christian," an interested woman said to a visiting pastor, "but I'm afraid I can't hold out. I'm sure to sin again!"

Turning to 1 John 1, the pastor said, "No doubt you *will* sin again, because God says, 'If we say that we have no sin, we deceive ourselves, and the truth is not in us' (v. 8). But if you *do* sin, God will forgive you if you will confess your sin to Him. But it isn't *necessary* for Christians to sin. As we walk in fellowship with God and in obedience to His Word, He gives us ability to resist and to have victory over temptation."

Then the pastor remembered that the woman had gone through surgery some months before.

"When you had your surgery," he asked, "was there a possibility of complications or problems afterward?"

"Oh, yes," she replied. "But whenever I had a problem, I went to see the doctor and he took care of it."

Then the truth hit her. "I see it!" she exclaimed. "Christ is always available to keep me out of sin or to forgive my sin!"

The life that is real is a life of *victory.*

The Bible says: "Ye are of God, little children, and have overcome them: because greater is He that is in you than he that is in the world" (1 John 4:4).

Also consider: Proverbs 4:14-15; James 1:12-16; 4:7-8; 1 John 1:7; 2:3.

Action assignment: Identify one or more areas in your life in which you continually fall into sin. Recognize God's ability to help you overcome temptation, and ask Him to enable you to keep these areas of your life pure.

SEAT OF POWER

The Christian really operates in two spheres: the human and the divine, the visible and the invisible. Physically, he is on the earth in a human body—but spiritually he is seated with Christ in the heavenly sphere. It is this heavenly sphere that provides the power and direction for the earthly walk.

The President of the United States is not always seated at his desk in the White House, but that executive chair represents the sphere of his life and power. No matter where he is, he is the President, because only he has the privilege of sitting at that desk. Likewise with the Christian; no matter where he may be on this earth, he is seated in the heavenlies with Jesus Christ, and this is the basis of his life and power.

The Christian's life is centered in heaven. His citizenship is in heaven; his name is written in heaven; his Father is in heaven; and his attention and affection ought to be centered on the things of heaven. Evangelist D.L. Moody used to warn about people who were so "heavenly minded they were no earthly good," but that is not what Paul is describing. "The heavenlies" (literal translation) describes that place where Jesus Christ is right now and where the believer is seated with Him. The battles we fight are not with flesh and blood on earth, but with satanic powers "in the heavenlies."

It's true! "God raised us up with Christ and seated us with Him in the heavenly realms in Christ Jesus" (Ephesians 2:6, NIV).

Read these verses to substantiate statements in paragraph three: Philippians 3:20; Luke 10:20; Colossians 3:1-4.

Action assignment: Get a good grasp on this truth and share it with a family member or friend. Ask God to help you explain it clearly.

WINNING OVER SIN

It is easy for Christians to get accustomed to sin. Instead of having a militant attitude that hates and opposes it, we gradually get used to sin, sometimes without even realizing it. The one thing that will destroy "the rest of our time" is sin. A believer living in sin is a terrible weapon in the hands of Satan. Peter presented several arguments to convince us to oppose sin in our lives.

Our Lord came to earth to deal with sin and conquer it forever. He dealt with the ignorance of sin by teaching the truth and by living it before men's eyes. He dealt with the consequences of sin by healing and forgiving; and, on the cross, He dealt the final deathblow to sin itself. He was armed, as it were, with a militant attitude toward sin, even though He had great compassion for lost sinners.

Our goal in life is to "cease from sin." We will not reach this goal until we die, or are called home when the Lord returns; but this should not keep us from striving.

As we yield ourselves to God and have the same attitude toward sin that Jesus had, we can overcome the old life and manifest the new life.

Scripture for today: "Jesus Christ, who is the faithful witness, the firstborn from the dead, and the ruler of the kings of the earth. To Him who loves us and has freed us from our sins by His blood, and has made us to be a kingdom and priests to serve His God and Father—to Him be glory and power for ever and ever!" (Revelation 1:5-6, NIV)

Other Scripture: 1 John 2:28; 3:9.

Action assignment: Meditate on what it cost Jesus to free you from the penalty of sin, and on how He is able to give you victory over the power of sin. Confess known sins to God, and thank Him for the blood of Christ that cleanses us from sin.

REMEMBER SODOM AND GOMORRAH

God made Sodom and Gomorrah an example to warn the ungodly that He does indeed judge sin. The citizens did not *occasionally* commit unnatural sexual sins; this was their way of life—and death!

The bent of their lives was constantly downward, indulging in unnatural acts. It is possible that the Sodomites were guilty not only of unnatural sex with each other, but also with animals, which would be "strange flesh" as mentioned in Jude 7. Both homosexuality and bestiality are condemned by God (Leviticus 18:22-25).

Sodom and Gomorrah, destroyed by fire from heaven, should indeed serve as an example and warning to ungodly people today. No one can read Genesis 18-19 without clearly seeing God's hatred for sin and, at the same time, His patience and willingness to postpone judgment. This certainly ties in with Peter's explanation for God's seeming delay in fulfilling the promise of Christ's return (2 Peter 3:8-18).

From Jude: "Sodom and Gomorrah and the surrounding towns gave themselves up to sexual immorality and perversion. They serve as an example of those who suffer the punishment of eternal fire" (Jude 7, NIV).

Read also: Genesis 18-19; 2 Peter 3:8-18.

Action assignment: To become more informed and to join forces with those warring against evil in our day, you might write to an organization such as the National Federation for Decency, P.O. Drawer 2440, Tupelo, MS 38803. Ask how you can become involved in the fight for decency. Pray for those who battle evil.

GRACE GIVING

During my years of ministry, I have endured many offering appeals. I have listened to pathetic tales about unbelievable needs. I have forced myself to laugh at old jokes that were supposed to make it easier for me to part with my money. I have been scolded, shamed, and almost threatened.

If our giving is motivated by grace, we will give willingly—not because we have been forced to give.

A friend of mine was leaving for a business trip, and his wife reminded him before church that she needed some extra money for household expenses. Just before the offering he slipped some money into her hand: she, thinking it was their weekly offering, put it all in the plate. It was the expense money for the week!

"Well," said my friend, "we gave it to the Lord and He keeps the records."

"How much did you *intend* to give?" asked their pastor, and my friend gave an amount. "Then that's what God recorded," said the pastor, "because He saw the intent of your heart!"

God sees not the portion, but the proportion. If we could have given more, and did not, God notes it. If we wanted to give more, and could not, God also notes that. When we give willingly, according to what we have, we are practicing "grace giving."

Verse for today: "Everyone must make up his own mind as to how much he should give. Don't force anyone to give more than he really wants to, for cheerful givers are the ones God prizes" (2 Corinthians 9:7, TLB).

Read more: Matthew 6:1-4; 1 Corinthians 16:2; 2 Corinthians 8:1-15, 9:6.

Action assignment: Set up a separate bank account and deposit the Lord's money in it as you deposit your paycheck in your regular account. Or devise another method to make sure you set aside a portion of your income for the Lord each time you are paid. Give regularly as the Lord directs you. Talk to God about how much He wants you to give, and ask Him to give you more wisdom in your use of money for His sake.

February

Be Renewed:

"We faint not; but though our outward man perish, yet the inward man is renewed day by day."

2 Corinthians 4:16

1

A MATTER OF LIFE AND DEATH

The writer of Psalm 73, Asaph, was able to evaluate time in the light of eternity and earth in the light of heaven. He looked at godless people and said, "They have more than heart could wish" (v. 7). But later he reverses that conclusion and realizes that because he has God, he has everything.

The ultimate test of life is death. We will die, but will have God as our portion forever! Our verse for today (see below) is the Old Testament version of Philippians 1:21—"For to me to live is Christ, and to die is gain." It is also a reminder of what missionary martyr Jim Elliot said: "He is no fool who gives what he cannot keep to gain what he cannot lose." Having the right values is a matter of life and death.

Psalm 73 teaches us some valuable lessons. To begin with, it encourages us to walk by faith and not by sight. God's Word is true no matter what our circumstances might look like. It also encourages us to get the "long view" of things and not to abandon the eternal for the temporal.

Most of all, Asaph reminds us that we need to spend time with God in worship and spiritual evaluation. We need to live "with eternity's values in view," and this comes from fellowship with the Lord. God's promises become real to us as we grow in our relationships with Him.

Verse for today: "My flesh and my heart faileth: but God is the strength of my heart, and my portion forever" (Psalm 73:26).

Also read: Psalms 37; 73:24-28; Proverbs 24:1-2; Matthew 16:26; 21:41.

Action assignment: When good things (like great fortunes and fame) happen to bad people, do you envy them? Or do you criticize God for blessing them and withholding from you? If so, ask God to forgive you and help you gain a fresh perspective as Asaph did. His faith increased so that he ended his psalm by declaring God's wonderful works. Write your own psalm which states any envy or criticism you might have, followed by your praise of the God who does everything right.

A WARNING TO YOUTH

Young people have to watch their hearts and their eyes, because either or both can lead them into sin (Num. 15:39; Prov. 4:23; Matt. 5:27–30). "Walk in the ways of your heart" (Eccles.11:9) is not an encouragement to go on a youthful fling and satisfy sinful desires (Jer. 17:9; Mark 7:20–23). It is rather a reminder for young people to enjoy the special pleasures that belong to youth and can never be experienced again in quite the same way. Older people need to remember that God expects young people to act like young people. The tragedy is that too many older people are trying to act like young people!

Solomon's warning is evidence that he doesn't have sinful pleasures in mind: "God will bring you into judgment" (Eccles. 11:9).

God does give us "richly all things to enjoy" (1 Tim. 6:17), but it is always wrong to enjoy the pleasures of sin. The young person who enjoys life in the will of God will have nothing to worry about when the Lord returns.

Yes, life is a school; and we must humble ourselves and learn all we can. Our textbook is the Bible, and the Holy Spirit is our Teacher (John 14:26; 15:26; 16:12–15). The Spirit can use gifted human teachers to instruct us, but He longs to teach us personally from His Word (Ps. 119:97–104). There are always new lessons to learn and new examinations to face as we seek to grow in grace and in the knowledge of our Savior (2 Peter 3:18).

Verse for Today: "Remember your Creator in the days of your youth, before the days of trouble come and the years approach when you will say, 'I find no pleasure in them'" (Eccles. 12:1, NIV).

Read: Ecclesiastes 11–12

Action assignment: Whether you are a young person or a senior citizen, list some of the things God has given you to enjoy. Thank God for them. Confess and determine to turn away from any pleasures that you believe are not pleasing to God.

3

NO LONGER GUILTY

In justification, God *declares* the believing sinner righteous; He does not *make* him righteous. Before the sinner trusts Christ, he stands guilty before God; but the moment he trusts Christ, he is declared not guilty and he can never be called guilty again!

Justification is not simply "forgiveness," because a person could be forgiven and then go out and sin and become guilty. Once you have been "justified by faith," you can never be held guilty before God.

Justification is also different from "pardon," because a pardoned criminal still has a record. When the sinner is justified by faith, *his past sins are remembered against him no more*, and God no longer puts his sins on record.

Finally, God justifies *sinners*, not "good people." Paul declares that God justifies "the ungodly" (Romans 4:5). The reason most sinners are not justified is because they will not admit they are sinners! And sinners are the only kind of people Jesus Christ can save.

When Peter separated himself from the Gentiles, he was denying the truth of justification by faith, because he was saying, "We Jews are different from—and better than—the Gentiles." Yet both Jews and Gentiles are sinners and can be saved only by faith in Christ.

Verse for today: "But now being made free from sin, and become servants to God, ye have your fruit unto holiness, and the end everlasting life" (Romans 6:22).

Other Scripture: Psalm 32:1-2; Romans 3:22-23; 4:1-8; 8:1, 30-34; Matthew 9:9-13; Luke 18:9-14. Justification leads to a changed life (read James 2).

Action assignment: Explain to someone the implications of justification. Ask God to help you realize the meaning of this truth in your own life.

STANDING TALL

You do not become patient and persevering by reading a book (even this one) or listening to a lecture. *You have to suffer.*

What were the believers in Thessalonica enduring? Paul used several words in 2 Thessalonians 1 to describe their situation: *persecutions*, which means "attacks from without," or "trials"; *tribulations*, which literally means "pressures," or afflictions that result from the trials; and *trouble* (v. 7), which means "to be pressed into a narrow place." No matter how we look at it, the Thessalonican Christians were not having an easy time.

God never wastes suffering. Trials work *for* us, not *against* us. If we trust God and yield to Him, then trials will produce patience and maturity in our lives. If we rebel and fight our circumstances, then we will remain immature and impatient.

God *permits* trials that He might build character into our lives. He can grow a mushroom overnight, but it takes many years—and many storms—to build a mighty oak.

Verse for today: "Dear friends, do not be surprised at the painful trial you are suffering, as though something strange were happening to you" (1 Peter 4:12, NIV).

Further reading: 2 Corinthians 4:15-18; James 1:1-5; 5:10-11; 1 Peter 4:13-19.

Action assignment: Think about the various hard times you have experienced and/or are experiencing in your life. What lessons have your learned as a result? Are you thankful to God for His being with you—even when His hand may not always have been clearly evident to you? Recommit all the hard times—past, present, and future—to Him, knowing that He is truly with you!

5

MORE IMPORTANT THAN TROPHIES

Phillips Brooks said, "The great purpose of life—the shaping of character by truth." Godly character and conduct are far more important than golf trophies or home-run records, though it is possible for a person to have both. Paul challenged Timothy to be as devoted to godliness as an athlete is to his sport. We are living and laboring for eternity.

A Christian, like an athlete, must make his body his servant and not his master. When I see high school football squads and baseball teams under the hot summer sun, going through their calisthenics, I am reminded that there are spiritual exercises that I ought to be doing. Prayer, meditation, self-examination, fellowship, service, sacrifice, submission to the will of others, witness—all of these can assist me, through the Spirit, to become a more godly person.

Spiritual exercise is not easy; we must "labor and suffer reproach" (1 Timothy 4:10). "For this we labor and strive" (NIV). The word translated "strive" is an athletic word from which we get our English word "agonize." It is the picture of an athlete straining and giving his best to win. A Christian who wants to excel must really work at it, by the grace of God and to the glory of God.

Verse for today: "Have nothing to do with godless myths and old wives' tales; rather, train yourself to be godly. For physical training is of some value, but godliness has value for all things, holding promise for both the present life and the life to come" (1 Timothy 4:7-8, NIV).

Also: 1 Corinthians 9:24-27; Hebrews 5:14; 1 Timothy 4:12.

Action assignment: Write down your spiritual purpose for life and the exercises you can do to obtain it. Ask God to help you maintain the right balance between spiritual and physical exercise.

OVERCOMING HYPOCRISY

Remember that hypocrisy robs us of reality in Christian living. We substitute reputation for character, mere words for true prayer, money for the devotion of the heart. No wonder Jesus compared the Pharisees to tombs that were whitewashed on the outside but filthy on the inside!

Hypocrisy not only robs us of character, it also robs us of spiritual rewards. Instead of the eternal approval of God, we receive the shallow praise of people. We pray, but there are no answers. We fast, but the inner person shows no improvement. The spiritual life becomes hollow and lifeless. We miss the blessing of God here and now, and the reward of God when Christ returns.

Hypocrisy also robs us of spiritual influence. The Pharisees were a negative influence; whatever they touched was defiled and destroyed. The people who admired them and obeyed the Pharisees' words thought they themselves were being helped, when in reality, they were being hurt.

The first step toward overcoming hypocrisy is to be honest with God in our secret life. We must never pray anything that we do not mean from the heart; otherwise, our prayers are simply empty words. Our motive must be to please God alone, no matter what men may say or do. We must cultivate the heart in the secret place. It has well been said, "The most important part of a Christian's life is the part that only God sees." When reputation becomes more important than character, we have become hypocrites.

Sad, but true of many: "The Lord says: 'These people come near to Me with their mouth and honor Me with their lips, but their hearts are far from Me. Their worship of Me is made up only of rules taught by men'" (Isaiah 29:13, NIV).

Other Scripture: Matthew 6:1-5, 16; Mark 7:7-8; Luke 6:46.

Action assignment: Write out a dictionary-type definition of the word *hypocrite*. Check your version against a good dictionary entry. Ask God to empower you daily to keep you from playing the role of a hypocrite in any situation.

7

A NEED FOR SEPARATION

There is a real sense in which the Christian must be separated from "the world"—and by that term, I mean "society without God." As the children of God, we are *in* the world physically but not *of* the world spiritually. We are sent *into* the world to let our lights shine and to win others to Christ. But it is only as we maintain our separation from the world—not being contaminated by it—that we can be successful servants of God.

The world wants to "spot" the Christian and start to defile him. First, there is "friendship of the world" which can lead to a love for the world. If we are not careful, we will become conformed to this world, and the result is being condemned with the world. This does not suggest that we lose our salvation, but that we lose all we have lived for.

Lot is an illustration of this principle. First he pitched his tent toward Sodom, and then moved into Sodom. Before long, Sodom moved into him and he lost his testimony even with his own family. When judgment fell on Sodom, Lot lost everything. It was Abraham, the separated believer, the friend of God, who had a greater ministry to the people than did Lot, the friend of the world. It is not necessary for the Christian to get involved with the world to have a ministry to the world. Jesus was "unspotted," and yet He was a friend of publicans and sinners. The best way to minister to the needs of the world is to be pure from the defilement of the world.

Verse to remember: "Religion that God our Father accepts as pure and faultless is this: to look after orphans and widows in their distress and to keep oneself from being polluted by the world" (James 1:27, NIV).

Related Scripture: John 14:30; 17:11-18; Luke 16:8; James 4:4; 1 John 2:15-17; Romans 12:1-2; 1 Corinthians 11:32.

Action assignment: Pray that God will keep you from defilement of the world and make you an effective minister for Christ in your world.

8

IN PURSUIT OF CONTENTMENT

Among the Jews in Solomon's day, a stillborn child was not always given a name. That way, it would not be remembered. It was felt that this would encourage the parents to get over their sorrow much faster. "It [the child] comes without meaning, it departs in darkness, and in darkness its name is shrouded" (Eccles. 6:4, NIV). In my pastoral ministry, brokenhearted parents and grandparents have sometimes asked, "Why did God even permit this child to be conceived if it wasn't going to live?" Solomon asked, "Why did God permit this man to have wealth and a big family if the man couldn't enjoy it?"

Some would argue that existence is better than nonexistence and a difficult life better than no life at all. Solomon might agree with them, for "a living dog is better than a dead lion" (Eccles. 9:4). But the problem Solomon faced was not whether existence is better than nonexistence, but whether there is any purpose behind the whole seemingly unbalanced scheme of things. As he examined life "under the sun," he could find no reason why a person should be given riches and yet be deprived of the power to enjoy them.

The ability to enjoy life comes from within. It is a matter of character and not circumstances. "I have learned, in whatever state I am, therewith to be content," Paul wrote to the Philippians (4:11, KJV). The Greek word *autarkes*, translated "content," carries the idea of "self-contained, adequate, needing nothing from the outside." Paul carried *within* all the resources needed for facing life courageously and triumphing over difficulties. "I can do all things through Christ who strengthens me" (Phil. 4:13).

Verse for Today: "I am not saying this because I am in need, for I have learned to be content whatever the circumstances" (Phil. 4:11, NIV).

Read: Ecclesiastes 6

Action assignment: As you face your responsibilities for the day, claim Philippians 4:13. And pray that you will learn to be content in the place where God has placed you.

BE READY FOR THAT DAY

We do not know *when* the Day of the Lord will happen, but we are told *what* will happen. Kenneth Wuest gives an accurate and graphic translation of 2 Peter 3:10: "The heavens with a rushing noise will be dissolved, and the elements being scorched will be dissolved, and the earth also and the works in it will be burned up."

For this reason, I do not personally believe that God will permit sinful men to engage in an earth-destroying atomic war. He will, I believe, overrule the ignorance and foolishness of men including well-meaning but unbelieving diplomats and politicians, so that He alone will have the privilege of "pushing the button" and dissolving the elements to make way for a new heaven and a new earth.

Of course, this great explosion and conflagration will not touch the "heaven of heavens" where God dwells. It will destroy the earth and the atmospheric heavens around it, the universe as we know it; this will make room for the new heavens and earth (2 Peter 3:13; Revelation 21:1).

Man's great works will also be burned up! All of the things man boasts about—his great cities, buildings, inventions, achievements—will be destroyed in a moment of time. When sinners stand before the throne of God, they will have nothing to point to as evidence of their greatness. It will all be gone.

Let us pause and consider: where will I be when God destroys the world? Is what I am living for only destined to vanish forever? Or am I doing the will of God so that my works will glorify Him forever?

Scripture for today: "Since everything will be destroyed in this way, what kind of people ought you to be? You ought to live holy and godly lives as you look forward to the Day of God and speed its coming. . . . But in keeping with His promise we are looking forward to a new heaven and a new earth, the home of righteousness" (2 Peter 3:11-13, NIV).

Also read: 2 Peter 3; Revelation 21:1; Matthew 24:43; 1 Thessalonians 5:3.

Action assignment: This is a timely topic. Get a firm grasp on it, enough to discuss it with a friend. Look at your life in light of this coming event.

CHASING AFTER THE WIND

Today's world is pleasure-mad. Millions of people will pay almost any amount of money to "buy experiences" and temporarily escape the burdens of life. While there is nothing wrong with innocent fun, the person who builds his or her life only on seeking pleasure is bound to be disappointed in the end.

Why? For one thing, pleasure-seeking usually becomes a selfish endeavor; and selfishness destroys true joy. People who live for pleasure often exploit others to get what they want, and they end up with broken relationships as well as empty hearts. *People are more important than things and thrills.* We are to be channels, not reservoirs; the greatest joy comes when we share God's pleasures with others.

If you live for pleasure alone, enjoyment will decrease unless the intensity of the pleasure increases. Then you reach a point of diminishing returns when there is little or no enjoyment at all, only bondage. For example, the more that people drink, the less enjoyment they get out of it. This means they must have more drinks and stronger drinks in order to have pleasure; the sad result is desire without satisfaction. Instead of alcohol, substitute drugs, gambling, sex, money, fame, or any other pursuit, and the principle will hold true: when pleasure alone is the center of life, the result will ultimately be disappointment and emptiness.

Verse for today: "Yet when I surveyed all that my hands had done and what I had toiled to achieve, everything was meaningless, a chasing after the wind; nothing was gained under the sun" (Eccles. 2:11, NIV).

Read: Ecclesiastes 2

Action assignment: What are three things that bring you great pleasure? What do you think the author of today's reading means when he writes, "The greatest joy comes when we share God's pleasures with others"?

11

MAKING LIFE A DAILY ADVENTURE

Solomon experimented with life and discovered that there was no lasting satisfaction in possessions, pleasures, power, or prestige. He had everything, yet his life was empty! There is no need for you and me to repeat these experiments. Let's accept Solomon's conclusions and avoid the heartache and pain that must be endured when you experiment in the laboratory of life. These experiments are costly and could even prove fatal.

When you belong to the family of God through faith in the Son of God, life is not monotonous: it is a daily adventure that builds character and enables you to serve others to the glory of God. Instead of making decisions on the basis of the vain wisdom of this world, you will have God's wisdom available to you (James 1:5).

As far as wealth and pleasure are concerned, God gives to us "richly all things to enjoy" (1 Tim. 6:17). Yes, "The blessing of the LORD makes one rich, and He adds no sorrow with it" (Prov. 10:22). The wealth and pleasures of the world do not satisfy, and the quest for power and position is futile. In Jesus Christ we have all that we need for life and death, time and eternity.

Verse for today: "But seek first the kingdom of God and his righteousness, and all these things shall be added to you" (Matt. 6:33).

Read: Ecclesiastes 1

Action assignment: Resolve to apply your knowledge of God's Word today in your decisions with no self-seeking or abrupt "short fuse" flare-ups. Strive for self-control, perseverance, and a thoughtful consideration of the feelings of others. Ask God for His enablement.

OUR SOVEREIGN GOD

John Wesley is said to have remarked that he read the newspaper "to see how God was governing His world," and this is certainly a biblical approach. God rules over kingdoms and nations (2 Chron. 20:6; Dan. 5:21). As A. T. Pierson used to say, "History is His story." This doesn't mean that God is to blame for the foolish or wicked decisions and deeds of government officials, but it does mean that He is on the throne and working out His perfect will.

The eminent British historian Herbert Butterfield said, "Perhaps history is a thing that would stop happening if God held His breath, or could be imagined as turning away to think of something else." The God who knows the number and the names of the stars (Ps. 147:4) and who sees when the tiniest bird falls to the ground dead (Matt. 10:29) is mindful of the plans and pursuits of the nations and is working out His divine purposes in human history.

Knowing that the Lord reigns over all things ought to encourage the people of God as we watch world events and grieve over the decay of people and nations. God's ways are hidden and mysterious, and we sometimes wonder why He permits certain things to happen, but we must still pray "Your will be done" (Matt. 6:10) and then be ready to obey whatever He tells us to do.

Today's Scripture: "But as for me, I watch in hope for the LORD, I wait for God my Savior; my God will hear me. Do not gloat over me, my enemy! Though I have fallen, I will rise. Though I sit in darkness, the LORD will be my light" (Mic. 7:7–8, NIV).

Read: Psalm 50

Action assignment: Pursue your meditation of God's Word throughout the day. Scan several psalms and write out some verses that will encourage you when world events trouble you. A few are Psalms 9:9, 27:5, 32:7, 138:7.

13

RICH PAUPERS!

She had gone down in history as "America's Greatest Miser." When she died in 1916, "Hetty" Green left an estate valued at over $100 million. She had eaten cold oatmeal because it cost to heat it; her son had suffered a leg amputation because she spent so long looking for a free clinic that his case became incurable. She was wealthy, yet she chose to live like a pauper.

Eccentric? Certainly! Crazy? Perhaps—but nobody could prove it. She was so foolish that she hastened her own death by bringing on an attack of apoplexy while arguing about the value of drinking skimmed milk! But Hetty Green is an illustration of too many Christian believers today. They have limitless wealth at their disposal, yet they live like paupers.

God the Father has made us rich in Jesus Christ! When you were born again into God's family, you were born rich. Through Christ, you share in the riches of God's grace, God's glory, God's mercy, and "the unsearchable riches of Christ." Our Heavenly Father is not poor, He is rich—and He has made us rich in His Son.

Think of it! "God has chosen to make known among the Gentiles the glorious riches of this mystery, which is Christ in you, the hope of glory" (Colossians 2:27, NIV).

Read: the following Ephesians passages and match them up with the last few lines of the reading: 1:7, 18; 2:4, 7; 3:8, 16.

Action assignment: Ask God to show you how to live less like a pauper and to make His spiritual blessings a greater reality to you.

NO LONGER BABIES

No one can escape coming into the world as a baby, because that is the only way to get here! But it is tragic when a baby fails to mature. No matter how much parents and grandparents love to hold and cuddle a baby, it is their great desire that the baby grow up and enjoy a full life as a mature adult. God has the same desire for His children. That is why He calls to us, "Go on to maturity!"

When I was in kindergarten, the teacher taught us our ABCs. (We didn't have television to teach us in those days.) You learn your ABCs so that you might read words, sentences, books—any literature. But you do not keep learning the basics. You must use the basics to go on to better things.

If we are going to make progress, we have to leave childhood behind and go forward in spiritual growth.

Verse for today: "Like newborn babies, crave pure spiritual milk, so that by it you may grow up in your salvation" (1 Peter 2:2, NIV).

Take time to read: 1 Corinthians 3:1-3; Hebrews 6:1-12; Ephesians 4:14.

Action assignment: What are the spiritual ABCs? List what you understand them to be. How many of these "basics" of the Christian faith have you mastered? Or more pointedly, how many have mastered you? Pray that God helps you to mature— according to His timetable.

15

A TIME FOR WAR

"Make love, not war!" may have been a popular slogan, but it is not always feasible. Doctors must make war against disease and death; sanitary engineers must war against filth and pollution; legislators must war against injustice and crime. And they all fight because of something they love!

The Apostle Paul waged war against false teachers because he loved the truth, and because he loved those whom he had led to Christ.

The test of a person's ministry is not popularity (Matthew 24:9-11) or miraculous signs and wonders (Matthew 24:23-24), but his faithfulness to the Word of God (see Isaiah 8:20; 1 Timothy 4; 1 John 4:1-6; also note that 2 John 7-11 warns us not to encourage those who bring false doctrine). Judaizers came along and substituted their false gospel for the true Gospel, and for this sin, Paul pronounced them accursed. The word he uses is *anathema;* which means "dedicated to destruction." No matter who the preacher may be—an angel from heaven or even Paul himself—if he preaches any other gospel, he is accursed!

Remember this: "Ye that love the Lord, hate evil" (Psalm 97:10). "Abhor that which is evil; cleave to that which is good" (Romans 12:9).

Also: Look up the Bible references listed in today's reading.

Action assignment: Ask God to make you more sensitive to evil and to help you war against it. Consider action you might take in your own community to help decrease the distribution of pornographic literature, for example. Visit your local Christian bookstore and ask for a book which could help you join forces with those who fight pornography or other evils.

WITH ETERNITY'S VALUES IN VIEW

Live expectantly today. This does not mean putting on a robe and sitting atop a mountain. But it does mean living in light of Christ's return, realizing that our works will be judged and that our opportunities for service on earth will end. It means to live "with eternity's values in view."

There is a difference between being ready to go to heaven and being ready to meet the Lord. Anyone who has sincerely trusted Christ for salvation is ready to go to heaven. Christ's sacrifice on the cross has taken care of that. But to be ready to meet the Lord at the Judgment Seat of Christ is quite another matter. Scripture indicates that some believers will not be happy to see Jesus Christ!

Having been a pastor for many years, I have had the sad experience of seeing believers deliberately disobey the Word of God. I recall one young woman who stubbornly chose to marry an unsaved man. When I tried to help her from the Bible, she said, "I don't care what you say. I don't care what the Bible says. I'm going to get married!" Will she be happy at the Judgment Seat of Christ?

Verse for today: "And now, little children, abide in Him; that, when He shall appear, we may have confidence, and not be ashamed before Him at His coming (1 John 2:28).

For further study: Review the last few verses of each chapter of 2 Thessalonians and note the practical results of living expectantly.

Action assignment: Ask the Lord to help you examine your heart in relation to the verses mentioned under "for further study."

17

WHEN WE GIVE AS JESUS GAVE

Jesus Christ is always the preeminent example for the believer to follow, whether in service, suffering, or sacrifice. Like Jesus Christ, the Macedonian Christians *gave themselves to God and to others.* If we give ourselves to God, we will have little problem giving our substance to God. If we give ourselves to God, we will also give ourselves for others. It is impossible to love God and ignore the needs of your neighbor. Jesus Christ gave Himself for us. Should we not give ourselves to Him? He died so that we might not live for ourselves, but for Him and for others.

Remember the Macedonians: "They gave not only what they could afford, but far more . . . because they wanted to, and . . . begged us to take the money so they could share in the joy of helping the Christians in Jerusalem. Best of all, they went beyond our highest hopes, for their first action was to dedicate themselves to the Lord and to us, for whatever directions God might give to them through us" (2 Corinthians 8:3-5, TLB).

Read: Galatians 1:4; 2:20; 2 Corinthians 5:15; 9:6-7.

Action assignment: If you have given yourself to God, write down ways your life has changed. If you haven't, write down ways your life would change if you did make such a commitment. Talk to God about your relationship to Him.

1.＿＿＿＿＿＿＿＿＿＿＿＿＿＿＿＿＿＿＿＿＿＿＿＿＿

2.＿＿＿＿＿＿＿＿＿＿＿＿＿＿＿＿＿＿＿＿＿＿＿＿＿

3.＿＿＿＿＿＿＿＿＿＿＿＿＿＿＿＿＿＿＿＿＿＿＿＿＿

4.＿＿＿＿＿＿＿＿＿＿＿＿＿＿＿＿＿＿＿＿＿＿＿＿＿

5.＿＿＿＿＿＿＿＿＿＿＿＿＿＿＿＿＿＿＿＿＿＿＿＿＿

SOLVING LIFE'S PROBLEMS

When Jesus watched His frustrated disciples as they tried to solve the problem of feeding the 5,000 (John 6), He taught them a lesson in faith and surrender. Here are the steps we must take in solving life's problems:

Start with what you have. Andrew found a lad who had a small lunch, and he brought the lad to Jesus.

Give what you have to Jesus. Was the boy willing to give up his lunch? Yes! God begins where we are and uses what we have. Jesus broke the bread and gave the pieces to the disciples.

Obey what He commands. The disciples had the people sit down as Jesus ordered and distributed the broken pieces. If we give what we have to Him, He will bless it and give it back to us to use in feeding others.

Conserve the results. Twelve baskets filled with leftovers were carefully collected so that nothing was wasted.

The Apostle John recorded a sermon on "the Bread of Life" that Jesus gave the next day in the synagogue in Capernaum (John 6:22-59). The people were willing to receive the physical bread, but they would not receive the living Bread—the Son of God come down from heaven. Each of us should make sure we are not in some degree like these people.

Meditate on this thought: "The disciples . . . said, 'This is a remote place, and it's already getting late. Send the crowds away, so they can go to the villages and buy themselves some food.' Jesus replied, 'They do not need to go away. You give them something to eat'" (Matthew 14:15-16, NIV).

Read: Matthew 14:13-21.

Action assignment: Consider the four steps above in relation to your own life. What kind of application can you make? Is there a matter you need to talk with the Lord about?

A CALL TO ARMS

What can we do practically to oppose the enemy and maintain the purity and unity of the church? For one thing, we must know the Word of God and have the courage to defend it. Every local church ought to be a Bible institute, and every Christian ought to be a Bible student. The pulpit needs to declare positive truth as well as denounce error.

Second, we must "watch and pray." The enemy is already here and we dare not go to sleep! Spiritual leaders in local congregations need to be alert as they interview candidates for baptism and church membership. Committees need to seek the mind of Christ as they appoint Sunday School teachers, youth sponsors, and other church leaders. Congregations must exercise discernment as they select officers.

Third, congregations and members must be careful where they send their money. "Should you help the wicked and love those who hate the Lord?" (2 Chronicles 19:2, NIV)

Finally, we must have the courage to maintain a position of biblical separation from those who deny Christ and the fundamental doctrines of the Word. This does not mean that we separate from fellow believers over minor doctrinal differences or that we practice "guilt by association." God's true army needs to stand together in the battle for truth.

Have you heeded the call to arms?

The Bible says: "Through Thy precepts I get understanding; therefore I hate every false way (Psalm 119:104).

Also consider: Psalms 5:4; 84:10; 101:3; Proverbs 8:13; Romans 16:17-20; 2 John 6-11.

Action assignment: Ask God for wisdom in determining what you can do to oppose the enemy and be better equipped as a student of His Word. Make a note of at least one thing you want to do.

GOD, THE AVENGER

The believer who seeks to obey God is going to have enemies. When our Lord was ministering on earth, He had enemies. No matter where Paul and the other apostles traveled, enemies opposed their work. Jesus warned His disciples that their worst enemies might be those of their own households. Unfortunately, some believers have enemies because they lack love and patience, not because they are faithful in their witness. There is a difference between sharing in "the offense of the Cross" and being an offensive Christian!

The Christian must not play God and try to avenge himself. Returning evil for evil, or good for good, is the way most people live. But the Christian must live on a higher level and return good for evil. This requires *love,* because our first inclination is to fight back. It also requires faith, believing that God can accomplish His will in our lives and in the lives of those who hurt us.

Verse for today: "Be joyful in hope, patient in affliction, faithful in prayer" (Romans 12:12, NIV).

Also read: Romans 12:17-21; Matthew 10:36; Galatians 5:11; 6:12-16; Deuteronomy 32:35.

Action assignment: Think about your most irritating enemy. Do you want to love him or fight him? Ask God to direct you in some specific action to show love to this enemy today. Precede this action with prayer for God's help and you'll be an overcomer of evil with good.

"DO GOOD TO ALL MEN"

We are to "do good unto all men" (see verse for today). This is how we let our light shine and glorify our Father in heaven. It is not only by *words* that we witness to the lost, but also by our *works*. In fact, our works pave the way for our verbal witness; they win us the right to be heard. It is not a question of asking, "Does this person deserve my good works?" Did *we* deserve what God did for *us* in Christ? Nor should we be like the defensive lawyer who tried to argue, "Who is my neighbor?" (Luke 10:25-37) Jesus made it clear that the question is not "Who is my neighbor?" but "To whom can I be a neighbor?"

As we "do good unto all men," we must give priority to "the household of faith," the fellowship of believers. This does not mean that the local church should become an exclusive clique with the members isolated from the world around them and doing nothing to help the lost. Rather, it is a matter of balance. A man always cares for his own family before he cares for others in the neighborhood (1 Timothy 5:8).

We must remember, however, that we share with other Christians so that all of us might be able to share with a needy world. The Christian in the household of faith is a receiver that he might become a transmitter. As we abound in love for one another, we overflow in love for all men (1 Thessalonians 3:12). This is how it was meant to be.

Verse for today: "As we have therefore opportunity, let us do good unto all men, especially unto them who are of the household of faith" (Galatians 6:10).

Other Scripture: Check out the references listed in today's reading.

Action assignment: Think of something good you can do for someone—and do it!

TRUE WITNESSING

A pastor got a phone call from an angry woman. "I have received a piece of religious literature from your church," she shouted, "and I resent your using the mails to upset people!"

"What was so upsetting about a piece of mail from a church?" the pastor asked calmly.

"You have no right to try to change my religion!" the woman stormed. "You have your religion and I have mine, and I'm not trying to change yours!" (She really was, but the pastor didn't argue with her.)

"Changing your religion, or anybody else's religion, is not our purpose," the pastor explained. "But we have experienced a wonderful new life through faith in Christ, and we want to do all we can to share it with others."

Many people, including some Christians, have the idea that "witnessing" means wrangling over differences in religious beliefs or sitting down and comparing churches. But witnessing means sharing our spiritual experiences with others—both by the lives we live and the words we speak.

Today's Scripture: "But sanctify the Lord God in your hearts: and be ready always to give an answer to every man that asketh you a reason of the hope that is in you with meekness and fear: having a good conscience; that, whereas they speak evil of you, as of evildoers, they may be ashamed that falsely accuse your good conversation in Christ" (1 Peter 3:15-16).

Also read: Matthew 5:13-16; Mark 5:19-20; James 3:13.

Action assignment: Be Christ's witness today by your life and your words. Be ready also to tell others why your life is different.

A CHARGE TO THE RICH

Paul wrote to Timothy about the danger of the love of money and added a special "charge" for Timothy to give the rich (see below). We may not think this charge applies to us, but it does. After all, our standard of living today would certainly make us "rich" in the eyes of Timothy's congregation!

If wealth makes a person proud, he understands neither himself nor his wealth. "But thou shalt remember the Lord thy God: for it is He that giveth thee power to get wealth" (Deuteronomy 8:18). We are not owners; we are stewards. If we have wealth, it is by the goodness of God and not because of any special merits on our part. The possessing of material wealth ought to humble a person and cause him to glorify God, not himself.

It is possible to be rich here and be poor in the next world. It is also possible to be poor in this world and rich in the next. Jesus talked about both. But if a believer is rich in this world, he can also be rich in the next, if he uses what he has to honor God. And a person who is poor in this world can use even his limited means to glorify God, thereby discovering great reward in the next world.

Paul instructed: "Charge them that are rich in this world, that they be not highminded; nor trust in uncertain riches, but in the living God, who giveth us richly all things to enjoy; that they do good, that they be rich in good works, ready to distribute, willing to communicate; laying up in store for themselves a good foundation against the time to come, that they may lay hold on eternal life" (1 Timothy 6:17-19).

Also read: Luke 16:19-31 and Matthew 6:19-34.

Action assignment: Search your heart and determine how well you are following the charge Timothy was instructed to give to the rich. List ways you can use money to glorify God.

FAST IN SECRET

It is not wrong to fast if we do it in the right way and with the right motive. Jesus fasted, and so did the members of the early church. Fasting helps to discipline the appetites of the body and keep our spiritual priorities straight. But it must never become an opportunity for temptation. Simply to deprive ourselves of a natural benefit (such as food or sleep) is not *of itself* fasting. We must devote ourselves to God and worship Him. Without the devotion of the heart there is no lasting spiritual benefit.

As with giving and praying, true fasting must be done in secret; it is between the believer and God. To "make unsightly" our faces (by looking glum and asking for pity and praise) would be to destroy the very purpose of the fast. Our Lord laid down a basic principle of spiritual living: Nothing that is truly spiritual will violate that which God has given us in nature. God usually does not tear down one good thing in order to build up another. If we have to look miserable to be considered spiritual, then there is something wrong with our view of spirituality.

Scripture says: "Moreover when ye fast, be not, as the hypocrites, of a sad countenance; for they disfigure their faces, that they may appear unto men to fast. Verily I say unto you, they have their reward. But thou, when thou fastest, anoint thine head, and wash thy face; that thou appear not unto men to fast, but unto thy Father which is in secret; and thy Father, which seeth in secret, shall reward thee openly" (Matthew 6:16-18).

Consider also: Matthew 4:1-4; Ezra 8:21-23; Joel 2:12-13.

Action assignment: Have you ever fasted? Prayerfully consider doing so. If God would have you fast, do it according to the guidelines of Scripture.

MORNING PEOPLE

Doctors tell us that some people are "morning people," while others are "evening people." That is, some people are wide awake before the alarm clock rings. They hit the floor running, and never have to yawn or throw cold water in their faces. Others, like myself, wake up slowly—first one eye, then the other—and gradually shift gears as they move into the day.

When it comes to the return of our Lord, we must all be "morning people"—awake, alert, sober, and ready for the dawning of that wonderful new day.

But for the unsaved crowd, reveling in drunkenness, the coming of Jesus Christ will mean the end of light and the beginning of eternal darkness.

A challenge: "Prepare your minds for action; be self-controlled; set your hope fully on the grace to be given you when Jesus Christ is revealed" (1 Peter 1:13, NIV).

Other verses: Acts 1:11; 1 Corinthians 1:7-8; 1 John 2:28.

Action assignment: If possible, turn in a hymnal to "Is It the Crowning Day?" Make it your song for the day. Thank God for the fact that Christ will return—perhaps today.

SPECIAL: TODAY!

As Christians, we must live a day at a time. No person, no matter how wealthy or gifted, can live *two* days at a time. God provides for us "day by day" as we pray to him (Luke 11:3). He gives us the strength we need according to our daily requirements. We must not make the mistake of trying to "store up grace" for future emergencies, because God gives us the grace we need *when* we need it. When we learn to live a day at a time, confident of God's care, it takes a great deal of pressure off our lives.

Yard by yard, life is hard!
Inch by inch, life's a cinch!

Your Father cares: "Let us therefore come boldly unto the throne of grace, that we may obtain mercy, and find grace to help in time of need" (Hebrews 4:16).

More evidence: Psalms 68:19, 107:8-9; Luke 12:6-7; John 14:13; 1 Corinthians 10:13; Philippians 4:19.

Action assignment: List things below that you really need to accomplish, and ask God for the strength and wisdom to accomplish them. Believe that He will help you moment by moment through the day.

1._____

2._____

3._____

4._____

5._____

POSTPONED PLEASURES

God is not going to *replace* suffering with glory; rather He will *transform* suffering into glory. Jesus used the illustration of a woman giving birth. The same baby that gave her pain also gave her joy. The pain was *transformed* into joy by the birth of the baby. The thorn in the flesh that gave Paul difficulty also gave him power and glory. The cross that gave Jesus shame and pain also brought power and glory.

Mature people know that life includes some "postponed pleasures." We pay a price *today* in order to have enjoyments in the *future*. The piano student may not enjoy practicing scales by the hour, but he looks forward to the pleasure of playing beautiful music one day. The athlete may not enjoy exercising and practicing his skills, but he looks forward to winning the game by doing his best. Christians have something even better: our very sufferings will one day be transformed into glory, and we will be "glad also with exceeding joy."

From the Word: "The sufferings of this present time are not worthy to be compared with the glory which shall be revealed in us" (Romans 1:18).

Also read: Romans 1:17; 2 Timothy 3:11; John 16:20-22; 2 Corinthians 12:7-10.

Action assignment: Think of some instance of suffering in your life that God transformed into glory. Ask God to give you a deeper understanding of this truth.

HEART TROUBLE

The heart of every problem is a problem of the heart. The people of Israel (with exceptions like Moses, Joshua, and Caleb) erred in their hearts, meaning that their hearts wandered from God and His Word. They also had evil hearts of unbelief; they doubted that God would give them victory in Canaan. They had seen God perform great signs in Egypt, but doubted He was adequate for the challenge of Canaan.

When a person has an *erring* and *disbelieving* heart, he will soon have a *hard* heart. This is a heart insensitive to the Word and work of God. So hard was the heart of Israel that the people even wanted to return to Egypt! Imagine wanting to exchange their freedom under God for slavery in Egypt!

Do you ever wish you weren't saved—that you could return to "Egypt"?

Verse for today: "I will give you a new heart and put a new spirit in you; I will remove from you your heart of stone and give you a heart of flesh" (Ezekiel 36:26).

Consider: Proverbs 4:23-27, Jeremiah 17:7-10; Matthew 5:8.

Action assignment: Think of something good you should do today, but do not really like to do—such as witnessing to a neighbor or colleague, cleaning the toilets, or visiting a sick friend. Ask Jesus to join you in the task, and do it with joy.

29

DESIRE THE BALANCED LIFE

It is important that we grow in a balanced way. The human body grows in a balanced way with the various parts functioning properly; likewise, the "spiritual man" must grow in a balanced way. We must grow in grace and knowledge, for example. We must keep a balance between worship and service, between faith and works.

A balanced diet of the whole Word of God helps us maintain a balanced life. The Holy Spirit empowers and enables us to keep things in balance. Before Peter was filled with the Spirit, he was repeatedly going to extremes. He would bear witness to Christ one minute and then try to argue with the Lord the next! (Matthew 16:13-23) He refused to allow Jesus to wash his feet, then wanted to be washed all over! (John 13:6-10) He promised to defend the Lord and even die with Him, yet he did not have the courage to *own* the Lord before a little servant girl! But when he was filled with the Spirit, Peter began to live a balanced life that avoided impulsive extremes.

What is the result of spiritual growth? Glory to God! "To Him be glory both now and forever." We glorify Jesus Christ when we keep ourselves separated from sin and error. It glorifies Him when we grow in grace and knowledge, for then we become more like Him.

Verse for today: "Grow in the grace and knowledge of our Lord and Saviour Jesus Christ. To Him be glory both now and forever!" (2 Peter 3:18, NIV)

Also read: Ephesians 2:19-22; 4:15.

Action assignment: How would you evaluate your spiritual diet? Is it helping you grow, or are there adjustments that need to be made? Talk it over with the Lord.

March

Be Renewed:

"[God] giveth power to the faint; and to them that have no might He increaseth strength."

Isaiah 40:29

1

THE BEST INVESTMENT

What is it that tempts people into unfaithfulness and dishonesty? The Lord stated that they want the praises of men instead of the approval of God. These words of Jesus are really convicting: "That which is highly esteemed among men is abomination in the sight of God" (Luke 16:15). Does this mean that it is a sin for a Christian to be rich? Of course not! Abraham and Job were wealthy men, yet God approved of them. But it is a sin for a Christian to *measure his worth* by riches. This explains why the Pharisees laughed at Jesus. They were covetous of riches and even used their religion to acquire riches from innocent people.

I wonder what our Lord would say about the present-day philosophy that says, "If you are a dedicated Christian, God will give you the very best! There is no reason why you shouldn't live in the best house, drive the best car, and make the best salary." Such blessings are not necessarily a proof of dedication and devotion. Throughout Bible history and church history many outstanding people were poor.

Money is a marvelous servant, but a terrible master. A person should use what he has in Christ's service.

Verse for today: "He that is faithful in that which is least is faithful also in much: and he that is unjust in the least is unjust also in much" (Luke 16:10).

Also read: Matthew 23:13-22; 1 Peter 4:10; Titus 1:7; 1 Corinthians 4:1-2,7.

Action assignment: In Luke 16:1-15 read the Parable of the Unjust Steward. When the Lord provides you with some extra money, what is your first response? Does being a faithful steward involve anything besides use of money? What about time and talent? Check out a good book from your church library on the subject of stewardship and let God speak to you through it.

WHAT'S THE ATTRACTION?

What is there about legalism that can so fascinate the Christian that he will turn from grace to law? For one thing, legalism appeals to the flesh. The flesh loves to be "religious"—to obey laws, to observe holy occasions, even to fast. Certainly there is nothing wrong with obedience, fasting, or solemn times of spiritual worship, *provided the Holy Spirit does the motivating and the empowering.* The flesh loves to boast about its religious achievements—how many prayers were offered, or how many gifts were given.

The person who depends on religious achievements can measure himself and compare himself with others. This is another fascination to legalism. But the true believer measures himself against Christ, not other Christians. There is no room for pride in the spiritual walk of the Christian who lives by grace, but the legalist constantly boasts about his achievements and his converts (Galatians 6:13-14).

Yes, there is a fascination to the Law, but it is only bait that leads to a trap; once the believer takes the bait, he finds himself in bondage. Far better to take God at His Word and rest on His grace. We were saved "by grace, through faith" and we must live "by grace, through faith." This is the way to blessing. The other way is the way to bondage.

Today's verse: "Through Him [Jesus] everyone who believes is justified from everything you could not be justified from by the Law of Moses" (Acts 13:39, NIV).

Also read: Romans 3:20-31; Galatians 4:9-11; 6:13-14; Ephesians 2:8-9; Colossians 2:20-23.

Action assignment: Make up lists with these headings: "Works I Can Boast About" and "Work that Christ Has Done for Me." How many items can you write in each column? Thank God that you do not have to justify yourself, and that you are justified through Christ.

3

GOD LOOKS AT THE HEART

To the Jews, the Gentiles were "uncircumcised dogs." The tragedy is that the Jews depended on this physical mark instead of the spiritual reality it represented (Deuteronomy 10:16; Jeremiah 9:26; Ezekial 44:9). A true Jew is one who has had an *inward* spiritual experience in the heart, and not merely an outward physical operation. People today make this same mistake with reference to baptism or the Lord's Supper, or even church membership.

God judges according to "the secrets of the heart"; He is not impressed with mere outward formalities. An obedient Gentile with no circumcision would be more acceptable than a disobedient Jew *with* circumcision. In fact, a disobedient Jew turned his circumcision into *un*circumcision in God's sight, for God looks at the heart. The Jews praised each other for their obedience to the Law, but the important thing is the "praise of God" and not the praise of men. When you recall that the name "Jew" comes from "Judah" which means "praise," this statement takes on new meaning.

The Bible says: "But the Lord said unto Samuel, 'Look not on his countenance, or on the height of his stature: because I have refused Him: for the Lord seeth not as man seeth: for man looketh on the outward appearance, but the Lord looketh on the heart" (1 Samuel 16:7).

Also consider: Deuteronomy 10:16; Jeremiah 9:26; Romans 2:16; 2 Corinthians 10:7; Genesis 29:35; 49:8; John 12:43.

Action assignment: Take a few minutes to consider what God's X-ray vision detects in your heart today. Confess your desire for *His* praise, rather than the praise of people.

GOD GIVES US POWER

By nature, none of us enjoys suffering. Even our Lord prayed, "Father, if Thou be willing, remove this cup from Me" (Luke 22:42). Paul prayed three times for God to remove his painful thorn in the flesh (2 Corinthians 12:7-8). But suffering is part of a faithful Christian life. Christians should not find themselves suffering because they have done wrong (1 Peter 2:20; 3:17); rather, they will sometimes suffer because they have done right and served God. When we suffer for doing good, we share Christ's sufferings (Philippians 3:10).

Years ago I read about a Christian who was in prison because of his faith. He was to be burned at the stake, and was certain he would never be able to endure the suffering. One night he experimented with pain by putting his little finger into a candle flame. It hurt, and he immediately withdrew it. "I will disgrace my Lord," he said to himself. "I cannot bear the pain." But when the hour came for him to die, he praised God and gave a noble witness for Jesus Christ. God gave him the power when he needed it, and not before.

Claim this for yourself: "God did not give us a spirit of timidity, but a spirit of power, of love and of self-discipline" (2 Timothy 1:7, NIV).

Look up and read each of the Bible verses listed in today's reading.

Action assignment: The power God has given us is the Holy Spirit Himself. Begin to rely on this divine power, and more and more quit doing things in your own power. Ask God to give you a greater understanding of this truth.

5

A BALANCED BODY

Each believer has a different gift or gifts, and God has bestowed these gifts so that the local body of Christ can grow in a balanced way. But Christians must exercise gifts by faith. We may not see the results of our ministries, but the Lord sees and He blesses. "Exhortation" (encouragement) is just as much a spiritual ministry as preaching or teaching. Giving and showing mercy are also important gifts. To some people, God has given the ability to rule, or to administer functions of the church. Whatever gifts we have must be dedicated to God and used for the good of the whole church.

It is tragic when any one gift is emphasized in a local church beyond all the other gifts. "Are all apostles? Are all prophets? Are all teachers? Do all work miracles? Do all have gifts of healing? Do all speak in tongues? Do all interpret?" (1 Corinthians 12:29-30) The answer to all these questions is no! For a Christian to minimize other gifts while he emphasizes his own is to deny the very purpose for which gifts are given: the benefit of the whole body of Christ.

Verse for today: "Now to each one the manifestation of the Spirit is given for the common good" (1 Corinthians 12:7, NIV).

Also read: 1 Corinthians 12:4-11; 29-30; Galatians 5:22-23; Philippians 2:1-4.

Action assignment: Are you contributing to your local body's growth? Be honest with yourself in your evaluation. Then pray for God's Spirit to give you the faith and knowledge you need to recognize your gift(s). Make definite plans to exercise your gift(s) for His glory and the good of the body. Otherwise your gifts may atrophy.

6

WHERE IS THE BURDEN?

It's difficult today to find people who are truly burdened about the sins of the nations and the sins of the church. Too many are like the rulers of Samaria or the members of the church of Laodicea, closing their eyes to reality and living on fantasy based on false theology. How many believers can honestly say, "Indignation has taken hold of me because of the wicked, who forsake Your law"? (Ps. 119:53). Or, "Rivers of water run down from my eyes, because men do not keep Your Law"? (v. 136). Too many Christians are laughing when they should be weeping (James 4:8–10) and tolerating sin when they should be opposing it (1 Cor. 5:2).

Dr. Vance Havner told of having dinner in an expensive restaurant with some friends, where he discovered that the dining room was dimly lighted. At first, he could scarcely read the menu, but then he found he could see fairly well. He said to his friends, "Isn't it strange how easy it is to become accustomed to the dark?" That's one of the problems in the church today: we've grown accustomed to the darkness, and our lights aren't shining brightly enough.

Verse for today: "You say, 'I am rich; I have acquired wealth and do not need a thing.' But you do not realize that you are wretched, pitiful, poor, blind and naked" (Rev. 3:17, NIV).

Read: Amos 6

Action Assignment: Start today by asking Jesus to help you be a light in your world. Sing the chorus "This Little Light of Mine" and really mean it.

7

THE GREAT SYMPATHIZER

When Charles Haddon Spurgeon was a young preacher in London, his successful ministry aroused the envy of some clergymen who attacked him through slander and gossip. His sermons were labeled "trashy," and he was called "an actor" and "a pulpit buffoon." Even after his ministry was established, Spurgeon was lied about in the press (including the *religious* press).

After one particularly nasty article in the press, Spurgeon fell before the Lord and prayed, "O Lord Jesus, Thou didst make Thyself of no reputation for me. I willingly lay my reputation down for Thy sake." From that time on, Spurgeon had peace in his heart. He knew that his Great High Priest understood his need and would give him the grace that he needed for each hour.

No matter what trials we meet, Jesus Christ is able to understand our needs and help us. We need never doubt His ability to sympathize and strengthen. Sometimes God puts *us* through difficulties that we might better understand the needs of others and become able to encourage them.

Verse for today: "For we do not have a high priest who is unable to sympathize with our weaknesses, but we have One who has been tempted in every way, just as we are—yet was without sin" (Hebrews 4:15, NIV).

For further reading: Job 22:29; Romans 12:15; 2 Corinthians 1:4, 8.

Action assignment: Think about two or three people you know who are sick or are experiencing personal tragedy of some kind. How can you show loving concern to these people? Make a point of calling them on the phone, writing them a note, or bringing them a gift of food or reading matter. Put your concern into action, praying for guidance as you minister to them in Jesus' name.

HOW TO SEEK THE LORD

What does it mean to "seek the Lord"? The Prophet Isaiah answers the question: "Seek the LORD while He may be found, call upon Him while He is near. Let the wicked forsake his way, and the unrighteous man his thoughts; let him return to the LORD, and He will have mercy on him; and to our God, for He will abundantly pardon" (Isa. 55:6–7).

To seek the Lord means first of all to change our thinking and abandon the vain thoughts that are directing our wayward lives. Disobedient children of God are thinking wrongly about God, sin, and life. They think God will always be there for them to turn to, but He may abandon them to their sins. They think they can sin and get away with it, but they forget that sinners reap what they sow. To walk "in the counsel of the ungodly" is folly indeed (Ps. 1:1), for it leads to a fruitless and joyless life.

When we return to the Lord, we also change direction: we "turn around" and start to move in the right direction. It means forsaking sin and turning to the Lord for mercy and pardon. Until we realize how heinous our sins are in the sight of God, we will never repent and cry out for mercy. To seek the Lord doesn't mean simply to run to God for help when our sins get us into trouble, although God will receive us if we're sincere. It means to loathe and despise the sin in our lives, turn from it, and seek the fellowship of God and His cleansing. "A broken and a contrite heart—these, O God, You will not despise" (Ps. 51:17).

James writes: "Come near to God and He will come near to you. Wash your hands, you sinners, and purify your hearts, you doubleminded" (James 4:8, NIV).

Read: James 4:8–10; Ezra 9:4–14

Action assignment: Talk to the Lord and tell Him you want Him to be in complete control of your life. Ask Him to show you any sin in your life that you need to confess and forsake.

MAKING THE BEST USE OF TIME

If you want to make the best use of "the rest of your time," live in the light of the return of Jesus Christ. All Christians may not agree on the details of the event, but we can agree on the demands of the experience. We shall someday actually stand before the Lord!

If we are sober-minded, we will "watch unto prayer." The word *watch* carries with it the idea of alertness and self-control. It is the opposite of being drunk or asleep. This admonition had special meaning to Peter, because he went to sleep when he should have been "watching unto prayer."

You find the phrase *watch and pray* often in the *King James Version* of the New Testament. It simply means to "be alert in our praying, to be controlled." There is no place in the Christian life for lazy, listless, routine praying. We must have an alert attitude and be on guard, just as the workers in Nehemiah's day were.

An expectant attitude toward Christ's return involves a serious, balanced mind and an alert, awake prayer life. The test of our commitment to the doctrine of Christ's return is not our ability to draw charts or discern signs, but is in our thinking and praying. If our thinking and praying are right, our living should be right.

Verse for today: "Let us not sleep, as do others; but let us watch and be sober" (1 Thessalonians 5:6).

Other Scripture: 1 Thessalonians 5:1-24; Mark 14:37-40; Ephesians 6:18.

Action assignment: Prepare a reminder that says, "Perhaps Today." Place it where you will frequently see it. Thank the Lord that someday He will return.

RICHES GALORE!

God's Word teaches that when we were unsaved, we owed God a debt we could not pay. Jesus makes this clear in His Parable of the Two Debtors in the Gospel of Luke. Two men owed money to a creditor, the one owing ten times as much as the other. But neither was able to pay, so the creditor "graciously forgave them both" (literal translation). No matter how much morality a man may have, he still comes short of the glory of God. Even if his sin debt is one-tenth that of others, he stands unable to pay, bankrupt at the judgment bar of God. God in His grace, because of the work of Christ on the cross, is able to forgive sinners, no matter how large their debt may be.

Thus when we trust Christ, *we become spiritually rich.* We now share in the riches of God's grace (Ephesians 1:7), the riches of His glory (Ephesians 1:18; Philippians 4:19), the riches of His wisdom (Romans 11:33), and the "unsearchable riches of Christ" (Ephesians 3:8). In Christ we have "all the treasures of wisdom and knowledge" (Colossians 2:3), and we are "complete in Him" (Colossians 2:10). Once a person is "in Christ," he has all he needs to live the kind of Christian life God wants him to live.

Verse for today: "The Spirit Himself testifies with our spirit that we are God's children. Now if we are children, then we are heirs—heirs of God and coheirs with Christ" (Romans 8:16-17, NIV).

Also read: Go back to the reading and look up the verses listed in the second paragraph.

Action assignment: From memory jot down on a piece of paper the riches mentioned above—plus any others you can think of. Keep the list handy and read it from time to time until you have it well in mind. Thank God for making you a joint heir with Christ.

HOW WILL YOU FARE?

As we live and work here on earth, it is relatively easy for us to hide things and pretend. But the true character of our works will ultimately be exposed at the Judgment Seat of Christ. He will reveal whether our works have been good or bad. The character of our service will be revealed as well as the motives that impelled us.

For those of us who have been faithful, it will be a time of rejoicing as we glorify the Lord by giving our rewards back to Him in worship and praise.

It behooves every Christian to examine his own life regularly to see if he is ready for the Judgment Seat of Christ. You will want to give a good account before Christ, so live today with that thought in mind.

From God's Word: "Every man shall receive his own reward according to his own labor.... Every man's work shall be made manifest: for the day shall declare it, because it shall be revealed by fire; and the fire shall try every man's work of what sort it is" (1 Corinthians 3:8, 13).

For further study: John 5:24; Romans 8:1; Revelation 20:11; 1 Corinthians 3:10-15, 4:1-5.

Action assignment: Consider what a great blessing it is to know that you won't be condemned for your sins. Talk to God and thank Him for that fact. What are the things in your life that Christ will reward you for? What are the things you can do today that Christ could count as "good works"?

NO LONGER A PHONY

A group of church members were discussing their new pastor.

"For some reason," said one man, "I really don't feel at ease with him. I believe he's a good man, all right—but something seems to stand between us."

Another member replied, "Yes, I think I know what you mean. I used to have that problem, but now I don't. The pastor and I have great fellowship."

"What did he do to make things better?"

"*He* didn't do anything," said the friend. "*I* did the changing. I decided to be open and honest about things, the way he is. There isn't one stain of hypocrisy in his life, and there was so much pretending in mine that we just weren't on the same wavelength. He and I both knew I was a phony. Since I've started to live an honest Christian life, *everything* is better."

One problem with dishonesty is that just keeping a record of our lies and pretenses is a full-time job! Abraham Lincoln said that if a man is going to be a liar, he'd better have a good memory. When a person uses up all his energy in *pretending*, he has nothing left for *living*, and life becomes shallow and tasteless. A person who pretends not only robs himself of reality, but keeps himself from growing; his true self is smothered under the false self.

The Scripture says: "Do not let kindness and truth leave you; bind them around your neck, write them on the tablet of your heart. So you will find favor and good repute in the sight of God and man" (Proverbs 3:3-4, NASB).

Also read: Proverbs 12:19, 22; Philippians 4:8.

Action assignment: Is there phoniness in your life? Confess it to the Lord and weed it out. Work on developing a more honest and Christlike you.

13

REMEMBER THE PROMISES

So often in the trials of life we fail to see the divine provisions God has made for us, and we forget the promises He has made to us. We open our hands to receive what we think we need instead of asking Him to open our eyes to see what we already have. The answer to most problems is close at hand, if only we have eyes to see (John 6:1–13; 21:1–6).

There are needy multitudes in the world today: wandering, weary, thirsty, blind, and giving up in despair. How we need to tell them the good news that the water of life is available and the well is not far away! (John 4:10–14; 7:37–39) God is kind and gracious to all who call on Him, because of His beloved Son, Jesus Christ.

Horatius Bonar wrote these words:

> I heard the voice of Jesus say,
> "Behold, I freely give
> The living water; thirsty one,
> Stoop down, and drink, and live."
> I came to Jesus, and I drank
> Of that life-giving stream;
> My thirst was quenched, my soul revived,
> And now I live in Him.

"If any man thirsts, let him come to Me and drink" (John 7:37). "And whoever desires, let him take the water of life freely" (Rev. 22:17).

Today's verse: "On the last and greatest day of the Feast, Jesus stood and said in a loud voice, "If anyone is thirsty, let him come to me and drink'" (John 7:37, NIV).

Read: John 6:1–13; 21:1–6

Action assignment: Do you really believe God's promises in His Word? Ask Him to help you claim a particular promise that you have read in your Bible. Ask Him to help you see the needs of others and make plans to share Christ with a needy friend.

ENGAGED!

Earnest is a fascinating word. In Paul's day it meant "the down payment to guarantee the final purchase of some commodity or piece of property." Paul used the term in writing to the Ephesian Christians: "Ye were sealed with that Holy Spirit of promise, which is the earnest of our inheritance until the redemption of the purchased possession" (Ephesians 1:13-14). Even today you will hear a real estate agent talk about "earnest money." The Holy Spirit is God's first installment to guarantee to His children that He will finish His work and eventually bring them to glory. The "redemption of the purchased possession" refers to the redemption of the body at the return of Christ (Romans 8:18-23; 1 John 3:1-3).

The word translated *earnest* also means "engagement ring." In Greece today you would find this word being used that way. And isn't an engagement ring an assurance—a guarantee—that the promises made will be kept? Our relationship to God through Christ is not simply a commercial one, but also a personal experience of love. He is the Bridegroom and His church is the bride. We know that He will come and claim His bride because He has given us His promise and His Spirit as the "engagement ring." What greater assurance could we want?

Today's Scripture: "Having believed, you were marked in Him [Christ] with a seal, the promised Holy Spirit, who is a deposit guaranteeing our inheritance until the redemption of those who are God's possession—to the praise of His glory" (Ephesians 1:13-14, NIV).

Other Scripture: Romans 8:18-23; 1 John 3:1-3; Ephesians 1:7.

Action assignment: Share the truth of this reading with someone today. If you are a woman—and especially if you are single—you might mention that you have an "engagement ring" from God.

15

THE FURNACE OF TESTING

One of the enemies of the life of faith is pride. When you win a victory, you may feel overconfident and start telling yourself that you can defeat *any* enemy at *any* time. You start depending on your past experience and your growing knowledge of the Word, instead of depending wholly on the Lord. This explains why the promise of 1 Corinthians 10:13 is preceded by the warning of verse 12: "Therefore let him who thinks he stands take heed lest he fall."

After you have won a great victory of faith, expect the enemy to attack you or the Lord to test you, or both. *This is the only way you can grow in your faith.* God uses the tough circumstances of life to build the muscles of your faith and keep you from trusting something other than His Word. *Don't try to run away from the problem.* It won't work.

When circumstances become difficult and you are in the furnace of testing, *remain where God has put you until He tells you to move.* Faith moves in the direction of peace and hope, but unbelief moves in the direction of restlessness and fear. "He that believeth shall not make haste" (Isa. 28:16, KJV). In times of testing, the important question is not, "*How* can I get out of this?" but, "*What* can I get out of this?" (See James 1:1–12.) God is at work to build your faith. God alone is in control of circumstances.

Today's verse: "These have come so that your faith of greater worth than gold, which perishes even though refined by fire may be proved genuine and may result in praise, glory and honor when Jesus Christ is revealed" (1 Peter 1:7, NIV).

Read: 1 Corinthians 10:1–13

Action assignment: Are you being tested in some way? Don't give up. Ask God to help you be patient and to get you through victoriously. Then when the pressure is off, give Him the glory. Find the song "Day by Day" and read it and sing it.

AN ETERNAL DIFFERENCE!

The great American statesman Daniel Webster was dining in Boston with a group of distinguished men, some of whom had Unitarian leanings. (The Unitarians deny the Trinity and the deity of both the Son and the Spirit.) When the subject of religion came up at the table, Webster boldly affirmed his belief in the deity of Jesus Christ and his confidence in His work of atonement.

"But, Mr. Webster," said one man, "can you comprehend how Christ could be both God and man?"

"No, sir, I cannot comprehend it," Webster replied. "If I could comprehend Him, He would be no greater than myself. I feel that I need a superhuman Saviour!"

Many false teachers argue, "But Jesus is the 'son of God' in the same way all of us are God's sons, made in the image of God! When Jesus claimed to be God's Son, He was not really claiming to be God." But when Jesus said to the Jews, "I and My Father are one," they threatened to stone Him! Why? Because He had blasphemed! "Because that Thou, being a man, makest Thyself God" (John 10:30-33). They knew what He meant when He called Himself the "Son of God" and claimed equality with God.

The Christian faith stands or falls on the doctrine of the deity of Jesus Christ. If He is only man, then He cannot save us, no matter how gifted or unique He might be. If He is not God in human flesh, then the Christian faith has no real validity. But Jesus is truly the Son of God and our faith in Him has glorious eternal implications!

Scripture for today: "This Man [Jesus], because He continueth ever, hath an unchangeable priesthood. Wherefore He is able also to save them to the uttermost that come unto God by Him, seeing He ever liveth to make intercession for them (Hebrews 7:24-25).

Additional Scripture: Colossians 1:17; 2 Timothy 1:9; Hebrews 13:8; 1 John 1:1-2.

Action assignment: Finish this sentence in as many ways as you can: "Since Jesus Christ *is* the eternal Son of God. . . ." Thank God for the fact that His Son makes an eternal difference in the lives of all who believe on Him.

MAKING IT IN A STORM

Many Christians have the mistaken idea that obedience to God's will produces "smooth sailing." But this is not true. As God's people, we are on the sea in the midst of a storm. Yet Jesus Christ is in heaven making intercession for us. He saw the disciples when they were in a storm and knew their plight (Mark 6:48), just as He sees us and knows our needs.

If you knew that Christ was in the next room, praying for you, it would give you new courage to endure the storm and do His will. He is not physically in the next room, but He is in heaven interceding for you. He sees your need, knows your fears, and is in control of the situation.

Often we feel that Jesus has deserted us when we are going through hard times. In the Psalms, David complained that God seemed far away and unconcerned. Yet he knew that God would ultimately rescue him. Even the great Apostle Paul got into a situation that was so difficult he felt "burdened excessively, beyond our strength, so that we despaired even of life" (2 Corinthians 1:8, NASB).

Jesus always comes to us in the storms of life. He may not come when we think He should, because He knows when we need Him the most.

Remember: "When thou passest through the waters, I will be with thee; and through the rivers, they shall not overflow thee: when thou walkest through the fire, thou shalt not be burned; neither shall the flame kindle upon thee (Isaiah 43:2).

Also claim these promises: Psalms 46:1; 50:15; 55:22; Isaiah 41:10.

Action assignment: Commit to memory one of the verses above. Quote it when you face a "storm." Thank the Lord for helping you through storms of the past.

FOUR KINDS OF PRAYER

First Timothy 2:1 mentions four terms related to talking to our Heavenly Father: supplications, prayers, intercessions, and giving of thanks.

Supplications carries the idea of "offering a request for a felt need."

Prayers is the commonest term for this activity, and it emphasizes the sacredness of prayer. We are praying *to God;* prayer is an act of worship, not just an expression of our wants and needs. There should be reverence in our hearts as we pray to God.

Intercessions is best translated *petitions.* This same word is translated "prayer" in 1 Timothy 4:5, where it refers to blessing the food we eat. (It is rather obvious that we do not *intercede* for our food in the usual sense of that word.) The basic meaning of the word is "to draw near to a person and converse confidently with him." It suggests that we enjoy fellowship with God so that we have confidence in Him as we pray.

Giving of thanks is definitely a part of worship and prayer. We not only give thanks for answers to prayer, but for who God is and what He does for us in His grace. We should not simply add our thanksgiving to the end of a selfish prayer! Thanksgiving should be an important ingredient throughout all of our prayers. In fact, sometimes we need to imitate David and present to God *only* thanksgiving with no petitions at all! (See Psalm 103.)

Good advice: "I exhort, therefore, that, first of all, supplications, prayers, intercessions, and giving of thanks, be made for all men" (1 Timothy 2:1).

Also: Psalm 103.

Action assignment: If you want peace in your heart, practice Philippians 4:6 today and every day!

19

HOW TO RECEIVE GOOD WAGES

If you serve a master, you can expect to receive wages. Sin pays wages—death! God also pays wages—holiness and everlasting life. In the old life, we produced fruit that made us ashamed. In the new life in Christ, we have the capacity to produce fruit that glorifies God and brings joy to our lives.

If a believer refuses to surrender his body to the Lord but uses its members for sinful purposes, then he is in danger of being disciplined by the Father, and this could mean death.

These three instructions need to be heeded each day that we live:

•*Know* that you have been crucified with Christ and are dead to sin;

•*Reckon* this fact to be true in your own life;

•*Yield* your body to the Lord to be used for His glory.

Now that you *know* these truths, *reckon* them to be true in *your* life—and then *yield* yourself to God.

Verse for today: "Do not be deceived: God cannot be mocked. A man reaps what he sows" (Galatians 6:7, NIV).

Also consider: Romans 6:1-10; Galatians 6:8-10; 1 John 5:17; 1 Corinthians 11:30.

Action assignment: Write the words *know, reckon,* and *yield* on separate lines on a piece of paper. Then write a statement opposite each that applies to you. Ask God to give you a clearer grasp of these terms and how they relate to your own life.

THE BROKEN WALL

There's a "broken wall" concerning salvation and God's grace.
If salvation were on the basis of merit, it would not be by grace. Grace implies God's sovereign choice of those who cannot earn and do not deserve His salvation (Ephesians 1:4-7 and 2:8-10). God saves us completely on the basis of the work of Christ, not because of anything we are or have.

The doctrine of God's grace, if we really believe it, forces us to relate to people on the basis of God's plan—not on the basis of human merit or social status. A "class church" is not a church that magnifies the grace of God. When He died, Jesus broke down the wall that separated Jews and Gentiles. In His birth and life, He broke down the walls between rich and poor, young and old, educated and uneducated. It is wrong for us to build those walls again; we cannot rebuild them if we believe in the grace of God.

Remember: "If you really keep the royal law found in Scripture, 'Love your neighbor as yourself,' you are doing right. But if you show favoritism, you sin and are convicted by the law as law-breakers" (James 2:8-9, NIV).

Other references: Romans 3:23-24; Ephesians 1:7; 2:11-22; Titus 3:7.

Action assignment: Are there any walls between you and others? If so, picture those walls; then picture Christ breaking them down. Thank God for His salvation by grace through faith, and for His power to break down walls.

WHAT DOES IT MEAN TO CONFESS?

A counselor was trying to help a man who had come forward during an evangelistic meeting. "I'm a Christian," the man said, "but there's sin in my life, and I need help." The counselor showed him 1 John 1:9 and suggested that the man confess his sins to God.

"O Father," the man began, "if we have done anything wrong—"

"Just a minute!" the counselor interrupted. "Don't drag *me* into your sin! Brother, it's not 'if' or 'we'—*you'd* better get down to business with God!"

The counselor was right.

Confession is not praying a lovely prayer, making pious excuses, or trying to impress God and other Christians. True confession is naming sin—calling it by name what God calls it: envy, hatred, lust, deceit, or whatever it may be. Confession simply means being honest with ourselves and with God, and if others are involved, being honest with them too. It is more than *admitting* sin. It means *judging* sin and facing it squarely.

When we confess our sins, God promises to forgive us. But this promise is not a "magic rabbit's foot" that makes it easy for us to disobey God!

The Bible commands: "Draw nigh to God, and He will draw nigh to you. Cleanse your hands, ye sinners; and purify your hearts, ye double minded. Be afflicted, and mourn, and weep: let your laughter be turned to mourning, and your joy to heaviness. Humble yourselves in the sight of the Lord, and He shall lift you up" (James 4:8-10).

Also read: Job 33:27-28; Isaiah 55:6-7; Revelation 3:19.

Action assignment: Think of three specific sins that God condemns, yet the world does not always consider wrong (gossip, for example). Try to see these sins through God's eyes and make a conscious effort to avoid them.

THE KINGDOM OF GOD

Many people have the idea that God is not reigning today—that Satan is in charge of things, and God will not rule until Jesus returns. I have heard sincere teachers say, "In the past, Jesus was the Prophet. Today in heaven, He is the Priest. When He returns, He will be the King." But this is not Bible doctrine.

There is a conflict in the world between the kingdom of God and the kingdom of Satan. When a sinner trusts Christ, he is delivered "from the power of darkness" and is "translated" into the kingdom of God's dear Son. The kingdom of darkness tries desperately to overcome the kingdom of light, but God is the victor. Christ completely vanquished Satan and his hosts when He died on the cross and rose again. As children in God's family, and subjects in God's kingdom, we share in that victory!

It is worth noting that the kingdom idea is a very important one. As Christians, we are prone to forget the kingship of our God, since we emphasize the fatherhood of God and the fact that Jesus is the Saviour. But He is King! Our Father is King!

Verse for today: "They shall speak of the glory of Thy kingdom and talk of Thy power; to make known to the sons of men His mighty acts, and the glorious majesty of His kingdom. Thy kingdom is an everlasting kingdom, and Thy dominion endureth throughout all generations" (Psalm 145:11-13).

Also read: Colossians 1:13; 2:14-15; Matthew 5:3-10; 6:10; 13:11-53; Luke 8:1; 23:50-51; Acts 1:3; 1 Corinthians 4:20; Ephesians 5:5; Revelation 11:15; 12:10.

Action assignment: In your relationship to God, do you often think of Him as a king? How do you relate to a king? Americans can relate to a president, but have no experience relating to kings. Ask God to show you how your relationship to Him will be enhanced as you view Him as your king. List the qualities that a loyal subject should maintain at all times, and subject yourself to the King of kings in a way you hadn't considered before.

23

SAVING FAITH

In the pilgrim life, you must go "from faith to faith" (Rom. 1:17) if you would go "from strength to strength" (Ps. 84:7). G. A. Studdert Kennedy said, "Faith is not believing in spite of evidence; it is obeying in spite of consequence." "By faith Abraham . . . obeyed" (Heb. 11:8). Faith without obedience is dead (James 2:14–26), and action without faith is sin (Rom. 14:23). God has wedded faith and obedience; like the two sides of a coin they go together.

This does not mean that sinners are saved by faith *plus* works, because Scripture declares that sinners are saved by faith alone (John 3:16–18; Eph. 2:8–9). Dr. H. A. Ironside, longtime pastor of Chicago's Moody Church, was told by a lady that she expected to get to heaven by faith plus her good works. "It's like rowing a boat," she explained. "It takes two oars to row a boat; otherwise you go around in a circle." Dr. Ironside replied, "That's a good illustration except for one thing: *I'm not going to heaven in a rowboat!*"

The faith that saves is the faith that proves itself in good works (Eph. 2:8–10; Titus 2:14; 3:8, 14). Abraham was saved by faith (Gen. 15:6; Rom. 4:1–5; Heb. 11:8), but his faith was made evident by his obedience (James 2:21–24).

Today's verse: "That is why I am suffering as I am. Yet I am not ashamed, because I know whom I have believed, and am convinced that He is able to guard what I have entrusted to Him for that day" (2 Tim. 1:12, NIV).

Read: Hebrews 11

Action assignment: Thank the Lord that by His grace He has saved you, that your salvation does not depend on your good works. But tell Him also that you believe in good works and to direct you today to be a blessing to someone through something that you can do.

THE RIGHTEOUS JUDGE

If God saved people only on the basis of their righteousness, nobody would ever be saved. God's mercy and compassion are extended according to God's will, not man's. All of us deserve condemnation—not mercy.

To illustrate these points in Romans 9:15, Paul quotes Exodus 33:19, which describes Israel's idolatry while Moses was on the mountain receiving the Law. The whole nation deserved to be destroyed, yet God killed only 3,000 people—not because the others were less wicked or less godly, but purely because of his grace and mercy.

Still, Paul asked, "Is there unrighteousness with God?" Then he replied, "God forbid!" (Romans 9:14) It is unthinkable that a holy God should ever commit an unrighteous act. God is sovereign in His work and acts according to His own will and purposes. The righteous Judge of this world does right.

Verse for today: "He is the rock, His works are perfect, and all His ways are just" (Deuteronomy 32:4, NIV).

More to consider: Romans 9:14-18; Exodus 9:16; 33; Job 37:23-24; Matthew 20:1-16; Isaiah 45:9-13.

Action assignment: Both God's love and His fairness are above our understanding. Still, we must be honest with our attitudes and feelings. Think of one instance in which God seemed unfair to you; then take a few minutes to pray earnestly for understanding. However weakly you understand His ways, express to God your trust in His wisdom by repeating a pledge like this: "I trust God's fairness beyond my own limited wisdom and knowledge. Amen."

COMFORT FOR THE HURTING

Dr. George W. Truett, who pastored the First Baptist Church of Dallas, Texas for nearly fifty years, told about an unbelieving couple whose baby died suddenly. Dr. Truett conducted the funeral and later had the joy of seeing them both trust Jesus Christ.

Many months later, a young mother lost her baby; again Dr. Truett was called to bring her comfort. But nothing he shared with her seemed to help. Then at the funeral service, the newly converted mother stepped to the girl's side and said, "I passed through this, and I know what you are passing through. God called me, and through the darkness I came to Him. He has comforted me, and He will comfort you!"

Dr. Truett said, "The first mother did more for the second mother than I could have done, maybe in days and months; for the first young mother had traveled the road of suffering herself." If we have experienced tribulations, they can help us identify with other sufferers and know better how they feel. We do not need to experience *exactly* the same trials in order to be able to share God's encouragement; but if we have known God's comfort, we can "comfort them which are in any trouble" (2 Corinthians 1:4).

Verse to Remember: "Praise be to the God and Father of our Lord Jesus Christ, the Father of compassion and the God of all comfort, who comforts us in all our troubles, so that we can comfort those in any trouble with the comfort we ourselves have received from God" (2 Corinthians 1:3-4, NIV).

Other verses: Psalm 140:12; 2 Corinthians 7:6; Galatians 6:2.

Action assignment: Recall two or three difficult experiences you have had. Consider how they have prepared you to minister to others. Ask God to enable you to help people who are going through similar experiences.

"LIGHT"-FOOTED

Walking in the light involves honesty, obedience, and love. That means following the example of Christ, walking as He walked when here on earth—and as He does right now in Heaven.

This has extremely practical applications in our daily lives. For example, what should a believer do when another believer sins against him? He should forgive, just as God for Christ's sake has forgiven them both.

Walking in the light—following the example of Christ—will also affect a home. Husbands are supposed to love and care for their wives, who, in turn, are to honor and obey their husbands.

In every area of life our responsibility is to do what Jesus would do. He is truly the one great example of the kind of life we should live.

Verse for today: "He that doeth righteousness is righteous, even as He is righteous" (1 John 3:7).

Also read: 1 John 1:5-8; 2:6; 3:3; 4:11; Ephesians 4:32; 5:1-2, 21-30; Colossians 3:13.

Action assignment: Rate the "health" of the following areas in your life, using a scale of 1 to 10, with 10 as "great":
- work
- church
- personal relationships
- marriage
- home and family life

Are the weaker areas (rated under 5) weak because you are not "walking in the light"—following Christ's example of honesty, obedience, and love? Do one thing today to reflect Christ's light in each weak area. Ask God to help you fully walk "in a manner worthy of the Gospel."

THE LIFE OF FAITH

First steps of faith are not always giant steps, which explains why Abraham did not fully obey God. Instead of leaving his family, as he was commanded, Abraham took his father and his nephew Lot with him when he left Ur; and then he stayed at Haran until his father died.

Whatever you bring with you from the old life into the new is likely to create problems. Terah, Abraham's father, kept Abraham from fully obeying the Lord; and Lot created serious problems for Abraham until they finally had to agree to part. Abraham and Sarah brought a sinful agreement with them from Ur (Gen. 20:13), and it got them into trouble twice (12:1–20; 20:1–18).

The life of faith demands total separation *from* what is evil and total devotion *to* what is holy (2 Cor. 6:14–7:1). As you study the life of Abraham, you discover that he was often tempted to compromise; and occasionally he yielded. God tests us in order to build our faith and bring out the best in us, but the devil tempts us in order to destroy our faith and bring out the worst in us.

When you walk by faith, you lean on God alone: His Word, His character, His will, and His power. You don't isolate yourself from your family and friends, but you no longer consider them your first love or your first obligation (Luke 14:25–27). Your love for God is so strong that it makes family love look like hatred in comparison! God calls us "alone" (Isa. 51:1–2), and we must not compromise.

Today's verse: "I have been crucified with Christ and I no longer live, but Christ lives in me. The life I live in the body, I live by faith in the Son of God, who loved me and gave Himself for me" (Gal. 2:20, NIV).

Read: Luke 14:25–27; 2 Corinthians 6:14–7:1

Action assignment: Perhaps God is calling you to serve Him in some special way but you feel inadequate. By faith, look to God to guide you. Or if you can step right into it, just do it—by faith.

WHAT ABOUT COMPETITION?

A man should "prove his own work," Paul wrote in Galatians 6:4, and it should be proved in the light of God's will and not in the shadows of somebody else's achievements. There is no place for competition in the work of God, unless we are competing against sin and Satan. When we see words like "best, fastest-growing, biggest, finest" applied to Christian ministries, we wonder who is getting the glory.

This does not mean that it is wrong to keep records. Charles Haddon Spurgeon used to say, "Those who criticize statistics usually have none to report." But we must be careful that we are not making others look bad just to make ourselves look good. And we should be able to rejoice at the achievements and blessings of others just as if they were our own. After all, if one member of the body is blessed, it blesses the whole body.

Verse to Remember: "Each one should test his own actions. Then he can take pride in himself, without comparing himself to somebody else, for each one should carry his own load" (Galatians 6:4-5, NIV).

Also consider: Psalm 133:1; Colossians 3:12-14; Galatians 5:13, 22, 26; 1 Thessalonians 4:9; 1 Peter 3:8.

Action assignment: Think about competition in its various forms—as you see it in others, as you see it in yourself. Determine whether you are letting competition turn you into an unloving person. Ask God to help you do all things in a way that pleases Him.

LET'S DEMONSTRATE THE FAITH

When my wife and I visited the Tower of London and saw the royal jewels, we noticed that the crowd was kept moving—and the guards stood still. They were constantly watching the visitors; nothing could move them from their appointed places. Similarly, you and I are helping to guard the "precious faith," and we must not be moved by the wiles of Satan nor the praises of men.

Too many Christians today emphasize *guarding* the truth, but downplay *living* the truth. One of the best ways to guard the truth is to put it into practice. It is good to be defenders of the faith, but we must not forget to be demonstrators of the faith. Lazarus did not have to give lectures on the resurrection. People had only to look at him and they believed. It is not enough to believe the truth and guard it; we must also practice it. If we hear the Word, but do not obey it, we are only fooling ourselves.

Today's verse: "Be ye doers of the Word, and not hearers only, deceiving your own selves" (James 1:22).

Also: James 1:23-27; 1 John 3:21-22, 24; 5:2-4.

Action assignment: Ask God to help you list five ways you can show your faith through obedience to His Word. List them here:

1._____

2._____

3._____

4._____

5._____

REPENTANCE: MORE THAN REGRET

Paul had written the Corinthians a stern message (2 Corinthians 7:8-9), and then had regretted it. But the letter achieved its purpose and the Corinthians repented, and this made Paul rejoice. Their repentance was not merely a passing regret; it was a true, godly sorrow for sin. The difference is seen in Judas and Peter. Judas "repented himself" (was full of regret) and went out and committed suicide; Peter wept and repented of his fall.

Do Christians need to repent? Jesus said that we do, and Paul agreed with Him. Four of the seven churches of Asia Minor, listed in Revelation 2-3, were commanded to repent. To repent simply means "to change one's mind"; disobedient Christians need to repent, not in order to be saved, but in order to restore their close fellowship with God.

Today's verse: "Godly sorrow brings repentance that leads to salvation and leaves no regret, but worldly sorrow brings death" (1 Corinthians 7:10, NIV).

Also: Matthew 26:75, 27:5; Luke 17:3-4; 2 Corinthians 12:21.

Action assignment: Spend a minute or two considering the difference between merely being sorry and truly repenting. Talk with God and ask Him to help you detect times when you need to repent to restore close fellowship with Him.

TWO APPROACHES TO LIFE

Today the cross is an accepted symbol of love and sacrifice. But in Jesus' day the cross was a horrible means of capital punishment. The Romans would not mention the cross in polite society. In fact, no Roman citizen could be crucified; this terrible death was reserved for Rome's enemies.

Jesus stated that He would be crucified (Matthew 20:17-19). Many of His teachings emphasized the cross. He presented to His disciples two approaches to life:

- deny yourself or live for yourself;
- take up your cross or ignore the Cross;
- follow Christ or follow the world;
- lose your life for His sake or save your life for your own sake;
- forsake the world or gain the world;
- keep your soul or lose your soul;
- share His reward and glory or lose His reward and glory.

To deny self does not mean to deny *things*. It means to give yourself wholly to Christ and share in His shame and death. To take up a cross does not mean to carry burdens or have problems. I once met a lady who told me her asthma was the cross she had to bear! To take up the cross means to identify with Christ in His rejection, shame, suffering, and death.

A challenge: "And He said to them all, 'if any man will come after Me, let him deny himself, and take up his cross daily, and follow Me' " (Luke 9:23).

Consider also: Romans 12:2; Philippians 3:7-10; Galatians 2:20.

Action assignment: If you haven't made a forthright commitment as outlined in Romans 12:1-2, perhaps this is the time to do it.

April

Be Renewed:

"Put on the whole armor of God,
that ye may be able to stand against
the wiles of the devil."

Ephesians 6:11

1

GOD'S CALL

"The God of glory appeared unto our father Abraham" (Acts 7:2). How God appeared to Abraham, we are not told; but it was the first of seven communications to Abraham recorded in Genesis. The revelation of God's glory would have shown Abraham the vanity and folly of the idol worship in Ur. Who wants to worship a dead idol when he has met the living God! First Thessalonians 1:9–10 and 2 Corinthians 4:6 describe this salvation experience.

But God also *spoke* to Abraham (Gen. 12:1–3), and the Word brought about the miracle of faith. "So then faith cometh by hearing, and hearing by the word of God" (Rom. 10:17, KJV). It was a call to separate himself from the corruption around him, and Abraham obeyed by faith (Heb. 11:8). True faith is based on the Word of God and leads to obedience. God could not bless and use Abraham and Sarah unless they were in the place of His appointment (2 Cor. 6:14–7:1).

Lost sinners today are not likely to receive a special revelation of God's glory as did Abraham and Sarah. But they can see His glory in the lives of His people (Matt. 5:16) and hear His Word of faith when they *share* their witness. God spoke to Abraham directly, but today we hear the truth of salvation through the witness of His people (Acts 1:8).

Christ's promise: "You will receive power when the Holy Spirit comes on you; and you will be My witnesses in Jerusalem, and in all Judea and Samaria, and to the ends of the earth" (Acts 1:8, NIV).

Read: Genesis 12:1–5; 1 Thessalonians 1:9–10

Action assignment: Perhaps God is calling you to separate yourself from some corrupting thing or influence, as He called Abraham to do. By faith, journey with God away from it. Whatever, talk to God and tell him you want to be obedient to Him in your daily walk.

2

GOD WRITES THE FINAL CHAPTER

We must not conclude that every trial will end with all problems solved, all hard feelings forgiven, and everybody "living happily ever after." It just doesn't always happen that way!

No matter what happens to us, *God always writes the last chapter.* Therefore, we don't have to be afraid. We can trust God to do what is right, no matter how painful our situation might be.

Job's greatest blessing was not the regaining of his health and wealth or the rebuilding of his family and circle of friends. His greatest blessing was *knowing God better and understanding His working in a deeper way.* As James wrote, "You have heard of the perseverance of Job and seen the purpose of the Lord, that the Lord is very compassionate and merciful" (James 5:11). And Hebrews 12:11 reminds us: "Now no chastening seems to be joyful for the present, but grievous; nevertheless, afterward it yields the peaceable fruit of righteousness to those who have been trained by it."

"In the whole story of Job," wrote G. Campbell Morgan, "we see the patience of God and endurance of man. When these act in fellowship, the issue is certain. It is that of the coming forth from the fire as gold, that of receiving the crown of life" (*The Answers of Jesus to Job*, Baker, p. 117).

No matter what God permits to come into our lives, He always has His "afterword." He writes the last chapter—and that makes it worth it all.

Therefore, BE PATIENT!

Today's verse: "Therefore, since we are surrounded by such a great cloud of witnesses, let us throw off everything that hinders and the sin that so easily entangles, and let us run with perseverance the race marked out for us" (Heb. 12:1, NIV).

Read: Job 42; 1 Peter 2:19–23

Action assignment: Underline one statement in today's reading that is especially meaningful to you in regard to God writing the "final chapter."

3

DEVELOPING A PRAYER LIST

Paul instructs that Christians should pray for "all men" (1 Timothy 2:1), making it clear that no person on earth is outside the influence of believing prayer. This means we should pray for the saved and the lost, for people near us and people far away, for enemies as well as friends. Paul urged the church to especially pray for those in authority. Godless Emperor Nero was on the throne at that time, and yet the believers were supposed to pray for him! Even when we cannot respect men or women in authority, we must respect their offices and pray for them. This can lead to peace, godliness, and holiness (1 Timothy 2:2).

To be sure, Paul has not named all the persons we can and should pray for, since "all men" covers the matter fully. We can't pray for everybody in the world by name, but we certainly ought to pray for those we know and know about. Why? Because it is a good thing to do, and because it pleases God.

Verse to remember: "I urge, then, first of all, that requests, prayers, intercession and thanksgiving be made for everyone—for kings and all those in authority, that we may live peaceful and quiet lives in all godliness and holiness. This is good, and pleases God our Saviour, who wants all men to be saved and to come to a knowledge of the truth" (1 Timothy 2:1-4, NIV).

Other Scripture: Daniel 9:3-19; Ephesians 1:15-19; 1 Thessalonians 3:10, 12-13.

Action assignment: Think about the people you should pray for—some daily, others less often. A prayer list for each day may help. Make it a habit to keep your list(s) handy and add names as God leads.

OUR SOURCE OF POWER

Anointing oil speaks of the presence and the working of the Holy Spirit in our lives. All believers have received the anointing of the Spirit (1 John 2:20, 27), and therefore we ought to be "a fragrance of Christ" to the Heavenly Father (2 Cor. 2:15). The more we are like Jesus Christ in character and conduct, the more we please our Father; and the more we please Him, the more He can bless and use us for His glory.

I once heard Dr. A. W. Tozer say, "If God were to take the Holy Spirit out of this world, much of what the church is doing would go right on; and nobody would know the difference." We have so much in human resources available to the church today that we manage to "serve the Lord" without the unction of the Holy Spirit working in our lives. But is that what God wants?

While here on earth, Jesus lived His life and did His work through the anointing of the Holy Spirit (Luke 4:16–19). If the spotless Son of God needed the Spirit's power, how much more do we! Do we dare pray in the energy of the flesh when the Spirit is present to assist us (Rom. 8:26; Eph. 2:18)? Do we try to witness for Christ without asking the Spirit to help us (Acts 1:8)? Can we fellowship with our Lord in His Word apart from the ministry of the Spirit of God (Eph. 1:15–23; 3:14–21)?

Today's verse: "And if the Spirit of Him who raised Jesus from the dead is living in you, He who raised Christ from the dead will also give life to your mortal bodies through his Spirit, who lives in you" (Rom. 8:11, NIV).

Read: 1 John 2:20–29; Acts 1:1–8

Action assignment: What are your answers to the three questions in the final paragraph of today's reading? Check out the Scripture referenced with each question.

5

TRAINING PERIOD

A faith that cannot be tested cannot be trusted. New believers must expect their faith to be tried, because this is the way God proves whether or not their decision is genuine. Faith, like a muscle, must be exercised to grow stronger. Tribulation and persecution are God's ways to strengthen our faith.

One of my favorite books is *Hudson Taylor's Spiritual Secret* by Dr. and Mrs. Howard Taylor. In it one reads how Hudson Taylor's faith in God grew from the first day he determined to live by faith in God alone. He learned to trust God for his salary and daily needs. As his faith was tested, he was able to trust God to supply for an entire missionary organization. Sometimes it seemed that God had forgotten, but Taylor continued to pray and trust—and God answered.

An easy life can lead to a shallow faith. The great men and women of faith in Hebrews 11 all suffered in one way or another, or faced tremendous obstacles, so that their faith could grow.

Verse for today: "My brethren, count it all joy when ye fall into divers temptations; knowing this, that the trying of our faith worketh patience" (James 1:2-3).

Also read: 1 Thessalonians 3:10; Philippians 4:19; 1 Peter 1:7.

Action assignment: Discuss with the Lord how you can exercise your faith through the challenges you face today. Thank God now for answering your prayer.

GOD'S LAST WORD

If the greatest sin is the corruption of the highest good, then Judah was guilty of great sin. Their highest good was to know the true God and worship Him, but they perverted that blessing and worshiped idols. They turned His temple into a den of thieves, persecuted His prophets, rejected His covenant, and disgraced His name. "God's name is blasphemed among the Gentiles because of you" (Rom. 2:24, NIV; see Ezek. 36:22). God patiently dealt with His people, seeking to woo them back, but they only hardened their hearts and turned deaf ears to His warnings.

Before we condemn the people of Judah, however, let's examine our own hearts and churches. Are there idols in our hearts? Do we give wholehearted devotion to the Lord, or is our devotion divided between Christ and another? When unsaved people visit our worship services, are they impressed with the glory and majesty of God (1 Cor. 14:23–25)? Do the worldly lives and questionable activities of professed believers disgrace God's name? Remember, God's "last word" to the church isn't the Great Commission; it's "Repent, or else!" (Rev. 2–3).

Isaiah challenges: "Seek the LORD while He may be found; call on Him while He is near. Let the wicked forsake his way and the evil man his thoughts. Let him turn to the LORD, and He will have mercy on him, and to our God, for He will freely pardon" (Isa. 55:6–7, NIV).

Read: Jeremiah 11

Action assignment: Think about it: Is there anything in your life that is displeasing to God? Determine now to turn from it and go to God for His pardon.

7

BROTHERLY LOVE AND BREAKFAST

The deepest kind of fellowship is not based on race or family relationship; it is based on the spiritual life we have in Christ. A church fellowship based on anything other than love for Christ and for one another simply will not last. Where there is true Christian love, there will also be *hospitality*. This was an important ministry in the early church because persecution drove many believers away from their homes. Many could not afford to stay in an inn; and since the churches met in homes, it was natural for a visitor to just stay with his host.

Moses records the story of Abraham showing generous hospitality to Jesus Christ and two of His angels. Abraham did not know who they were when he welcomed them; it was only later that he discovered the identities of his illustrious guests. You and I may not entertain angels in a literal sense, but *any* stranger could turn out to be a messenger of blessing to us. Often we have had guests in our home who have turned out to be messengers of God's blessings.

The Bible says: "Share with God's people who are in need. Practice hospitality" (Romans 12:13, NIV).

For further study: 1 Thessalonians 4:9-10; 1 Peter 1:22; 2 Peter 1:7.

Action assignment: Thank God for someone who exhibited Christian love and hospitality to you recently. Show hospitality and brotherly love to a family you know this week.

IN HIS IMAGE

"But we all, with open face beholding as in a glass the glory of the Lord, are changed into the same image from glory to glory, even as by the Spirit of the Lord" (2 Corinthians 3:18). This verse says that you and I can share the image of Jesus Christ and go "from glory to glory" through the ministry of the Spirit of God!

Under the Old Covenant, only Moses ascended the mountain and had fellowship with God; but under the New Covenant, all believers have the privilege of communion with Him. Through Jesus Christ, we may enter into the very holy of holies, and we don't have to climb a mountain!

The "mirror" is a symbol of the Word of God. As we look into God's Word and see God's Son, the Holy Spirit transforms us into the very image of God. It is important, however, that we hide nothing from God. We must be open and honest with Him and not "wear a veil."

The word translated *changed* is the same word translated *transfigured* in the accounts of our Lord's transfiguration (Matthew 17; Mark 9). It describes a change on the outside that comes from the inside.

Moses *reflected* the glory of God, but you and I may *radiate* the glory of God. When we meditate on God's Word and in it see God's Son, then the Spirit transforms us! We become more like the Lord Jesus Christ as we grow "from glory to glory." *This wonderful process cannot be achieved by keeping the Law.* The glory of the Law faded away, but the glory of God's grace continues to increase in our lives.

Verse: Meditate on 2 Corinthians 3:18 in a translation other than the *King James Version* as rendered above.

Read: Hebrews 10:19-20; James 1:22-25; Mark 9:1-8.

Action assignment: List characteristics of Jesus that you would like in your life; talk to God about your becoming more Christlike.

9

GOD'S TEMPLE—YOUR BODY

Why does the Lord want your body? To begin with, the believer's body is God's temple; God wants to use it for His glory. But Paul wrote that the body is also God's tool and God's weapon. God wants to use the members of the body as tools for building His kingdom and weapons for fighting His enemies.

The Bible tells of people who permitted God to use their bodies for the fulfilling of His purposes. God used the rod in Moses' hand and conquered Egypt. He used the sling in David's hand to defeat the Philistines. He used the mouths and tongues of the prophets. Paul's dedicated feet carried him from city to city as he proclaimed the Gospel. The Apostle John's eyes saw visions of the future, his ears heard God's message, and his fingers wrote it all down in a book we can read.

Have you given over your body for God's use?

Today's verse: "Do not offer the parts of your body to sin, as instruments of wickedness, but rather offer yourselves to God, as those who have been brought from death to life; and offer the parts of your body to Him as instruments of righteousness" (Romans 6:13, NIV).

Other Scripture: 1 Corinthians 6:19-20; Philippians 1:20-21.

Action assignment: Think of ways in which your brain, eyes, mouth, hands, and feet can be used by God. How can they be used today? Commit your body to God in a definite act.

GRACE AND GLORY

No matter how difficult the fiery trial may become, a Christian always has hope. In his first epistle, Peter gave reasons for this hopeful attitude.

• *We have God's grace.* Our salvation is because of His grace. He called us before we called on Him. We have tasted that the Lord is gracious (1 Peter 2:3), so we are not afraid of anything that He purposes for us. His grace is "manifold" and meets every challenge. As we submit to Him, He gives us the grace we need. In fact, He is "the God of all grace." He has grace to help in every time of need. "He giveth more grace" and we must stand in that grace.

• *We know we are going to glory.* He has "called us unto His eternal glory by Christ Jesus" (5:10). This is the wonderful inheritance into which we were born. Whatever begins with God's grace will always lead to God's glory. If we depend on God's grace when we suffer, that suffering will result in glory. The road may be difficult, but it leads to glory, and that is all that really counts.

Today's Scripture: "For the Lord God is a sun and shield; the Lord will give grace and glory: no good thing will He withhold from them that walk uprightly" (Psalm 84:11).

See also: Ephesians 2:8-9; 1 Peter 1:10; 4:10; 5:12.

Action assignment: Write your own psalm to the Lord, thanking Him for His grace and the glory that will be yours as a believer in Him.

11

THE REMEDY FOR IDOLS

Instead of separating themselves from the evil practices of the nations, as Moses had instructed (Deut. 7:1–11), Israel gradually imitated those practices and began to worship pagan gods. But these gods were worthless, manufactured by craftsmen, "like a scarecrow in a melon patch" (Jer. 10:5, NIV). They can't speak or walk, and they have to be carried around (see Ps. 115). If only the people would contemplate the glory and majesty of the true and living God—the everlasting God who created the heavens and the earth by the Word of His power!

In *Knowledge of the Holy* (p. 11), A. W. Tozer reminds us that "the essence of idolatry is the entertainment of thoughts about God that are unworthy of Him." It means worshiping and serving the creature rather than the Creator (Rom. 1:25), the gifts rather than the Giver. The idols were senseless, and so were the people (Jer. 10:8), because we become like the god we worship (Ps. 115:8).

Our contemporary idols aren't as ugly as the pagan idols in Jeremiah's day, but they capture just as much affection and do just as much damage. Whatever we worship and serve other than the true and living God is an idol, whether it's an expensive house or car, the latest stereo equipment, a boat, a library, a girlfriend or boyfriend, our children, a career, or a bank account. That on which I center my attention and affection and for which I am willing to sacrifice is my god, and if it isn't Jesus Christ, then it's an idol. "Little children, keep yourselves from idols" (1 John 5:21).

The remedy for idolatry is for us to get caught up in the majesty and grandeur of God, the true God, the living God, the everlasting King.

Today's Verse: "Correct me, LORD, but only with justice not in your anger, lest You reduce me to nothing" (Jer. 10:24, NIV)

Read: Jeremiah 10

Action assignment: As you pray, ask God to convict you about any idol in your life. Think of your relationship to God: Does He really have first place?

TRUE RICHES

A distraught wife sought out a Christian marriage counselor and told her sad story of a marriage about to dissolve. "But we have so much!" she kept saying, "Look at this diamond ring on my finger. Why, it's worth thousands! We have an expensive mansion in an exclusive area. We have three cars, and even a cabin in the mountains. Why, we have everything money can buy!"

The counselor replied "It's good to have the things money can buy, provided you don't lose the things money *can't* buy. What good is an expensive house if there's no home? Or an expensive ring if there's no love?"

In Christ, you and I have "the things money can't buy," and these spiritual riches open up to us all the wealth of God's vast creation. We enjoy the gifts because we know and love the Giver. It is a source of great encouragement to know that Father, Son, and Holy Spirit are all working on my behalf to make me rich. God not only gives us "richly all things to enjoy" (1 Timothy 6:17), but He gives us eternal riches without which all other wealth is valueless.

Verse for today: "Praise be to the God and Father of our Lord Jesus Christ, who has blessed us in the heavenly realms with every spiritual blessing in Christ" (Ephesians 1:3, NIV).

Also: Read all of Ephesians 1 and note the riches mentioned.

Action assignment: Make a note to obtain a copy of *Be Rich*, from which today's reading comes. Study it chapter by chapter during the coming weeks. Take time now to praise God for the spiritual blessings which He has showered on you and other believers.

13

THE MEANING OF THE RESURRECTION

We must never underestimate the importance of the resurrection of Jesus Christ. The world believes that Jesus died, but not that He arose from the dead. What is the significance of the Resurrection?

It proves that Jesus is God's Son. Jesus stated that He had authority to lay down His life and to take it up again (John 10:17-18).

It verifies the truth of Scripture. Both in the Old Testament and in the teaching of Jesus, His resurrection is clearly taught (Psalm 16:10).

It ensures our own future resurrection. Because Jesus rose again, we shall one day be raised (1 Thessalonians 4:13-18).

It is proof of a future judgment. "Because He hath appointed a day, in the which He will judge the world in righteousness by that Man whom He hath ordained; whereof He hath given assurance unto all men, in that He hath raised Him from the dead" (Acts 17:31).

It is the basis for Christ's heavenly priesthood. Because He lives by the power of an endless life, He is able to intercede for us (Hebrews 7:23-28).

It gives power for Christian living. We cannot live for God by our own strength. It is only as His resurrection power works in and through us that we can do His will and glorify His name.

It ensures our future inheritance. Because we have a living hope, we can experience hopeful living.

Today's verse: "Jesus said unto her, 'I am the resurrection, and the life; he that believeth in Me, though he were dead, yet shall he live" (John 11:25).

Action assignment: Go back through the reading for today and look up the references listed. Take time to let the truth of the Resurrection grip you. Thank God for what it means to you.

AVOIDING LEGALISM

What really is "legalism"? It is the belief that I can become holy and please God by obeying laws. It is measuring spirituality by a list of do's and don'ts. The weakness of legalism is that it sees *sins* (plural) but not *sin* (the root of the trouble). It judges by the outward, not the inward. Furthermore, the legalist fails to understand the real purpose of God's Law and the relationship between Law and grace.

Believers who try to live by rules and regulations discover that their legalistic system only arouses more sin and creates more problems. The churches in Galatia were very legalistic, and they experienced all kinds of trouble. "But if ye bite and devour one another, take heed that ye be not consumed one of another" (Galatians 5:15). Their legalism did not make them more spiritual; it made them more sinful! Why? Because the Law arouses sin in our nature.

From the Word: "You who are trying to be justified by law have been alienated from Christ; you have fallen away from grace" (Galatians 5:4, NIV).

Also consider: Romans 4:4-5, 16; Ephesians 2:8.

Action assignment: Write out what you are trusting in to make you a member of God's family. Thank God that salvation is by His grace, not by your efforts.

15

PURE PRAISE

Psalm 145 was written with one purpose in mind: to praise the Lord. Notice that there are no requests and no confessions of sin in Psalm 145. It is pure praise!

Just listen to the psalmist as he speaks to the Lord! "I will extol [exalt] Thee. . . . I will bless Thy name. . . . I will praise Thy name" (vv. 1-2). He is not satisfied to wait until he gets to heaven, where he will praise God forever. He starts by expressing his praise to God every day! Praise is one earthly occupation we will continue in heaven, so we all ought to begin practicing now.

Some Christians praise the Lord and some do not. Perhaps the difference is this: the believers who praise the Lord have their eyes of faith fixed on Him, while the silent saints look only at themselves. When God is the center of our lives, we can praise Him every day, because we will always find blessings no matter how difficult your circumstances. To a praising saint, the circumstances of life are a window through which he sees God. To a complaining saint, these same circumstances are only a mirror in which he sees himself. That is why he complains.

Verse for today: "I will bless the Lord at all times; His praise shall continually be in my mouth" (Psalm 34:1).

Also read: Psalms 145:1-10; 146:1-2; Matthew 11:25; 21:16; Luke 19:37-38; Acts 16:25; Hebrews 13:15; Revelation 19:5.

Action assignment: Do those close to you call you "negative" or "positive"? If you have a positive personality, it will be easy for you to learn the habit of praise; but if you are negative in your outlook it might be more difficult. Give the act of praising God a priority in your prayertime today. Then carry over this attitude of praise into every area of your life, today and every day. Thus you will establish an earthly pattern that will continue in heaven.

THE PROOF OF LOVE

Obedience to God's Word is proof of our love for Him. There are three motives for obedience: We can obey because we *have to,* because we *need to,* or because we *want to.*

A slave obeys because he *has* to. If he doesn't obey he will be punished. An employee obeys because he *needs* to. He may not enjoy his work, but he *does* enjoy getting his paycheck! He needs to obey because he has a family to feed and clothe. But a Christian is to obey his Heavenly Father because he *wants* to—for his relationship with God is one of love.

This is the way we learned obedience when we were children. First we obeyed because we *had* to. If we didn't obey, we were punished! But as we grew up, we discovered that obedience meant enjoyment and reward; so we started obeying because it met certain *needs* in our lives. It was a mark of real maturity when we started obeying because of love.

"Baby Christians" must constantly be warned or rewarded. Mature Christians listen to God's Word and obey it simply because they love Him.

Jesus said: "If ye love Me, keep My commandments" (John 14:15).

Also read: 1 John 2:4-5; 1 John 5:2-3; Psalm 119:10.

Action assignment: Spend a few minutes telling God you love Him. Thank Him for His love for you. Perhaps you can think of an area in your life in which you have not obeyed Him; ask God to help you be obedient.

17

KEPT FOR ETERNITY!

God's purpose in our redemption is not simply to rescue us from hell, as great a work as that is. His ultimate purpose in our salvation is that for all eternity the church might praise God for His grace (Ephesians 1:6, 12, and 14). If God has an eternal purpose for us to fulfill, He will keep us for all eternity. Since we have not been saved by our good works, we cannot be lost by our bad works. Grace means salvation completely apart from any merit or works on our part. Grace means that God does it all for Jesus' sake! Our salvation is the gift of God, not a reward.

Salvation cannot be "of works" because the work of salvation has already been completed on the cross. This is the work that God does for us, and it is a finished work. We can add nothing to it; we dare take nothing from it. When Jesus died, the veil of the temple was torn in two, from the top to the bottom, signifying that the way to God was now open. There is no more need for earthly sacrifices. One sacrifice—the Lamb of God—has finished the great work of salvation. God did it all, and He did it by His grace.

Scripture for today: "God raised us up with Christ and seated us with Him in the heavenly realms in Christ Jesus, in order that in the coming ages He might show the incomparable riches of His grace, expressed in His kindness to us in Christ Jesus" (Ephesians 2:6-7, NIV).

Also read: Ephesians 1:6, 12, 14; John 17:1-4; 19:30; Hebrews 10:1-14.

Action assignment: On the left side of a sheet of paper, list things some people are depending on to make themselves right with God or some false god they might worship. Then on the right side, write out what you are depending on for salvation. Put a big X through the list on the left. Thank God for his finished work of salvation.

ARE YOU USING YOUR GIFT?

Each Christian has at least one spiritual gift that he or she must use to the glory of God and the building up of the church. We are stewards; God has entrusted these gifts to us that we might use them for the good of His church. He even gives us the spiritual ability to develop our gifts and be faithful servants of the church.

There are speaking gifts and there are serving gifts, and both are important to the church. Not everybody is a teacher or preacher, though all can be witnesses for Christ. There are those "behind-the-scenes" ministries that help make the public ministries possible. God gives us the gifts, the abilities, and the opportunities to use the gifts—and He alone must get the glory.

Scripture to remember: "Be devoted to one another in brotherly love. Honor one another above yourselves. Never be lacking in zeal, but keep your spiritual fervor, serving the Lord" (Romans 12:10-11, NIV).

Other Scripture: Romans 12:1-13; 1 Corinthians 12.

Action assignment: Sing a song of service to Christ, such as "How I Praise Thee, Precious Saviour." Talk to God about using your gift or gifts in His service to others.

19

LIVING TRUE

One of the marks of a true servant of God is his honesty and integrity: he practices what he preaches. This does not mean he is sinlessly perfect, but that he sincerely seeks to obey the Word of God. He tries to maintain a good conscience.

A conscience can become "seared" or "cauterized." Just as a person's flesh can be "branded" so that it becomes hard and without feeling, so a person's conscience can be deadened. Whenever we affirm with our lips something that we deny with our lives (whether people know it or not), we deaden our consciences just a little more. Jesus made it clear that it is not religious talk or even performing miracles that shows a person is qualified for heaven, but doing God's will in everyday life (Matthew 7:21-29). *Believing* and *behaving* always go together.

Today's verse: "Fight the good fight, holding on to faith and a good conscience. Some have rejected these and so have shipwrecked their faith" (1 Timothy 1:19-20, NIV).

Read: 1 Timothy 1:3-7; 4:1-5; Matthew 7:21-29.

Action assignment: Consider some things that could happen to you today that would call for you to choose between right and wrong. Determine now that your choice will please God. Invite the Holy Spirit to give you the "follow-through" allowing you to live in a way that doesn't have to be regretted.

THE PROMISE OF GOD'S BLESSING

God becomes our Father when we trust Jesus Christ as our Saviour, but He cannot *be to us* a Father unless we obey Him and fellowship with Him. He longs to receive us in love and treat us as His precious sons and daughters. *Salvation* means we share the Father's life, but *separation* means that we enter fully into the Father's love.

God blesses those who separate themselves from sin and unto the Lord. Abraham, for example, separated himself from Ur of the Chaldees and God blessed him. When Abraham compromised and went to Egypt, God had to chasten him. As long as Israel was separated from the sinful nations in Canaan, God blessed them; but when they began to mingle with the heathen, God had to discipline them.

Because of God's gracious promises, we have some spiritual responsibilities. We must cleanse ourselves once and for all of anything that defiles us. It is not enough to ask God to cleanse us; we must clean up our own lives and get rid of those things that make it easy for us to sin.

But cleansing ourselves is only half of the responsibility; we must also be "perfecting holiness in the fear of God" (2 Corinthians 7:1). This is a constant process as we grow in grace and knowledge. It is important to be balanced. The Pharisees were keen on putting away sin, but they neglected to perfect holiness. It is foolish to try to perfect holiness if there is known sin in our lives.

Remember this: "Whoever has My commands and obeys them, He is the one who loves Me. He who loves Me will be loved by My Father, and I too will love him and show Myself to him" (John 14:21), NIV).

And these verses: Ezra 9:10-15; Nehemiah 9:2; 2 Corinthians 7:1.

Action assignment: Talk with God, asking Him to search your heart and help you separate yourself from anything that is keeping you from a closer relationship to Him.

21

NEEDED: A FIFTH FREEDOM

At the close of an important speech to Congress on January 6, 1941, President Franklin D. Roosevelt shared his vision of the kind of world he wanted to see after the war was over. He envisioned four basic freedoms enjoyed by all people: freedom of speech, freedom of worship, freedom from want, and freedom from fear. To some degree, these freedoms have been achieved on a wider scale than in 1941, but our world still needs a fifth freedom: People need to be free from themselves and the tyranny of a sinful nature.

The legalists thought they had the answer to the problem in laws and threats, but Paul explained that no amount of legislation can change man's basic sinful nature. It is not law on the *outside*, but love on the *inside* that makes the difference. We need another power within, and that power comes from the Holy Spirit of God.

It is the Holy Spirit in the heart who gives assurance of salvation, and it is the Holy Spirit who enables us to live for Christ and glorify Him. The Holy Spirit is not simply a "divine influence"; He is a divine Person, just as are the Father and the Son. What God the Father *planned* for you, and God the Son *purchased* for you on the cross, God the Spirit *personalizes* for you and applies to your life as you yield to Him.

Verse to remember: "We have not received the spirit of the world but the Spirit who is from God, that we may understand what God has freely given us" (1 Corinthians 2:12, NIV).

Also read: John 14:16-17, 26; 16:7-14; Galatians 5:5, 16-18, 22-25.

Action assignment: Stop to consider how wonderful it is to be a Christian and have the Holy Spirit as your guide. Thank God for the ministry of the Holy Spirit and tell Him of your desire to let Him control you.

THY WILL BE DONE

Our minds control our bodies, and our wills control our minds. Many people think they can control their will by "willpower," but they usually fail. This was Paul's experience as recorded in Romans 7:15-21. It is only when we yield our wills to God that His power can take over and give us the willpower (and the "won't" power) we need to be victorious Christians.

A disciplined prayer life is the method whereby a surrendered will can properly function. A sincere "Not my will, but Thy will be done" allows God to have His will in everything that involves us and our wills.

Verse for today: "And be not conformed to this world: but be ye transformed by the renewing of your mind, that ye may prove what is that good, and acceptable, and perfect, will of God" (Romans 12:2).

Also read: Psalm 40:8; Isaiah 1:18-20; 43:26; Matthew 26:39; John 5:30.

Action assignment: Jesus is our supreme example, and He prayed, "Not My will, but Thy will be done." Prepare a list of the things in your life that you know represent resistance to God's will. Ask God to help you surrender each one to His perfect will.

IS ANGER ALWAYS WRONG?

When the Prophet Nathan told King David the story about "the stolen ewe lamb" (2 Samuel 12), the king became angry—but at the wrong person. "Thou art the man," said Nathan (v. 7), and David then confessed, "I have sinned" (v. 13). In the garden, Peter was slow to hear, swift to speak, and swift to anger—and he almost killed a man with a sword (Matthew 26:51). Many church fights are the result of short tempers and hasty words. There is a godly anger against sin; and if we love the Lord, we must hate sin. But man's anger does not produce God's righteousness. In fact, anger is just the opposite of the patience God wants to produce in our lives as we mature in Christ.

I once saw a poster that read, "Temper is such a valuable thing, it is a shame to lose it!" It is temper that helps to give steel its strength. The person who cannot get angry at sin does not have much strength to fight it. James warns us against getting angry at God's Word because it reveals our sin to us. Like the man who broke the mirror because he disliked the image in it, people rebel against God's Word because it tells the truth about them and their sinfulness.

Remember: "He that is slow to wrath is of great understanding: but he that is hasty of spirit exalteth folly" (Proverbs 14:29).

Also: 2 Samuel 12; Proverbs 14:17; 15:1, 16:32; Ephesians 4:26-27; James 1:3-4, 19.

Action assignment: List ways that sin harms people. What would be number one on your list? How bothered or angry are you about sin? How much are you considering sin from God's viewpoint? Talk to God about the matter.

RADICAL SURGERY

A Christian doctor had tried to witness to a very moral woman who belonged to a church that denied the need for salvation and the reality of future judgment. "God loves me too much to condemn me," the patient would reply. "I cannot believe that God would make such a place as a lake of fire."

The woman became ill and the doctor discovered that cancer had attacked her body. An operation was necessary. "I wonder if I really should operate," the doctor said to her in her hospital room. "I really love you too much to cut into you and give you pain."

"Doctor," said the patient, "if you really loved me, you would do everything possible to save me. How can you permit this awful thing to remain in my body?"

It was easy then for him to explain that what cancer is to the body, sin is to the world; and both must be dealt with radically and completely. Just as a physician cannot love health without hating disease and dealing with it, so God cannot love righteousness without hating sin and judging it. In fact, God demands radical surgery when a Christian sins: He commands, "Cut it out!"

Today's verse: "I acknowledged my sin unto Thee, and mine iniquity have I not hid. I said, I will confess my transgressions unto the Lord; and Thou forgavest the iniquity of my sin" (Psalm 32:5).

Other verses: Psalms 41:4; 51:2-5; 69:5; Luke 15:17-21; 1 John 1:8-10.

Action assignment: Talk to God and ask Him to enable you to first of all recognize sin in your life, and then to "cut it out."

GET AN EARLY START

It is good to lay the foundations of faith in childhood and youth. For some Christians, the "golden years" are really "leaden years" because they wasted their youth and did not lay solid foundations of faith. This does not mean that an older person who has missed his opportunities to live for Christ is automatically a failure. It is never too late to serve God. But the best time to start sowing the seed for a "late harvest" of blessing is in our younger years. The writer of Psalm 71 had a real burden to share this truth with the next generation. His greatest concern was that he not be put to shame. He wanted to end well to the glory of God. I heard about a preacher who used to pray, "Lord, deliver me from becoming a mean old man!" A friend said to me, "As I grow into old age, I want to become mellow, not rotten."

As we enter our mature years, we need not fear, because God will protect us. He will be our shelter in the storm, our fortress in the battle. As we continually abide in Him, He will strengthen us and enable us to praise Him; that praise will keep us from criticizing and complaining. The wicked may accuse, threaten, and attack us, but God will surround and sustain us. He will not always prevent troubles, but He will protect us in troubles and eventually bring us out better than when we went in.

Verse for today: "Now also when I am old and grayheaded, O God, forsake me not; until I have showed Thy strength unto this generation" (Psalm 71:18).

Also read: Deuteronomy 32:20; Psalm 71; 2 Timothy 1:5-7; 4:7-8.

Action assignment: We live in a youth-oriented culture. Advertising and the media glorify youth and often make fun of the old. Ask God to increase your awareness of someone older who may need your attention. Then make the effort to fill his or her need. That need may be for someone to listen; ask that older person to tell you about his or her spiritual experience, which may also help you lay better foundations for your own faith.

GOD ALONE JUDGES

In Matthew 6:22-23, Jesus used the illustration of the eye to teach us how to have a spiritual outlook on life. One truth presented in that passage is this: *We must not pass judgment on others' motives.* We should examine their actions and attitudes, but we cannot judge their motives—for only God can see their hearts. It is possible for a person to do a good work with a bad motive. It is also possible to fail in a task and yet be very sincerely motivated. When we stand before Christ at the last judgment, He will examine the secrets of the heart and reward us accordingly.

The image of the eye teaches us another truth: *We must exercise love and tenderness when we seek to help others.* I have had extensive eye examinations, and once had surgery to remove an imbedded speck of steel; I appreciated the tenderness of the physicians. Like eye doctors, we should minister with tender, loving care to people we want to help. We can do more damage than a speck of dirt in the eye if we approach others with impatience and insensitivity.

The Bible commands: "Therefore judge nothing before the time, until the Lord come, who will bring to light the hidden things of darkness, and will make manifest the counsels of the hearts; and then shall every man have praise of God" (1 Corinthians 4:5).

Also read: Matthew 6:22-23; 7:1-5; James 4:11-12.

Action assignment: Instead of examining the motives of others today, examine the motivation of your own heart. Seek always to bring glory and honor to God alone, not to yourself.

27

AFTER THE BUFFETING

The mystery of human suffering will not be solved completely in this life. Sometimes we suffer simply because we are human. Our bodies change as we grow older, and we are susceptible to the normal problems of life. The same body that can bring us pleasure can also bring us pain. The same family members and friends who delight us can also break our hearts. This is a part of the "human comedy."

Sometimes we suffer because we are foolish and disobedient to the Lord, who may see fit to chasten us in His love. King David suffered greatly because of his sin with Bathsheba. In His grace, God forgives our sins; but in His government, He must permit us to reap what we sow.

Suffering also is a tool God uses for building godly character. Certainly Paul was a man of rich Christian character because he permitted God to mold and make him in the painful experiences of his life.

When you walk along the shore of the ocean, you notice that the rocks are sharp in the quiet coves, but polished in those places where the waves beat against them. God can use the "waves and billows" of life to polish us, if we will let Him.

Verse for today: "I want to know Christ and the power of His resurrection and the fellowship of sharing in His sufferings" (Philippians 3:10, NIV).

Consider: Psalm 51; Romans 5:1-5; 2 Corinthians 12:9; Hebrews 12:3.

Action assignment: Considering the four types of suffering described in the entry, try to label your sufferings accordingly. Which have been the easiest to bear? Why? Which have been the hardest to bear, and why? Commit your sufferings to the Lord, who says, "Cast your burdens on Me, for I care for you."

PRAISING THE CREATOR-GOD

If the twenty-four elders of Revelation typify the people of God in heaven, then we must ask, "Why should God's people praise God the Creator?" If the heavens are declaring the glory of God (Psalm 19), why shouldn't God's heavenly people join the chorus? Creation bears constant witness to the power, wisdom, and glory of God. Acknowledging the Creator is the first step toward trusting the Redeemer (see Acts 14:8-18; 17:22-31).

But sinful man worships and serves the creature rather than the Creator, and this is idolatry (Romans 1:25). Furthermore, sinful man has polluted and destroyed God's wonderful creation; and he is going to pay for it (see Revelation 11:18). Creation is for God's praise and pleasure, and man has no right to usurp that which rightfully belongs to God. Man plunged creation into sin, so that God's *good* creation is today a *groaning* creation (Romans 8:22); but because of Christ's work on the cross, it will one day be delivered and become a *glorious* creation (Romans 8:18-24).

It is unfortunate that the church today often neglects to worship the God of Creation. The real answer to the ecological problem is not financial or legal, but spiritual. It is only when man acknowledges the Creator and begins to use creation to God's glory that the problems will be solved.

Scripture to remember: "Praise the Lord in song, for He has done excellent things; let this be known throughout the earth. Cry aloud and shout for joy, O inhabitant of Zion, for great in your midst is the Holy One of Israel" (Isaiah 12:5-6, NASB).

Additional Scripture: Look up and read the Scripture listed as part of today's reading.

Action assignment: Meditate on the wonders of God's creation. List your selection of the "Ten Wonders of the World" created by God. Make your prayer one of praise to the Creator.

WHEN YOU ARE TEMPTED

Satan would convince us that our Father is holding out on us, that He does not really love us and care for us. When Satan approached Eve, he suggested that if God really loved her, He would permit her to eat of the forbidden tree. When Satan tempted Jesus, he raised the question of hunger: "If Your Father loves You, why are You hungry?"

The goodness of God is a great barrier against yielding to temptation. Since God is good, we do not need any other person (including Satan) to meet our needs. It is better to be hungry in the will of God than full outside the will of God. Once we start to doubt God's goodness, we will be attracted to Satan's offers; and the natural desires within will reach out for his bait. Moses warned Israel not to forget God's goodness when they began to enjoy the blessings of the Promised Land. We need this warning today.

Next time you are tempted, meditate on the goodness of God in your life. If you think you need something, wait on the Lord to provide it. Never toy with the devil's bait. Remember that one purpose for temptation is to teach us patience. David was tempted twice to kill King Saul and hasten his own coronation, but he resisted the temptation and waited for God's time.

Remember this: "If you, then, though you are evil, know how to give good gifts to your children, how much more will your Father in heaven give good gifts to those who ask Him!" (Matthew 7:11, NIV)

Also read: Deuteronomy 6:10-15; Jeremiah 9:24; James 1:5, 17.

Action assignment: List several possible situations that Satan could use to tempt you. Determine now what you would do. As you decide, think of God's goodness in your life. How might patience help you in a given instance of temptation?

BLESSED ASSURANCE!

Why is it so important that we *know* we have been born of God? There are two kinds of children in this world: the children of God and the children of the devil. You would think that a "child of the devil" would be a person who lives in gross sin, but such is not always the case. An unbeliever is a "child of the devil." He may be moral and even religious; he may be a counterfeit Christian. But because he has never been "born of God" and experienced spiritual life personally, he is still Satan's "child."

A counterfeit Christian—and they are common—is something like a counterfeit ten-dollar bill. Suppose you have a counterfeit bill and think it is genuine. You use it to pay for a tank of gas. Eventually, it reaches the bank, where the teller says, "I'm sorry, but this bill is a counterfeit." That ten-dollar bill may have done a lot of good while in circulation, but when it arrived at the bank it was exposed for what it *really* was—and put out of circulation.

So it is with a counterfeit Christian. He may do many good things in his life, but when he faces the final judgment he will be rejected. Each of us must ask himself honestly, "Am I a true child of God, or am I a counterfeit Christian? Have I truly been born of God?"

The Bible says: "Many will say to Me in that day, 'Lord, Lord, have we not prophesied in Thy name? And in Thy name have cast out devils? And in Thy name done many wonderful works?' And then I will profess unto them, 'I never knew you: depart from Me, ye that work iniquity'" (Matthew 7:22-23).

Consider also: all of 1 John.

Action assignment: Examine your own life for signs of one who is an authentic believer. Make certain that you have been "born of God." If you know you have been, you can make "Blessed Assurance" your song for today.

May

Be Renewed:

"But we have this treasure
in jars of clay to show that this
all-surpassing power is from
God and not from us."

2 Corinthians 4:7, NIV

CALL TO OBEDIENCE

Because He is the sinless, eternal Son of God, and because His was the perfect, or "complete," sacrifice, Jesus Christ is the "author of eternal salvation" (Hebrews 5:9). No Old Testament priest could offer *eternal* salvation to anyone, but that is exactly what we have in Jesus Christ. Through His earthly sufferings, Christ was equipped for His heavenly ministry as our High Priest. He is able to save, keep, and strengthen us.

What do *we* have to do? Hebrews 5:9 says He is the "author of eternal salvation unto all them that *obey.*" Once we have put our faith in Jesus Christ, and thus obeyed His call, we experience His eternal salvation. It's simple, but profound.

Verse for today: "In You our fathers put their trust; they trusted and You delivered them. They cried to You and were saved; in You they trusted and were not disappointed" (Psalm 22:4-5, NIV).

Also read: Romans 6:17; Galatians 5:7; 1 Thessalonians 5:23-24; 1 Peter 1:22.

Action assignment: On a scale of 1 to 10, rate yourself in the following categories:

How much I trust God	____	How much I praise God	____
How much I obey God	____	How much I serve God	____
How much I love God	____	How much I love others	____
How much I thank God	____	How much I serve others	____
		How much I love myself	____

Pray for wisdom and the will to improve your overall "score."

FAITH IS THE VICTORY

I don't recall too many chapel messages from my years as a seminary student, but Vance Havner gave a message that has stayed with me and often encouraged me. Speaking from Hebrews 11, he told us that because Moses was a man of faith, he was able to "see the invisible, choose the imperishable, and do the impossible." I needed that message then and I still need it today.

What was true for Moses centuries ago can be true for God's people today, but men and women of faith seem to be in short supply. Whatever our churches may be known for today, they're not especially known for glorifying God by great exploits of faith. "The church used to be known for its good deeds," said one wit, "but today it's better known for its bad mortgages."

"For whatever is born of God overcomes the world. And this is the victory that has overcome the world—our faith" (1 John 5:4). Christians are either overcome because of their unbelief or overcomers because of their faith. And remember, faith doesn't depend on how we feel, what we see, or what may happen. The Quaker poet John Greenleaf Whittier put it this way in "My Soul and I":

> Nothing before, nothing behind;
> The steps of faith
> Fall on the seeming void, and find
> The rock beneath.

Remember: "Fight the good fight of faith. Take hold of the eternal life to which you were called when you made your good confession in the presence of many witnesses" (1 Tim. 6:12, NIV).

Read: Hebrews 11

Action assignment: Write out your definition of faith, completing the sentence: "My faith in God means. . . ." Take time to talk to God about your belief in Him. Ask Him to help you grow in faith. Bring some concern to Him and begin trusting Him to act in response to your faith.

3

TRUTH IN WORD AND CHARACTER

Swearing is not the sin of "cursing," but the sin of using oaths to affirm that what is said is true. The Pharisees used all kinds of tricks to sidestep the truth, and oaths were among them. They would avoid using the holy name of God, but would come close by using the city of Jerusalem, heaven, earth, or some part of the body.

Jesus taught that our conversation should be so honest, and our character so true, that we would not need "crutches" to get people to believe us. Trust depends on character, and oaths cannot compensate for a poor character. "In the multitude of words there wanteth not sin; but he that refraineth his lips is wise" (Proverbs 10:19). The more words a man uses to convince us, the more suspicious we should be.

The Bible commands: "But above all things, my brethren, swear not, neither by heaven, neither by the earth, neither by any other oath: but let your yea be yea; and your nay, nay; lest ye fall into condemnation" (James 5:12).

Also consider: Matthew 5:33-37; Deuteronomy 23:21-23.

Action assignment: Be conscious of speaking the truth with simplicity today. Strive to be a person of integrity whose words are believable. Commit your day—and your speech—to God.

JUST A JAR OF CLAY

The Christian is simply a "jar of clay"; it is the treasure *within the vessel* that gives the vessel its value. God has made us the way we are so that we can do the work He wants us to do. God said of Paul, "He is a chosen vessel unto Me, to bear My name before the Gentiles" (Acts 9:15). No Christian should ever complain to God because of his lack of gifts or abilities, or because of his limitations or handicaps. Our very genetic structure is in the hands of God. Each of us must accept himself and be himself.

The important thing about a vessel is that it be clean, empty, and available for service. Each of us must seek to become a vessel so that God might use us. We are earthen vessels, so we need to depend on God's power and not our own.

We must focus on the treasure, not on the vessel. Paul was not afraid of suffering or trial, because he knew God would guard the vessel as long as Paul was guarding the treasure. Sometimes God permits our vessels to be jarred so that some of the treasure will spill out and enrich others.

Remember this: "But we have this treasure in jars of clay to show that this all-surpassing power is from God and not from us" (2 Corinthians 4:7, NIV).

Read: Psalm 139:13-16; 2 Timothy 2:20-21.

Action assignment: In your own words, describe:
1. The Treasure_____

_____
2. The "jar of clay"_____
3. How some of the treasure could spill out from you should you be "jarred"_____

_____

Then talk with God.

5

A BIBLICAL HOPE

In the Bible the concept of *hope* does not involve a self-produced feeling of encouragement that is imaginary. Nor is it "wishful thinking" of the "hope-so" variety. A Christian's hope is built on the solid foundation of the character of God and the Word of God. It is this term that Job used when he said of God, "Though He slay me, yet will I trust [hope] in Him" (Job 13:15).

The Hebrew word for *hope* used in our verse for today (below) means a long and patient waiting in spite of delay and disappointment. It is a hope that is strengthened with bright expectation; we know God is going to meet our needs and accomplish His purposes. The opposite of this hope is a feeling of fear and dread.

What is a believer's source of hope? It is God! We have hope because God has saved us and certainly will not abandon us. We have hope because of the Spirit who lives within us and because of the Word He has given us. Jesus Christ is our hope.

The result of this is "I will . . . praise Thee more and more." What an optimistic outlook on life! Instead of finding more and more things to complain about, the psalmist found more and more blessings for which to praise God!

Verse for today: "I will hope continually, and will yet praise Thee more and more" (Psalm 71:14).

Also read: Romans 5:1-2; 8:31-32; 15:4, 13; 1 Timothy 1:1; Psalms 42:11; 119:49, 81, 114; Philippians 1:20.

Action assignment: Compose a prayer of thanksgiving about your source of hope. Start by thanking God for Himself, for His gift of salvation through Jesus Christ, for His gifts of the Holy Spirit and the Bible. Then express your faith that God will meet your needs and accomplish His purposes in your life.

GIFTED BY GRACE

Each Christian must know what his spiritual gifts are and what ministry (or ministries) he is to have in the local church. It is not wrong for a Christian to recognize gifts in his own life and in the lives of others. What *is* wrong is the tendency to have a false evaluation of ourselves. Nothing causes more damage in a local church than a believer who overrates himself and tries to perform a ministry that he cannot do. (Sometimes the opposite is true, and people undervalue themselves; both attitudes are wrong.)

Gifts come because of God's grace. They must be accepted and exercised by faith. We were saved "by grace, through faith," and we must live and serve "by grace, through faith." Since our gifts are from God, we cannot take the credit for them. All we can do is accept them and use them to honor His name.

Verse for today: "So we, being many, are one body in Christ, and every one members one of another. Having then gifts differing according to the grace that is given to us" (Romans 12:5-6).

Also read: 1 Corinthians 12; 15:10; Ephesians 2:8-9; 4:7-16.

Action assignment: Make a list of your duties and services in your church. Are you performing well in each one? If not, ask God to redirect your thinking and give you faith for new directions in service. By His grace your gifts will be honed for the good of your church.

A MATURE LOVE FOR GOD

Why do we have a joyful attitude as we face trials? Because we love God, and He loves us, and He will not harm us. Why do we have an understanding mind? Because He loves us and has shared His truth with us, and we love Him in return. Why do we have a surrendered will? Because we love Him. Where there is love, there is surrender and obedience. Why do we have a believing heart? Because love and faith go together. When we love someone, we trust him, and do not hesitate to ask him for help.

But there is another factor involved: love keeps us faithful to the Lord. The double-minded person is like an unfaithful husband or wife: he wants to love both God and the world. James admonished, "Purify your hearts, ye double minded" (4:8). The Greek word translated by the word *purify* literally means "make chaste." The picture is that of an unfaithful lover.

God's purpose in trials is maturity. "Let patience have her perfect work, that ye may be perfect and entire, wanting nothing" (1:4). The Charles B. Williams translation says it graphically: "But you must let your endurance come to its perfect product so that you may be fully developed and perfectly equipped."

Verse for Today: "Hold fast the form of sound words, which thou hast heard of me, in faith and love which is in Christ Jesus" (2 Timothy 1:13).

Also read: James 1:5-8; 4:8; 2 Timothy 3:16-17.

Action assignment: A sound biblical hope is developed by sound Bible study. Visit a Christian bookstore and consider the Bible study books displayed there; the right one may be there for you. As you give Bible study a priority in your life and pray for wisdom as you study, you can gain true maturity in all phases of your walk with God.

IT PAYS!

As Christians, we must live for eternity and not just for the present. In fact, walking by faith and not by sight makes our Christian lives meaningful today.

This brings to mind the story of two farmers, one a believer and the other an atheist. When harvest season came, the atheist taunted his believing neighbor because it seemed God had not blessed him too much. The atheist's family had not been sick, his fields were rich with harvest, and he was sure to make a lot of money.

"I thought you said it paid to believe in God and be a Christian," said the atheist.

"It *does* pay," replied the Christian. "But God doesn't always pay His people in September."

What kind of future does the unbeliever face? Paul used dramatic terms to describe it: tribulation, vengeance, flaming fire, punishment, and everlasting destruction. The Christ-rejecting world will receive from God exactly what it gave God's people! When God recompenses, He pays in kind—for there is a law of compensation that operates in human history.

God promises: "Be thou faithful unto death, and I will give thee a crown of life" (Revelation 2:10).

Consider: Luke 6:22-23, 35; 16:10-12; Romans 2:6-11; 2 Thessalonians 1:3-12; Hebrews 11:26; Revelation 22:12.

Action assignment: Look up the word *faithful* in a good dictionary. Consider how you could be more faithful to God. Talk to Him about any problem you may have with faithfulness and with living "with eternity's values in view."

9

SAYING NO TO LUST

Sexual impurity begins in the desires of the heart. Jesus did not say that lustful desires are identical to lustful deeds, so that a person might just as well go ahead and commit adultery. The desire and the deed are not identical, but spiritually speaking, they are equivalent. The "look" Jesus mentioned was not a casual glance, but *a constant stare with the purpose of lusting.* It is possible for a man to glance at a beautiful woman and know that she is beautiful, but not lust after her. The man Jesus described, saying he should pluck out his eye, looks at a women *for the purpose of feeding his inner sensual appetites* as a substitute for the act. It is not accidental; it is planned.

How can we defeat lust? By purifying the desires of our hearts— appetite leads to action—and disciplining the actions of our bodies. Obviously our Lord is not talking about literal surgery; this would not solve the problem in the heart. The eye and the hand are usually the two "culprits" when it comes to sexual sins, so they must be disciplined. Jesus said, "Deal immediately and decisively with sin! Don't taper off—cut off!" Spiritual surgery is more important than physical surgery, for the sins of the body can lead to eternal judgment.

The Bible commands: "Do not offer the parts of your body to sin, as instruments of wickedness, but rather offer yourselves to God, as those who have been brought from death to life; and offer the parts of your body to Him as instruments of righteousness" (Romans 6:13, NIV).

Read also: Colossians 3:5; Romans 13:13-14; Matthew 5:27-30.

Action assignment: If you need "spiritual surgery" in the area of lust, take care of it today. Ask God to help you see this sin as He sees it, and to help you avoid it in any circumstance.

THE BENEFITS OF WISDOM

A newspaper cartoon shows an automobile balancing precariously over the edge of a cliff, with an embarrassed husband at the wheel and his disgusted wife sitting next to him. Meekly, he says to his wife, "Honey, there's got to be a lesson here somewhere."

There's a lesson there all right, and it's this: *The only way to end up at the right destination is to choose the right road.* If you've ever made a wrong turn in a strange place and found yourself lost, then you know how important that lesson is.

The Bible frequently exhorts us to choose the right path, but the contemporary world thinks there are "many ways to God" and any path you sincerely follow will eventually take you there.

Jesus made it clear that in this life we can take only one of two ways, and each of them leads to a different destination. Everybody has to choose either the crowded road that leads to destruction or the narrow road that leads to life (Matt. 7:13–14). There's no middle way.

In the Book of Proverbs, the words "path" and "way" (and their plurals) are found nearly one hundred times (KJV). Wisdom is not only a person to love, but a path to walk, and the emphasis in chapters 2, 3, and 4 is on the blessings God's people enjoy when they walk on Wisdom's path. The path of Wisdom leads to life, but the way of Folly leads to death; when you walk on the path of Wisdom, you enjoy three wonderful assurances: Wisdom *protects* your path, *directs* your path, and *perfects* your path.

Never forget: "The LORD gives wisdom, and from His mouth come knowledge and understanding" (Prov. 2:6, NIV).

Read: Proverbs 2

Action assignment: In Proverbs 2, what does the writer challenge you to hide? What happens if you seek wisdom and understanding? What happens when wisdom enters into your heart?

LOOK AT THE WINNERS!

The heroes of faith listed in Hebrews 11 are referred to as a "great . . . cloud of witnesses" in the next chapter. These men and women now in heaven are not watching us as we run the race, like people seated in a stadium; the word *witnesses* does not mean "spectators." Our English word *martyr* comes directly from the Greek word translated "witness." These people are not witnessing what we are doing; rather, they are bearing witness *to us* that God can see us through. God bore witness to them, and they are bearing witness to us through the Old Testament. The believer who has to admit, "I rarely read the Old Testament, except for Psalms and Proverbs," is missing a great deal of spiritual help (see verse for today).

One of the best ways to develop endurance and encouragement is to get to know the godly men and women of the Old Testament who ran the race—and won.

Verse for today: "For everything that was written in the past was written to teach us, so that through endurance and the encouragement of the Scriptures we might have hope" (Romans 15:4, NIV).

Also read: Hebrews 11:1-2, 4-5, 39; 12:1; 2 Timothy 3:16-17.

Action assignment: If you are having problems with your family, read about Joseph. If you think your job is too big for you, study the life of Moses. If you are tempted to retaliate, see how David handled this problem.

EXAMINATION TIME

Haman could send out the death warrants for thousands of innocent people and then sit down to a banquet with a king! What a calloused heart he had! He was like the people the Prophet Amos described "who drink wine in bowls, and anoint [themselves] with the best ointments, but are not grieved for the affliction of Joseph" (Amos 6:6). However, in the end, it was his own death warrant that Haman had sealed; for within less than three months, Haman would be a dead man (Esther 8:9).

Helen Keller said, "Science may have found a cure for most evils, but it has found no remedy for the worst of them all—the apathy of human beings" (*My Religion*, p. 162). Jesus vividly illustrated that apathy in the Parable of the Good Samaritan (Luke 10:25–37). He pointed out that two religious men, a priest and a Levite, ignored the needs of the dying man, while the Samaritan, a hated outsider, sacrificed to take care of him. Jesus also made it clear that loving the Lord ought to make us love our neighbor, and our neighbor is anyone who needs us.

Therefore, before we condemn wicked Haman, let's examine our own hearts. Billions of lost sinners in today's world are under a sentence of *eternal* death, and most Christians do very little about it. We can sit at our church banquets and Sunday dinners without even thinking about helping to get the message out that "the Father has sent the Son as the Savior of the world" (1 John 4:14).

Today's verse: "Again Jesus said, 'Peace be with you! As the Father has sent Me, I am sending you'" (John 20:21, NIV).

Read: Esther 3

Action assignment: Determine if there is anything you can do today or this week to speed the Good News to the lost. Can you use your tongue, pen, computer, or money? Pray for those have been sent to bring the Good News to others.

13

"LORD, MAKE US BLESSABLE"

Many years ago, I was in a prayer meeting with a number of Youth for Christ leaders, among them Jacob Stam, brother of John Stam who, with his wife Betty, was martyred in China in 1934. We had been asking God to bless this ministry and that project, and I suppose the word "bless" was used scores of times as we prayed. Then Jacob Stam prayed, "Lord, we've asked you to bless all these things; but, please, Lord, *make us blessable.*" Had Naomi been in that meeting, she would have had to confess, "Lord, I'm not blessable."

Whenever we have disobeyed the Lord and departed from His will, we must confess our sin and return to the place of blessing. Abraham had to leave Egypt and go back to the altar he had abandoned (Gen. 13:1–4); Jacob had to go back to Bethel (35:1). The repeated plea of the prophets to God's people was that they *turn* from their sins and *return* to the Lord. "Let the wicked forsake his way, and the unrighteous man his thoughts, and let him return to the LORD, and He will have compassion on him; and to our God, for He will abundantly pardon" (Isa. 55:7, KJV).

"He who covers his sins will not prosper, but whoever confesses and forsakes them will have mercy" (Prov. 28:13). When we try to cover our sins, it's proof that we really haven't faced them honestly and judged them according to God's Word. True repentance involves honest confession and a brokenness within. "The sacrifices of God are a broken spirit, a broken and contrite heart—these, O God, You will not despise" (Ps. 51:17). Instead of brokenness, Naomi had bitterness.

Today's verse: "'Ever since the time of your forefathers you have turned away from My decrees and have not kept them. Return to Me, and I will return to you,' says the LORD Almighty" (Mal. 3:7, NIV).

Read: Ruth 1

Action assignment: Concentrate on any side track you may have recently taken in your spiritual journey and accept God's plan for a quick return to the main road. Talk to God about it.

PURIFIED BY BLOOD

The word *covenant* not only means "an agreement," but also carries the idea of a last will and testament. If a man writes his will, that will is not in force until he dies. It was necessary for Jesus Christ to die so that the terms of the New Covenant might be enforced. Even the Old Covenant was established on the basis of blood. The book of the Law was sprinkled with blood, and so were the people and the tabernacle and its furnishings.

Blood was also used in the administration of the tabernacle service. Under the Old Covenant, people and objects were purified by blood, water, or fire. This was ceremonial purification; it meant that the persons and objects were now acceptable to God. The purification did not alter the nature of the person or object. God's principle is that blood must be shed before sin can be forgiven.

Since God has ordained that remission of sins is through the *shedding* of blood, and since purification comes through the *sprinkling* of blood, it is necessary that blood be shed and applied if the New Covenant is to be in force.

The Bible says: "But if we walk in the light, as He is in the light, we have fellowship one with another, and the blood of Jesus Christ His Son cleanseth us from all sin" (1 John 1:7).

Also consider: Hebrews 9:14-23; Exodus 24:3-8.

Action assignment: Take time to confess your sin to God. Ask Him to purify your thoughts so that the things you do today will flow out of obedience.

15

BEING HONEST WITH GOD

Laodicea in Asia Minor was known for its wealth and its manufacture of a special eye salve, as well as of a glossy black wool cloth. It was also located near Hieropolis, where there were famous hot springs, and Colossae, known for its pure, cold water.

As with some of the previous churches, the Lord adapted His words to something significant about the city in which the assembly was located. To the Laodicean church in Revelation, the Lord presented Himself as "the Amen," which is an Old Testament title for God. He is the truth and speaks the truth, because He is "the faithful and true witness" (Revelation 3:14). The Lord was about to tell this church the truth about its spiritual condition; unfortunately, they would not believe His diagnosis.

"Why is it that new Christians create problems in the church?" a young pastor once asked me.

"They don't create problems," I replied. "They *reveal* them. The problems have always been there, but we've gotten used to them. New Christians are like children in the home: they tell the truth about things!"

The Laodicean church was blind to its own needs and unwilling to face the truth. Yet honesty is the beginning of true blessing, as we admit what we are, confess our sins, and receive from God all that we need. If we want God's best for our lives, churches, and nation, we must be honest with God and let God be honest with us.

Scripture to remember: "If My people, who are called by My name, will humble themselves and pray and seek My face and turn from their wicked ways, then will I hear from heaven and will forgive their sin and will heal their land" (2 Chronicles 7:14, NIV).

Additional Scripture: Psalms 32:5; 79:9; Titus 2:14; Hebrews 9:13-14; 1 John 1:8-9.

Action assignment: Before God, search your heart. Confess any sin in your life that the Holy Spirit shows you. Come to God as a representative of your nation and confess national sins.

WHEN IT'S LAW VS. THE BIBLE

As Christian citizens, we should submit to the authority vested in human government. But Scripture does not say we must blindly obey every law. When Daniel and his three friends refused to obey the king's dietary regulations, for example, they disobeyed; but the *way* they did it proved that they honored the king and respected the authorities (Daniel 1). They were not rebels; they were careful not to embarrass the official in charge or get him into trouble; yet they stood their ground. They glorified God, and at the same time honored the authority of the king.

Peter and the other apostles faced a similar challenge shortly after Pentecost (Acts 4–5). The Jewish council commanded them to stop preaching in the name of Jesus, but Peter and his associates refused to obey. They did not cause a rebellion or in any way question or deny the authority of the council. They submitted to the institution but refused to stop preaching. They showed respect to their leaders even though these men were opposed to the Gospel.

It is important that we respect the office even if we cannot respect the man or woman in the office. As much as possible we should seek to cooperate with the government and obey its laws; but we must never allow any law to make us violate our Christian conscience or disobey God's Word.

Scripture commands: "Everyone must submit himself to the governing authorities, for there is no authority except that which God has established. The authorities that exist have been established by God" (Romans 13:1; NIV).

Other Scripture: Romans 13:1-10; Acts 4:19; 5:29.

Action assignment: Take time right now to pray for those in authority—city, county, state, and federal officials. Use names of the officials where possible.

17

LOOKING TO JESUS CHRIST!

When the dying Jews looked to the uplifted serpent in the wilderness, they were healed (Numbers 21:4-9). This is an illustration of our salvation through faith in Christ. "Looking unto Jesus" (Hebrews 12:2) describes an *attitude* of faith and not just a single act. "To look" means "to trust."

When our Lord was here on earth, He lived by faith. The mystery of His divine and human natures is too profound for us to understand fully, but we do know that He had to trust His Father in heaven as He lived day by day. The fact that Jesus *prayed* is evidence that He lived by faith. Our Lord endured far more than did any of the heroes of faith named in Hebrews 11, and therefore He is a perfect example for us to follow. On the cross He suffered for *all* the sins of *all* the world! Yet He endured and finished the work the Father gave Him to do.

Scripture says: "And as Moses lifted up the serpent in the wilderness, even so must the Son of man be lifted up; that whosoever believeth in Him should not perish, but have eternal life" (John 3:14-15).

Also read: John 3:16; 7:4, Hebrews 2:13; Isaiah 8:17.

Action assignment: Express your devotion to Christ for enduring the Cross for you. Determine to look to—trust in—Him as your perfect example.

THE MARK OF A CHRISTIAN

There are four basic words for *love* in the Greek language. *Eros* refers to physical love; it gives us our English word *erotic*. *Eros* love does not have to be sinful, but in Paul's day its main emphasis was sensual. This word is never used in the New Testament. Another word, *storge* (pronounced STOR-gay), refers to *family love*, the love of parents for their children. This word is also absent from our New Testament, though a related word is translated "kindly affectioned" in the *King James Version* in Romans 12:10.

The two words most used for love are *philia* (fil-E-uh) and *agape* (a-GAH-pay). *Philia* is the love of deep affection, such as friendship or even marriage. But *agape* is the love God shows toward us. It is not simply a love based on feeling; it is expressed in our wills. *Agape* love treats others as God would treat them, regardless of feelings or personal preferences.

The word *philadelphia* is translated "brotherly love." Because Christians belong to the same family, and have the same Father, they should love one another.

Christ taught: "A new commandment I give unto you, that ye love one another" (John 13:34).

Other Scripture: Romans 5:5; 12:10, 1 John 4:19; 1 Thessalonians 3:12.

Action assignment: Ask God to bring to mind someone for whom you can do something in love. Find the hymn by Charles Wesley, "Love Divine, All Loves Excelling," and make it part of your prayer.

19

A HIGH PRIVILEGE

In his worship, David not only sought the Lord and gazed upon His glory, but also praised Him in song. He brought the "sacrifice of praise" to the Lord, a privilege we have as the priests of God. How easy it is to plead with the Lord in the midst of battle and then forget to praise Him after He has given us victory. Victories on the battlefield are won in the prayer closet. "Praying always with all prayer and supplication in the Spirit" is as much a part of spiritual victory as putting on the armor and using the sword.

Without satisfying worship, there can be no successful warfare. How did David know that God was a light, a deliverer, and a fortress? He learned it while gazing on God's glory in his time of worship and meditation. David envied the priests who were privileged to dwell close to God's house and even enter the courts and the holy place. Perhaps the priests envied David for his exploits and travels, but how David longed to leave the battlefield and dwell in God's house! But wherever he was he took time to come into God's presence, meditate on God's gracious kindness, and contemplate the person of God.

Verse for today: "One thing have I desired of the Lord, That will I seek after; that I may dwell in the house of the Lord all the days of my life, to behold the beauty of the Lord, and to inquire in His temple" (Psalm 27:4).

Also read: Hebrews 13:15; 1 Peter 2:5; Psalm 91:1-4.

Action assignment: Worship is an exercise of discipline. It takes patience to wait on the Lord for His strength and courage to help in the battles of life. An awareness of God's attributes could motivate you to such a discipline. If this is a need in your life, ask God to provide a Bible study on His attributes, or begin a study on your own. Read a book on the topic of worship; ask your pastor to recommend one to you.

TRUE FAITH INVOLVES ACTION

Rahab was a harlot, an unlikely person to put faith in the true God of Israel! The other inhabitants of her city were marked for death, but God in His mercy and grace permitted Rahab to live. She knew that Jehovah had delivered Israel from Egypt and that He had opened the Red Sea. She also knew God had defeated the other nations during Israel's wilderness wanderings. "For the Lord your God, He is God" (Joshua 2:11). That was her testimony of faith, and God honored it.

True faith must always show itself in good works. Rahab protected the spies, put the cord in the window as directed, apparently won her family to the true faith, and in every way obeyed the Lord. Not only was she delivered from judgment, but she became a part of the nation of Israel. She married Salmon and gave birth to Boaz, who was an ancestor of King David. Imagine a pagan harlot becoming part of the ancestry of Jesus Christ! That is what faith can do!

Rahab is certainly a rebuke to unsaved people who give excuses for not trusting Christ. A condemned, heathen harlot, she knew very little spiritual truth—but she acted on what she did know. She stands as one of the great women of faith in the Bible.

Verse for today: "By faith the harlot Rahab perished not with them that believed not, when she had received the spies with peace" (Hebrews 11:31).

Look up: Joshua 2:8-21, 6:25; James 2:20-26.

Action assignment: Think of the excuses you've heard for not trusting Christ, and note how Rahab's actions refute each excuse. Pray for someone you know who may be using some defense today.

AN "A" FOR ABIDING

Imagine imitating the life of Jesus Christ with the poor equipment we have as mere human beings. A man with two broken legs might as well try to play baseball like a big league star. We would give the man an "E for effort," but he would nevertheless fail in his attempt.

The only way to walk as Christ walked is to abide in Him. Jesus Himself taught His disciples the meaning of abiding in Him. He said that just as a branch gets its life by remaining in contact with the vine, so believers receive their strength by maintaining fellowship with Christ.

To abide in Christ means to depend completely on Him for all we need in order to live for Him and serve Him. It is a living relationship. As He lives out His life through us, we are able to follow His example and walk as He walked. This is the secret of spiritual victory.

Verse for today: "He that saith he abideth in Him ought himself also so to walk, even as He walked" (1 John 2:6).

More to consider: John 15; Galatians 2:20; 2 Corinthians 5:17; 1 John 3:6.

Action assignment: List 2 or 3 successes and failures you have had:

SUCCESSES

1. _____ 2. _____ 3. _____

FAILURES

1. _____ 2. _____ 3. _____

What accounted for your successes and failures? Were you "abiding in Christ" when you had these successes and failures? What difference did Christ make? Ask the Lord to help you depend more fully on Him—no matter what the cost, no matter whether you achieve outward "success" or "failure."

GETTING READY

Sin in our lives keeps us from serving Christ as we should; this means a loss of reward. Lot is a good example of this truth. Unlike his uncle Abraham, Lot was not walking with the Lord and thus lost his testimony—even with his own family. When the judgment finally came, Lot was spared the fire and brimstone. But everything he lived for was burned up.

How does the Christian prepare for the Judgment Seat of Christ? By making Jesus Christ Lord of his life and faithfully obeying Him. Instead of judging other Christians, we had better judge our own lives and make sure *we* are ready to meet Christ.

Verse for today: "And now, dear children, continue in Him, so that when He appears we may be confident and unashamed before Him at His coming" (1 John 2:28, NIV).

Also read: Luke 12:41-48; Hebrews 13:17; Genesis 18–19; Revelation 3:21.

Action assignment: We don't want to be ashamed when we meet Jesus; we desire to please Him. Think about Jesus accompanying you through your day's activities, and seek to please Him in what you do. List four specific activities in which His presence will make an important difference:

1. _____

2. _____

3. _____

4. _____

23

GOD HAS SPOKEN THROUGH HIS SON

Several years ago, my wife, younger daughter, and I visited Great Britain and found ourselves in Lichfield, where we learned that Queen Elizabeth was coming to dedicate a new school for exceptional children. We interrupted our plans and stood on the curb, waiting patiently for the motorcade, which finally appeared. We stood perhaps ten feet from the Queen as she slowly rode by with her lady-in-waiting, waving to the crowd in her distinctive manner.

Now, suppose she had rolled down the window and called, "Hello, Warren! Hello, Betty and Judy! I'll tell my guards to take care of you!" If that had happened, everybody would have been duly impressed with our importance and perhaps asked for our autographs. Imagine, here are three American citizens to whom the Queen speaks personally!

Queen Elizabeth has never spoken to me, and probably never will; *but Almighty God has spoken to me in Jesus Christ and through His Word!* "God . . . has in these last days spoken to us by His Son" (Heb. 1:1–2). In spite of all that a world of sinners has done to the Lord, He still speaks to us in His grace. He not only speaks the word of salvation, but He also gives us the guidance we need for everyday life. Just as Boaz instructed Ruth, so the Lord also shares His Word of wisdom to direct our daily lives. He is the "Lord of the harvest" and assigns to us our place in His field.

Today's verse: "In the past God spoke to our forefathers through the prophets at many times and in various ways, but in these last days He has spoken to us by His Son, whom He appointed heir of all things, and through whom He made the universe" (Heb. 1:12, NIV).

Read: Ruth 2

Action assignment: Has God spoken to you today through His Word? Daily, as you read God's Word, pray and ask Him to speak to you, to give you some "take away" for the day.

THE GIFT OF DESIRE

The normal desires of life were given to us by God and, of themselves, are not sinful. Without these desires, we could not function. Unless we felt hunger and thirst, we would never eat and drink, and we would die. Without fatigue, the body would never rest and would eventually wear out. Sex is a normal desire; without it the human race could not continue.

It is when we want to satisfy these desires in ways outside God's will that we get into trouble. Eating is normal; gluttony is sin. Sleep is normal; laziness is sin. "Marriage is honorable in all, and the bed undefiled; but whoremongers and adulterers God will judge" (Hebrews 13:4).

The secret is in constant control. These desires must be our servants and not our masters; and this we can do through Jesus Christ.

Verse for today: "Every good gift and every perfect gift is from above, and cometh down from the Father of lights, with whom is no variableness, neither shadow of turning" (James 1:17).

Also read: Psalm 37:4-5; James 1:13-18; 1 John 5:15.

Action assignment: Thank God for His gift of desire. In your prayer today, be honest with God and yourself. If there is a problem area where your desire has become a master, ask God to help you turn that desire around to becoming a servant. Make a commitment to one particular change that is needed in your life—something you know is causing you to act in an immature way. The blessings that result will far outweigh any pain the change may cause.

ALL SHOOK UP!

God is speaking to us today through His Word and His providential workings in the world. We had better listen! If God shook things at Sinai and those who refused to hear were judged, how much more responsible are we today who have experienced the blessings of the New Covenant! God today *is* shaking things. (Have you read the newspapers lately?) He wants to tear down the "scaffolding" and reveal the unshakable realities that are eternal. Alas, too many people, including Christians, are building their lives on foundations that can shake.

As events draw nearer to our Lord's return, we shall see more shaking in this world. But a Christian can be confident, for he shall receive an unshakable kingdom. In fact, he is a part of God's kingdom today.

What shall we do as we live in a shaking world? Listen to God speak, and obey Him. Receive grace day by day to serve Him. Do not be distracted or frightened by the tremendous changes going on around you. Keep running the race with endurance (Hebrews 12:1). Keep looking to Jesus Christ. Remember that your Father loves you, and draw on His enabling grace.

While others are being frightened—you can be confident!

The Bible says: "God is our refuge and strength, a very present help in trouble. Therefore will not we fear, though the earth be removed, and though the mountains be carried into the midst of the sea" (Psalm 46:1-2).

Also consider: Isaiah 40:31; 41:10; Haggai 2:6; Hebrews 12:25-29.

Action assignment: Think of a change that could threaten to shake you today. Focus on the seven reminders given here to produce in you God's unshakable reality. Go back and underline them.

IS IT YOUR NATURE TO LOVE?

Have you noticed that animals do *instinctively* what is necessary to keep them alive and safe? Fish do not attend classes to learn how to swim (even though they swim in schools), and birds by nature put out their wings and flap them in order to fly. It is *nature* that determines action. Because a fish has a fish's nature, it swims; because a hawk has a hawk's nature, it flies. And because a Christian has God's nature, he loves, because "God is love" (1 John 4:8).

You can never have too much Christian love. Paul prayed that the Thessalonians' love might "increase and abound" (1 Thessalonians 3:12); and God answered that prayer (see 2 Thessalonians 1:3).

How does God cause our love to "increase more and more"? By putting us into circumstances that force us to practice Christian love. Love is the "circulatory system" of the body of Christ, but if our spiritual muscles are not exercised, the circulation is impaired. The difficulties that we believers have *with one another* are opportunities for us to grow in our love. This explains why Christians who have had the most problems with each other often end up loving one another deeply, much to the amazement of the world.

Paul's prayer: "The Lord make you to increase and abound in love one toward another, and toward all men, even as we do toward you" (1 Thessalonians 3:12).

More love verses: 2 Thessalonians 1:3; 1 Timothy 6:2; Hebrews 13:1-3.

Action assignment: Quote John 3:16 from memory and emphasize the words *so loved.* Consider how you can put *giving* love into effect in a relationship with someone. Talk to God about how you can love more deeply.

27

FINDING HARMONY

We belong to one family of God and share the same divine nature. We are living stones in one building, priests serving in one temple. We are citizens of the same heavenly homeland. It is Jesus Christ who is the source and center of this unity. If we center our attention and affection on Him, we will walk and work together; if we focus on ourselves, we will only cause division.

Unity does not eliminate diversity. Not all children in a family are alike, nor are all the stones in a building identical. In fact, it is diversity that gives beauty and richness to a family or building. The absence of diversity is not *unity*; it is *uniformity*, and uniformity is dull. It is fine when the choir sings in unison, but most of us prefer that they sing in harmony.

Christians can differ and still get along. All who cherish the "one faith" and who seek to honor the "one Lord" can love each other and walk together. God may call us into different ministries, or to use different methods, but we can still love each other and seek to present a united witness to the world.

After all, one day all of us will be together in heaven; so it might be a good idea if we learned to love each other down here!

St. Augustine said it perfectly: "In essentials, unity; in nonessentials, liberty: in all things, charity."

Today's Scripture: "Beloved, let us love one another: for love is of God; and everyone that loveth is born of God and knoweth God" (1 John 4:7).

Also read: Romans 12:18; John 17:20-24; Ephesians 4:1-6.

Action assignment: Begin memorizing 1 Corinthians 13, if you do not already know it. Ask God to enable you to show love to someone today.

FOR MATURE ADULT BELIEVERS ONLY!

Chastening is evidence of the Father's love. Satan wants us to believe that the difficulties of life are proof that God does *not* love us, but just the opposite is true. Sometimes God's chastening is seen in His *rebukes* from the Word or through circumstances. At other times He shows His love by *punishing* us with some physical suffering. Whatever the experience, we can be sure that His chastening hand is controlled by His loving heart. The Father does not want us to be pampered babies; He wants us to become mature adult sons and daughters who can be trusted with the responsibilities of life.

All of us had a father; if this father was faithful, he had to discipline us. If a child is left to himself, he grows up to become a selfish tyrant. A father chastens *only his own sons and daughters,* and this is proof that they *are* his children. We may feel like spanking the neighbors' children (and our neighbors may feel like spanking ours), but we cannot do it. God's chastening is proof that we are indeed His children.

The Bible says: "Know then in your heart that as a man disciplines his son, so the Lord your God disciplines you" (Deuteronomy 8:5, NIV).

Also read: Ephesians 1:4-7; Hebrews 12:7-11; 1 John 3:1-2.

Action assignment: Think of a current difficulty God has allowed in your life. Thank Him that whatever He allows is controlled by His loving heart.

PLASTIC SURGERY

"My wife is going to have plastic surgery," a man said to his friend. "I'm taking away all her credit cards!" How easy it is to purchase things we do not need with money we do not have. Then we lose not only our credit, but also our good Christian witness. "If therefore you have not been faithful in the use of unrighteous mammon [money] who will entrust the true riches to you?" (Luke 16:11, NASB) Churches and Christians who defend their orthodoxy but do not pay their bills have no orthodoxy to defend.

Paul urged: "Study to be quiet, and to do your own business, and to work with your own hands, as we commanded you; that ye may walk honestly toward them that are without, and that ye may have lack of nothing" (1 Thessalonians 4:11-12).

Also consider: Luke 6:31; Acts 24:16; 2 Corinthians 7:2; 8:1-9; 1 Peter 2:12.

Action assignment: If you feel there's often more outgo than income in your household, consider working out a budget. Talk with a friend who lives by a budget. Talk to the Lord about your use of money; ask Him to help you avoid damaging your testimony by helping you not to fall behind in paying your debts.

A WIDENESS TO HIS MERCY AND GRACE

Jesus Christ, our Great High Priest, is enthroned in heaven. He is also ministering mercy and grace to those who come for help. *Mercy* means that God does not give us what we deserve; *grace* means that He gives us what we do not deserve.

As believers in Jesus Christ, we can run to our High Priest at any time, in any circumstance, and find the help we need. Not only that, but we can come boldly into the presence of God. No trial is too great, no temptation is too strong, but that Christ can give us the mercy and grace that we need, when we need it.

"But He is so far away!" we may argue. "And He is the perfect Son of God! What can He know about the problems of weak sinners like us?"

But that is a part of His greatness! When He was ministering on earth in a human body, He experienced all that we experience, *and even more,* yet He did not sin.

If we fail to hold fast our confession, we are not proving that Jesus Christ has failed. We are only telling the world that *we failed* to draw on His grace and mercy when it was freely available to us.

Verse for today: "The Lord is slow to anger, abounding in love and forgiving sin and rebellion" (Numbers 14:18, NIV).

More from God's Word: Psalms 57:1-7; 106:1; 2 Chronicles 5:13; Romans 9:15-18; 12:1; Ephesians 2:4-5; James 2:12-13.

Action assignment: Using the definitions of *mercy* and *grace* listed in this entry, give three ways God has shown mercy and grace to you. For example, "I was speeding in my car, but I didn't get caught" could go under *mercy* (and foolhardiness too!). Thank God for His mercy and grace, and ask His forgiveness for those times when you should have been "caught" but weren't.

WHAT ABOUT BAPTISM?

The Flood of Noah's day pictures death, burial, and resurrection. The waters buried the earth in judgment, but they also lifted Noah and his family up to safety. The early church saw in the ark a picture of salvation. Noah and his family were saved by faith because they believed God and entered into the ark of safety. So sinners are saved by faith when they trust Christ and become one with Him.

When Peter wrote that Noah and his family were "saved by water," he was careful to explain that this illustration does not imply salvation by baptism. Baptism is a "figure" of that which does save us, namely, "the resurrection of Jesus Christ" (1 Peter 3:21). Water on the body, or the body placed in water, cannot remove the stains of sin. Only the blood of Jesus Christ can do that. However, baptism does save us from one thing: a bad conscience. Peter told his readers that a good conscience is important to a successful witness, and a part of that "good conscience" is being faithful to our commitment to Christ as expressed in baptism.

Today's verse: "Water symbolizes baptism that now saves you also—not the removal of dirt from the body but the pledge of a good conscience toward God. It saves you by the resurrection of Jesus Christ" (1 Peter 3:21, NIV).

Also read: 1 John 1:7–2:2, 1 Peter 3:16-22.

Action assignment: Write out what you believe about baptism. Tell God that you are trusting the blood of Christ to cleanse you. If you have not been baptized, determine what you should do about it.

June

Be Renewed:

"Blessed are they that hear
the Word of God and keep it."

Luke 11:28

1

HOW WELL DO YOU LISTEN?

The Lord Jesus repeatedly warned people about the wrong kind of hearing, and His warnings are still needed. "Who hath ears to hear, let him hear" (Matthew 13:9). In other words, "Take heed *that* you hear." Use every opportunity you have to hear the Word of God.

But He gave another warning in Mark 4:24. "Take heed *what* ye hear" (italics added). How often believers hear the Word of God in Sunday School and church—then get into their cars, turn on their radios, and listen to programs that help erase the impressions made by the Word. When we visited congregations in Great Britain, my wife and I were impressed with their practice of sitting down after the benediction to meditate on the Word and allow the Spirit to minister to them. This is far better than rushing out of church and joking with friends.

Our Lord's third warning is in Luke 8:18: "Take heed therefore *how* ye year" (italics added). Many people are careless hearers and cannot apply themselves to listen to the teaching of God's Word.

How do we appropriate the Word? By understanding it and receiving it into our hearts, and by meditating on it so that it becomes part of our inner selves. Meditation is to the spiritual life what digestion is to the physical life. If you did not digest your food, you would die. It takes time to meditate, but it is the only way to appropriate the word and grow.

Jesus said: "Blessed are they that hear the Word of God, and keep it" (Luke 11:28).

For further study: Matthew 7:24-25; John 2:22; 6:63; 15:3; Ephesians 5:26.

Action assignment: Select one of the verses above and commit it to memory. Thank God for His Word.

ACTIVE PATIENCE

Patience is an important characteristic of the maturing Christian life. If we do not learn to be patient, we are not likely to learn anything else. As believers, we are able to rejoice even in our tribulations, because we know that tribulation brings about patience; and patience, experience; and experience, hope (Romans 5:3-4).

We must never think that patience is complacency. Patience is *endurance in action.* It is not the Christian sitting in a rocking chair, waiting for God to do something. It is the soldier on the battlefield, keeping on when the going is tough. It is the runner on the race track, refusing to stop because he wants to win the race.

Too many Christians have a tendency to quit when circumstances become difficult. The saintly Dr. V. Raymond Edman, late president of Wheaton College near Chicago, used to remind students, "It is always too soon to quit."

I have often thought of that statement when I find myself in the midst of trying circumstances. It is not talent or training that guarantees victory: it is perseverance. "By perseverance the snail reached the ark," said Charles Spurgeon.

Verse for today: "You need to persevere so that when you have done the will of God, you will receive what He has promised" (Hebrews 10:36, NIV).

Also read: 1 John 5:4; Romans 5:3-4; 8:35-39; Hebrews 12:1.

Action assignment: Learning to be patient is not easy, because it usually involves frustrations and disappointments. What causes you to want to give up? Consider that "nothing can separate you from the love of God," and make that your motto as you anchor your hope in Him.

3

GOD'S JUDGMENT

In New Testament times, the national and religious pride of the Jews encouraged them to despise the "Gentile dogs" and have nothing to do with them. Paul used this judgmental attitude to prove the guilt of the seemingly pious; the very things they condemned in the Gentiles, they themselves were practicing! They thought they were free from judgment because they were God's chosen people, but Paul affirmed that God's election of the Jews made their responsibility and accountability even greater.

God's judgment is according to truth. He does not have one standard for Jews and another for Gentiles. One who reads the list of sins in Romans 1:29-32 cannot escape the fact that each of us is guilty of at least one of them. There are "sins of the flesh and of the spirit." There are "prodigal sons" and "elder brothers." In condemning the Gentiles for their sins, the Jews were really condemning themselves. How often are we guilty of the same thing? As the old saying puts it, "When you point your finger at somebody else, the other three are pointing at you."

The Bible commands: "Since we have these promises, dear friends, let us purify ourselves from everything that contaminates body and spirit, perfecting holiness out of reverence for God" (2 Corinthians 7:1, NIV).

Also read: Romans 1:29-32; 3:23; Ephesians 2:8-9; Luke 15:11-32.

Action assignment: Study the list of sins in Romans 1:29-32. Search your heart and ask God to forgive you for any of the sins you find there.

THE WISE PILGRIM

God wants us to turn loose from the things of this world and stop depending on them. He wants us to center our attention on the world to come. This means that we "hang loose" as far as this world is concerned, and start living for the eternal values of the next world.

Abraham, a wealthy man, could have lived in an expensive house in any location he chose. But he was first of all God's servant, a pilgrim and a stranger—which meant living in tents. Lot chose to abandon the pilgrim life and move into the evil city of Sodom. Which of these two men had true security? It would appear that Lot was safer in the city than Abraham was in his tents on the plain. But Lot became a prisoner of war—and Abraham had to rescue him.

Instead of heeding God's warning, Lot went back into the city. When God destroyed Sodom and Gomorrah, Lot lost everything. Lot survived, but he trusted in the things of this world instead of trusting the Word of God.

Like Abraham, we should be wise pilgrims following God's beckoning voice.

Verse for today: "But our citizenship is in heaven. And we eagerly await a Saviour from there, the Lord Jesus Christ" (Philippians 3:20, NIV).

Further reading: Colossians 3:1-4; 1 Corinthians 15:42-58; Isaiah 26:7-9.

Action assignment: Too often we are possessed by our possessions. Today give something that you consider precious to someone else. Do not buy a gift, but give what means something to you. Let this be an expression of your desire to share and to test your ability to be less attached to things.

5

DEVELOPING A GOOD CONSCIENCE

Our word *conscience* comes from two Latin words: *con,* meaning "with," and *scio,* meaning "to know." We "know with" the conscience. It is the internal judge that witnesses to us, that either approves our actions or accuses us. Conscience may be compared to a window that lets in the light of God's truth. If we persist in disobeying, the window gets dirtier and dirtier until the light cannot enter. This leads to a "defiled conscience". A "seared conscience" is one that has been so sinned against that it no longer is sensitive to what is right and wrong. It is even possible for the conscience to be so poisoned that it approves things that are bad and accuses when the person does good! This the Bible calls "an evil conscience." For example, a criminal feels guilty if he "squeals" on his friends, but happy if he succeeds in his crime!

Conscience depends on knowledge, the "light" coming through the window. As a believer studies the Word, he better understands the will of God, and his conscience becomes more sensitive to right and wrong. A "good conscience" is one that accuses when we think to do wrong and approves when we do right. It takes "exercise" to keep the conscience strong and pure. Are you exercising your conscience?

From Paul: "I strive always to keep my conscience clear before God and man" (Acts 24:16, NIV).

Look up: Romans 2:14-15; Titus 1:15; 1 Timothy 4:2; Hebrews 10:22.

Action assignment: Take a minute to consider how well your conscience functions. Ask God to make your conscience even more sensitive to right and wrong.

HOW TO DO GOD'S WILL

The Word of God has in it the power to accomplish the will of God. "For nothing is impossible with God" (Luke 1:37, NIV). It has well been said, "God's commandments are God's enablements." Jesus commanded the crippled man to stretch out his hand—the very thing the man could not do. Yet that word of command gave him the power to obey. He trusted the word, obeyed, and was made whole (Mark 3:1-5). When we believe God's Word and obey, He releases power—divine energy—that works in our lives to fulfill His purposes.

The Word of God in us is a great source of power in times of testing and suffering. If we appreciate the Word in our hearts, appropriate the Word in our minds, and apply the Word with our wills, we will be controlled by God's Word—and He will give us victory.

Know this: "Wherewithal shall a young man cleanse his way? By taking heed thereto according to Thy Word.... Thy Word have I hid in mine heart, that I might not sin against Thee" (Psalm 119:9, 11).

Meditate on these verses: Psalms 19:7-11; 40:8; 119:18, 24, 35; Luke 11:28.

Action assignment: Try to imagine what your life would be like if you had no knowledge of God's Word. Thank God for what it means to you and ask Him to help you to apply it to your life today.

A GRACE GARMENT

Along with patience, we need *long-suffering*. This word means "self-restraint" and is the opposite of revenge. Patience has to do primarily with circumstances, while long-suffering has to do with people. God is long-suffering toward people because of His love and grace. Long-suffering is one fruit of the Spirit. It is among the "grace garments" that the believer should wear on his soul.

It is amazing how people can patiently endure trying circumstances, only to lose their tempers with a friend or loved one. Moses was patient during the contest with Pharaoh in Egypt. But he lost his temper with his own people and, as a result, forfeited his right to enter the Promised Land.

Patience and long-suffering go together if we are growing spiritually. Paul listed them as the marks of the true minister of Jesus Christ. Certainly, Paul displayed these graces in his own life. The great example of patience and long-suffering in the Old Testament is Job. In the New Testament, of course, it is Jesus Christ.

Verse for today: "He that hath no rule over his own spirit is like a city that is broken down, and without walls" (Proverbs 25:28).

Also read: 2 Corinthians 6:4-6; 2 Timothy 3:10-12; 2 Peter 3:9; Galatians 5:22; Colossians 3:12-13.

Action assignment: If God had not been long-suffering with us, would we be saved? Loving relationships call for us to wear the grace garment of long-suffering. Pray for God to give you a great measure of this fruit for His honor and glory.

OPEN-HEART SURGERY

God sees our hearts, but *we* do not always know what is there. God uses the Word to enable us to see the sin and unbelief in our own hearts. The Word *exposes* our hearts like a sharp scalpel. If we trust God, the Word then *enables* our hearts to obey God and claim His promises. This is why each believer should be diligent to apply himself to hear and heed God's Word. In the Word we see God, and we also see how God sees us. We see ourselves as we really are.

This experience enables us to be honest with God, to trust His will, and to obey Him. By trusting His Word and obeying His will, we may enter into His rest and thus claim our rich inheritance in Christ. Our hearts have been made right by His divine surgery, but we need to keep them *unclogged* day by day!

Verse for today: "The Word of God is living and active. Sharper than any double-edged sword, it penetrates even to dividing soul and spirit, joints and marrow; it judges the thoughts and attitudes of the heart" (Hebrews 4:12, NIV).

Also consider: Hebrews 4:13; Jeremiah 17:9; Ephesians 5:8-16; James 1:22-25.

Action assignment: Take time to honestly reflect on any aspects of God's Word that have ever made you uncomfortable. Why did you feel this way? What did you do about it? If you have yet to come to terms with this, let God gently perform spiritual surgery on your heart. Give yourself time to heal before comparing your reaction to those "penetrating" aspects of God's Word.

9

THE NEED FOR WASHING

Every day in the United States, 450 billion gallons of water are used for homes, factories, and farms, enough water to cover Manhattan to a depth of ninety-six feet. In the East, the heat and the dust made frequent washing a necessity; but the water was not always plentiful. With regard to the Jews, the Law of Moses required ceremonial washings, and taking a bath and changing clothes usually preceded a special event (Gen. 35:1–3). Naomi told Ruth to act like a bride preparing for her wedding (Ruth 3:3; Ezek. 16:9–12).

If we want to enter into a deeper relationship with our Lord, we must "cleanse ourselves from all filthiness of the flesh and spirit, perfecting holiness in the fear of God" (2 Cor. 7:1). Whenever we sin, we must pray, "Wash me" (Ps. 51:2, 7); but sometimes God says to us, "Wash yourselves, make yourselves clean" (Isa. 1:16). When we seek forgiveness, God washes the record clean (1 John 1:9); but God will not do for us what we must do for ourselves. Only we can put out of our lives those things that defile us, and not rush into God's presence until we have cleansed ourselves of the sins that rob us of God's blessing. Is it any wonder that our worship is often an empty routine and that the power of God doesn't come to our meetings?

Remember this: "Since we have these promises, dear friends, let us purify ourselves from everything that contaminates body and spirit, perfecting holiness out of reverence for God" (2 Cor. 7:1, NIV).

Read: Ruth 3

Action assignment: Think of ways that you can cleanse yourself, "perfecting holiness in the fear of God." Make your prayer time more than "an empty routine."

GROWING IN GRACE

It is not we who work for God; it is God who works in us and through us to produce the fruit of His grace. Christian service is the result of Christian devotion. The work that we do is the outflow of the life that we live. It is by abiding in Christ that we can produce fruit.

God must make the worker before He can do the work. God spent thirteen years preparing Joseph for his ministry in Egypt, and eighty years preparing Moses to lead Israel. Jesus spent three years teaching His disciples how to bear fruit; and even the learned Apostle Paul needed a "post-graduate course" in Arabia before he could serve God with effectiveness. A newborn babe can cry and make its presence known, but it cannot work. A new Christian can witness for Christ and even win others—but he must be taught to walk and learn God's wisdom before he is placed in an office of responsible ministry.

Verse for today: "For it is God which worketh in you both to will and to do of His good pleasure" (Philippians 2:13).

Also read: Colossians 1:10; Ephesians 4:1; Philippians 1:27; 1 Thessalonians 2:11-12; 4:1.

Action assignment: Read John 15 and then write an essay about the Christian "producer." Relate this to yourself. Pray that you will learn the lesson of abiding in Christ so that you can become fruitful in every good work.

TRUE FREEDOM

Freedom without authority is anarchy. Authority without freedom is slavery. True freedom is *liberty under authority*. It is a vain thing to think that man can be free without God. The history of man is the record of new "freedoms" that led only to new slavery. Every step man has taken to break free from God's moral law has only brought him into more bondage. Why? Because man is made in the image of God; so, when he rebels against God, he is rebelling against himself as well!

God maintains His authority whether men accept it or not. God is still the supreme Ruler of the universe; His laws are still in force; His judgments are certain. If man cooperates with the laws of God, he will succeed. If he resists those laws, he will fail and be destroyed. God is speaking today in nature, in His Word, and in the human conscience; yet man will not listen. God is speaking today in grace, but one day He will begin to speak in judgment.

The athlete cannot find the freedom to use his skills unless he learns to submit to his coach. The student must submit to the teacher, the apprentice to the master craftsman. True freedom is found not in doing whatever you want to do, but in being all that God wills for you.

Verse for today: "I delight to do Thy will, O my God: yea, Thy law is within my heart" (Psalm 40:8).

Also read: Jeremiah 26:13; Matthew 8:27; Hebrews 5:9; 13:17; 1 Peter 4:17.

Action assignment: Are you aware of any rebellion in your life? If not, thank God for the marvelous freedom and peace He has given you. If freedom and peace elude you, ask God to show you any lack of submission to His will that you may have. Decide to make obedience to God and His commands a priority. He will bless you with joyous freedom as you do His will.

HOW IMPORTANT IS THE BIBLE TO YOU?

Would you rather have God's Word than *money?* The believer who wrote Psalm 119 made it clear that God's Word meant more to him than "all riches" (v. 14), "thousands of gold and silver" (v. 72), "fine gold" (v. 127), and even "great spoil" (v. 162).

I recall a young couple I sought to help in one of my churches. They had a lovely little son, but were very careless about attending church and Sunday School; the little boy was not getting the Christian training he needed. A visit to the home told me why: the father wanted more money, so he worked on Sundays to make double time. He did not *have* to work on the Lord's Day, but he wanted the money rather than God's Word. He earned more money, but he was never able to keep it. The son became ill and the extra money went to doctors.

Would you rather have God's Word than *sleep?* "My eyes anticipate the night watches, that I may meditate on Thy Word" (Psalm 119:148, NASB). The Jews had three night watches: sunset to 10, 10 to 2, and 2 until dawn. The psalmist gave up sleep three times each night that he might spend time with the Word. But some Christians cannot get out of bed on Sunday morning to study the Word.

If we are going to be victorious in suffering, we must appreciate the Word.

From the Bible: "Thy Word is a lamp unto my feet, and a light unto my path" (Psalm 119:105).

For further thought: Psalms 19:7-11; 43:3; 119:11, 18; Isaiah 34:16; 55:10-11.

Action assignment: Think about how God's Word in your heart keeps you from sin.

13

IN GOOD HANDS

The sober-minded believer has a calm, sane outlook on life. He is not complacent, but neither is he frustrated and afraid. He hears the tragic news of the day, yet he does not lose heart. He experiences the difficulties of life, but he does not give up. He knows his future is secure in God's hands, so he lives each day creatively, calmly, and obediently. Outlook determines outcome; and when your outlook is the *uplook,* then your outcome is secure.

Believe this: "The Lord God will help me; therefore shall I not be confounded: therefore have I set my face like a flint, and I know that I shall not be ashamed" (Isaiah 50:7).

Also: Micah 7:7; Romans 8:28; Hebrews 4:16.

Action assignment: List several concerns you have, and ask God to give you peace to live each day with the assurance that you are in His hands.

1._____

2._____

3._____

4._____

5._____

HOW TO ESCAPE IMPURITY

Paul devoted a great deal of space to the theme of sexual purity because it was a critical problem in the church of his day. It is also a critical problem in the church today. For many people, marriage vows are no longer considered sacred; divorce, even among believers, is no longer governed by the Word of God. There are "gay churches" where homosexuals and lesbians "love one another" and claim to be Christians. Premarital sex and pornography are accepted by many who go to church regularly.

How does the Spirit of God help us live a clean life, free from sexual impurity? To begin with, He creates holy desires in us so that we have an appetite for God's pure Word—not for the garbage of the flesh. Also, He teaches us the Word and helps us to recall God's promises in times of temptation. As we yield to the Spirit, He empowers us to walk in holiness and not be detoured into the lusts of the world and the flesh. The fruit of the Spirit overcomes the works of the flesh.

Fight back: "Take the helmet of salvation and the sword of the Spirit, which is the Word of God. And pray in the Spirit on all occasions with all kinds of prayers and requests. With this in mind, be alert" (Ephesians 6:17, NIV).

Consider: Romans 13:12-14; 1 Peter 2:1-3; John 14:26

Action assignment: Study Galatians 5:16-26. How can you avoid gratifying the desires of the sinful nature? What is the battle described in verse 17? List any acts of the sinful nature that may trouble you. Talk with God about how to cultivate the fruit of the Spirit in your life.

ROOM FOR VARIETY

Just as the whole of the Law is summed up in love, so the whole of human relationships is fulfilled in love. This applies to every Christian and to every area of life.

This love is evidenced by a *unity of mind*. Unity does not mean uniformity; it means cooperation in the midst of diversity. The members of the body work together in unity, even though they are all different. Christians may differ on *how* things are to be done, but they must agree on *what* is to be done and *why*. A man criticized D. L. Moody's methods of evangelism, and Moody said, "Well, I'm always ready for improvement. What are *your* methods?" The man confessed that he had none. "Then I'll stick to my own," said Moody.

Whatever methods we use, we must seek to honor Christ, win the lost, and build the church. Some methods are definitely not scriptural, but there is plenty of room for variety in the church.

The Bible says: "If you have any encouragement from being united with Christ, if any comfort from His love, if any fellowship with the Spirit, if any tenderness and compassion, then make my joy complete by being like-minded, having the same love, being one in spirit and purpose" (Philippians 2:1-2, NIV).

Also read: Philippians 2:1-11; Ephesians 4:1-6.

Action assignment: Are you at odds with some brother or sister in Christ? Spend time praying for that person and your relationship.

KNOWING GOD'S WILL

The *general* will of God for all His children is given clearly in the Bible. The *specific* will of God for any given situation must always agree with what He has already revealed in His Word. The better we know God's general will, the easier it will be to determine His specific guidance in daily life.

Paul did not encourage the Colossians to seek visions or wait for voices. He prayed that they might get deeper into God's Word and thus have greater wisdom and insight concerning God's will. He wanted them to have "all wisdom"—not that they would know everything, but that they would have all the wisdom necessary for making decisions and living to please God.

Spiritual intelligence is the beginning of a successful, fruitful Christian life. God puts no premium on ignorance. Great men of God like Charles Spurgeon, G. Campbell Morgan, and H.A. Ironside never had the privilege of formal Bible training. But they were devoted students of the Word, learning its deeper truths through hours of study, meditation, and prayer. The first step toward fullness of life is spiritual intelligence—growing in the will of God by knowing the Word of God.

Verse for today: "Study to show thyself approved unto God, a workman that needeth not be ashamed, rightly dividing the Word of truth" (2 Timothy 2:15).

Also read: Colossians 1:9-10; Ephesians 5:17; John 14:26; 15:13-15.

Action assignment: Resolve to know God's will by consistently studying His Word. Pray for God to grant you the discipline it will take. His Holy Spirit will be your constant helper.

OUR FAITHFUL HELPER

What happens when we who have become members of God's family through Jesus Christ are tempted to sin? Jesus stands ready to help us! He was tempted when He was on earth, but no temptation ever conquered Him. Because He has defeated every enemy, He is able to give us the grace we need to overcome temptation. The word "succour" (Hebrews 2:18) literally means "to run to the cry of a child." It means "to bring help when it is needed." Angels are able to *serve* us, but they are not able to *succour* us in our times of temptation. Only Jesus Christ can do that, and He can do it because He became a man and suffered and died.

Verse to remember: "There hath no temptation taken you but such as is common to man, but God is faithful, who will not suffer you to be tempted above that ye are able; but will with the temptation also make a way to escape, that ye may be able to bear it" (1 Corinthians 10:13).

Also read: Hebrews 2:18; Romans 8:15-17; 2 Corinthians 1:3-4; 1 Peter 2:21-25.

Action assignment: Are you willing to be a partner with Jesus in others' sufferings and temptations, giving them strength? Call up or visit two people you know who are going through a trial of some kind. Spend more time listening to them than talking. Close your conversation with prayer. Put it on your calendar to call or visit them again in three days.

MAKING THE MOST OF OPPORTUNITIES

Ruth became a part of God's wonderful plan for Israel to bring the Savior into the world, and Esther helped save the nation of Israel so that the Savior could be born.

God can use poor peasants and powerful queens to accomplish His divine purposes in this world. The question is not "*Where* do I live and work?" but "*For whom* do I live and work, for myself or my Lord?" Most of us are familiar with the famous statement of Socrates, "Know thyself." However, we need to get acquainted with a statement by Pittacus, one of the Seven Wise Men of Greece: "Know thine opportunities." God gave Esther the opportunity to surrender herself and serve Him and His people, and she seized that opportunity. Ambrose Bierce defined opportunity as "a favorable occasion for grasping a disappointment." Not so for the dedicated Christian! Opportunity is for us a favorable occasion for grasping *His appointment* and accomplishing His purposes.

We must never think that the days of great opportunities are all past. Today, God gives to His people many exciting opportunities to "make up the hedge, and stand in the gap" (Ezek. 22:30, KJV), if only we will commit ourselves to Him. Not only in your church, but in your home, your neighborhood, your place of employment, your school, even your sickroom, God can use you to influence others and accomplish His purposes, if only you are fully committed to Him.

Today's verse: "I know your deeds. See, I have placed before you an open door that no one can shut. I know that you have little strength, yet you have kept my word and have not denied my name" (Rev. 3:8, NIV).

Read: Ruth 4

Action assignment: Remember, unexpected happenings in your daily routine often bring special opportunities for committed service. Today look for opportunities whereby God can use you to influence others for His glory and honor, whether by speech or manner of conduct.

19

BY FAITH—VICTORY

God's people today stand in a valley between two mounts—Mount Calvary, where Jesus died for our sins, and Mount Olivet, where He will return in power and great glory (Zech. 14:4). The Old Testament prophets saw the Messiah's suffering and glory, but they did not see the "valley" between this present age of the church (1 Peter 1:10–12). Believers today aren't living under the curse of the Law, because Jesus bore that curse "on a tree" (Gal. 3:10–14). In Christ believers are blessed with "every spiritual blessing" (Eph. 1:3) because of the grace of God.

However, because Christians "are not under the Law, but under grace" (Rom. 6:14; 7:1–6), it doesn't mean that we can live any way we please and ignore the Law of God or defy it. We aren't saved by keeping the Law, nor are we sanctified by trying to meet the demands of the Law; but "the righteousness of the Law" is "fulfilled in us" as we walk in the power of the Holy Spirit (Rom. 8:4). If we put ourselves under Law, we forfeit the enjoyment of the blessings of grace (Gal. 5). If we walk in the Spirit, we experience His life-changing power and live so as to please God.

Let's give thanks that Jesus bore the curse of the Law for us on the cross and that He bestows all the blessings of the heavenlies on us through the Spirit. By faith we can claim our inheritance in Christ and march forth in victory!

Today's verse: "For sin shall not be your master, because you are not under law, but under grace" (Rom. 6:14, NIV).

Read: Romans 7:1–6

Action assignment: Thank God that you can claim victory through Him. Find the song "Faith Is the Victory" and sing it. Note what the song says about a banner and about God's Word. Check your armor (Eph. 6:10–18) and see if you are properly attired for victory. Encourage yourself by reviewing 1 Corinthians 15:57–58.

A RICH WELCOME

The hope of seeing Christ and going to heaven is not only a motivation for faith and love, but also for holy living. When I was a young Christian, an older friend warned me, "Don't be caught doing anything that would embarrass you if Jesus returned!" That is a rather negative view of the promise of heaven, even though it does have some merit. In fact, John warns us that if we do not abide in Christ (keep in fellowship with Him in obedience), we may be ashamed when He returns.

But there is a positive side to this truth. We should keep our lives clean so that when Jesus Christ *does* return, nothing will cloud our first meeting with Him. We will enter into the joy and glory of His presence with confidence and love! Peter called this a "rich welcome" into the everlasting kingdom (2 Peter 1:11, NIV).

Verse for today: "Beloved, now are we the sons of God, and it doth not yet appear what we shall be: but we know that, when He shall appear, we shall be like Him; for we shall see Him as He is. And every man that hath this hope in him purifieth himself, even as He is pure" (1 John 3:2-3).

Also read: 1 John 2:28; 1 Peter 1:4-9: Colossians 1:5; Hebrews 6:19.

Action assignment: Do you think with great joy about that "rich welcome" into heaven? If not, ask God to reveal any unholy living that has crept into your life—remembering that neglecting to do His will is also sin. Then trust in Christ's shed blood for cleansing and renewed grace for pure living.

THE REAL THING

The New Covenant Christian has *reality!* We are not depending on a high priest on earth who annually visits the holy of holies in a temporary sanctuary. We depend on the heavenly High Priest who has entered once and for all into the eternal sanctuary. There He represents us before God, *and He always will.*

Beware of trusting anything that is made with hands for your spiritual life. It will not last. The tabernacle was replaced by Solomon's temple, and that temple was destroyed by the Babylonians. When the Jews returned to their land after the Captivity, they rebuilt their temple; King Herod, in later years, expanded and embellished it. But the Romans destroyed that temple, and it has never been rebuilt. Furthermore, since the genealogical records have been lost or destroyed, the Jews are not certain who can minister as priests. These things that are made with hands are perishable, but the things not made with hands are eternal.

Remember this: "While we look not at the things which are seen, but at the things which are not seen: for the things which are seen are temporal; but the things which are not seen are eternal" (2 Corinthians 4:18).

Consider: 2 Corinthians 5:1; Hebrews 9:24; 1 Peter 1:13-14.

Action assignment: Think of one or two examples of something made with hands that you might be trusting in rather than God. Now ask God to help you trust only in those things which will last forever.

A TAILOR-MADE YOKE

Jesus said, "*Come.*" The Pharisees all said, "Do!" and tried to make the people follow Moses and the traditions. But true salvation is found only in a person, Jesus Christ. To come to Him means to trust Him. This invitation is open to those who are exhausted and burdened down. That is exactly how the people felt under the yoke of pharisaical legalism.

"*Take.*" This is a deeper experience. When we come to Christ by faith, *He gives* us rest. When we take His yoke and learn, *we find* rest, that deeper rest of surrender and obedience. The first is "peace *with* God"; the second is "the peace *of* God." To "take a yoke" in that day meant to become a disciple. When we submit to Christ, we are yoked to Him. The word "easy" means "well-fitting"; He has just the yoke that is tailor-made for our lives and needs.

"*Learn.*" The first two commands represent a crisis as we come and yield to Christ; but this step is into a *process.* As we learn more about Him, we find a deeper peace, because we trust Him more. Life is simplified and unified around the person of Christ.

Verse for today: "Come unto Me, all ye that labor and are heavy laden, and I will give you rest" (Matthew 11:28).

Also read: Matthew 11:25-30; 23:2-5; Acts 15:10; Romans 5:1; Philippians 4:6-8; 1 John 5:3.

Action assignment: Thank God for your tailor-made yoke. Then list some areas that are very hard for you right now. Ask the Lord to direct you in your Bible study so that your trust in His yoke will give you the peace you need.

UNION AND COMMUNION

The fact of God's presence with us is ensured by His promise, but the experience of His presence depends on how we relate to Him in faith, love, obedience, and desire. There is a difference in the Christian life between "union" (belonging to Christ) and "communion" (enjoying fellowship with Christ).

A father and mother might possibly forsake a child, but it is not likely. God is to us a devoted and faithful Father, and also tenderly deals with us as would a loving mother. As children in God's family, we have a Saviour who is closer than a brother, and a Father who is both father and mother to us in all the demands of life.

As we walk the path of life, we need direction and guidance. The enemy is always present to trip us up and get us on attractive detours. No matter what the contour of the land might be, God wants to lead us on a level (plain) path so that we will not trip and fall. Satan wants to lead us on crooked paths that are uneven and treacherous.

Verse for today: "When Thou saidst, 'Seek ye My face,' my heart said unto Thee, 'Thy face, Lord, will I seek'" (Psalm 27:8).

Other verses: Psalms 27:11-12; 103:13; Isaiah 49:15; John 14:16-18.

Action assignment: God's path for your life becomes clear as you experience His presence. Ask Him to make Himself real to you as you prayerfully obey him. Fellowship with Him will give you joy and strength to resist the attacks of Satan. Today, decide to practice the presence of Christ throughout your day's activities. Thank Him for the *fact* of His presence as you experience daily communion with Him. Memorize John 14:23: "If a man love Me, he will keep My words; and My Father will love him, and We will come unto him, and make Our abode with him."

THE WALK OF FAITH

During most of the year, the Jordan River was about a hundred feet wide; but at the spring flood season, the river overflowed its banks and became a mile wide. As soon as the priests bearing the ark put their feet into the river, the water stopped flowing and stood like a wall about twenty miles away upstream, near a city called Adam. It was a miracle of God in response to faith.

Unless we step out by faith (Josh.1:3; 3:14–17) and "get our feet wet," we're not likely to make much progress in living for Christ and serving Him. Each step that the priests took opened the water before them until they were standing in the midst of the river on dry ground. They stood there as the people passed by; and when the whole nation had crossed, the priests walked to the shore and the flow of the water resumed.When God opened the Red Sea, He used a strong wind that blew the whole night before (Exod. 14:21–22). This was not an accident, for the wind was the blast of God's nostrils (15:8). When Moses lifted his rod, the wind began to blow; and when he lowered the rod, the waters flowed back and drowned the Egyptian army (14:26–28). When Israel crossed the Jordan River, it was not the obedient arm of a leader that brought the miracle but the obedient feet of the people. Unless we are willing to step out by faith and obey His Word, God can never open the way for us.

If you want to claim your spiritual inheritance in Christ, believe the Word of faith and *get your feet wet!* Step out in a walk of faith.

The Bible says: "Without faith it is impossible to please God, because anyone who comes to him must believe that he exists and that he rewards those who earnestly seek him" (Heb. 11:6, NIV).

Read: Joshua 3

Action assignment: Ask yourself, "Am I willing to get my feet wet today for Christ?" Be prepared to respond in a Christlike way to that emergency request from a neighbor or some other interruption to your carefully planned schedule. Surrender to God's leading and reap the resulting joy and satisfaction of faithful service. Think about it: "Worry is unbelief parading in disguise."

25

SAVING FAITH

Saving faith involves the mind, the emotions, and the will. With the mind we understand the truth of the Gospel, and with the heart we feel conviction and the need to be saved. But it is only when we exercise the will and commit ourselves to Christ that the process is complete. Faith is not mental assent to a body of doctrines, no matter how true those doctrines may be. Faith is not emotional concern. *Faith is commitment to Jesus Christ.*

When missionary John G. Paton was translating the Bible in the Outer Hebrides, he searched for the exact word to translate *believe.* Finally, he discovered it: the word meant "lean your whole weight upon." That is what saving faith is—leaning your whole weight upon Jesus Christ.

The false teachers who had come to Colossae tried to undermine the saints' faith in Christ and the Word. This same kind of undermining goes on today. Any religious teaching that dethrones Jesus Christ, or that makes salvation other than an experience of God's grace through faith, is anti-Christian and born of Satan.

Verse for today: "Rooted and built up in Him, and established in the faith, as ye have been taught, abounding therein with thanksgiving" (Colossians 2:7).

Also read: Colossians 2:3-10; Ephesians 2:8-10; Romans 5:1-2.

Action assignment: Examine your commitment to Jesus Christ. Are you leaning your whole weight (your mind, emotions and will) upon Him? If so, thank Him for the great privileges you have as a Christian. The daily study of His Word gives assurance and encourages growth so that faith becomes steadfast and established.

THE FINISHED WORK

A teenage boy whose mother was away on a visit found himself with time on his hands. He decided to read a book from the family library. His mother was a devout Christian, so the boy knew there would be a sermon at the beginning and an application at the end of the book, but there would also be some interesting stories in between.

While reading the book, he came across the phrase, "the finished work of Christ." It struck him with unusual power: "the finished work of Christ."

"Why does the author use this expression?" he asked himself. "Why not say the atoning or the propitiatory work of Christ?" (You see, he knew all the biblical terms. He just did not know the Saviour!) Then the words "It is finished" flashed into his mind, and he realized afresh that the work of salvation was accomplished.

"If the whole work was finished and the whole debt paid, what is there left for me to do?" He knew the answer, and fell to his knees to receive the Saviour and full forgiveness of sins. That is how J. Hudson Taylor, founder of the China Inland Mission, was saved.

Scripture says: "I have glorified Thee on the earth: I have finished the work which Thou gavest Me to do" (John 17:4).

Also read: John 19:30; Hebrews 12:2.

Action assignment: Take time now to thank God for paying the whole debt for your sins. Think of a teenager you know, and ask God to make this truth real in his or her life.

LET THE LORD BE LORD

Some standards and practices in our local churches are traditional but not necessarily scriptural. Can you remember when dedicated Christians opposed Christian radio "because Satan was the prince of the power of the air?" Some people still make Bible translation use a test of orthodoxy. The church is divided and weakened because Christians will not allow Jesus Christ to be Lord.

Think about it. No Christian has the right to "play God" in another Christian's life. We can pray, advise, and even admonish, but we cannot take the place of God. What is it that makes a dish of food "holy" or a day "holy"? It is the fact that we relate it to the Lord. Paul carefully emphasized the believer's union with Christ: "Whether we live or die, we belong to the Lord" (Romans 14:8, NIV). Our first responsibility is to the Lord. If Christians went to the Lord in prayer instead of to their brothers with criticism, our churches would certainly have a renaissance of fellowship.

Verse for today: "For this very reason, Christ died and returned to life so that He might be the Lord of both the dead and the living" (Romans 14:9, NIV).

Take time to read: Romans 14:1-23; 1 Corinthians 10:23-33; Galatians 5:13-26.

Action assignment: Which is more important to you: letting Christ be Lord or maintaining your own view of things? What happens when the two seem to conflict? Which is victor?

Mentally list several issues that have divided or have the potential of dividing your church or fellowship group. What did you do, or what can you do, to alleviate the tensions arising as the result of these issues? Ask God to help you be more sensitive to His truth and His grace, the combination that brings love and freedom to every situation.

DEBT FREE!

God has forgiven us. Redemption and forgiveness go together. The word translated *forgiveness* means "to send away" or "to cancel a debt." Christ has not only set us free and transferred us to a new kingdom, but He has canceled every debt so we cannot be enslaved again. Satan cannot find anything in the files that will indict us!

In recent years, the church has rediscovered the freedom of forgiveness. God's forgiveness of sinners is an act of His grace. We did not deserve to be forgiven, nor can we earn forgiveness. Knowing that we are forgiven makes it possible for us to fellowship with God, enjoy His grace, and seek to do His will. Forgiveness is not an excuse for sin; rather, it is an encouragement for obedience. And, because we have been forgiven, we can forgive others. The Parable of the Unforgiving Servant makes it clear that an unforgiving spirit always leads to bondage.

Verse for today: "In whom we have redemption through His blood, the forgiveness of sins, according to the riches of His grace" (Ephesians 1:7).

Also read: Matthew 18:21-35; Colossians 1:14; 3:13-14; Luke 6:37.

Action assignment: Memorize Ephesians 4:32—"And be ye kind one to another . . . even as God for Christ's sake hath forgiven you." Make a list of those whom you need to forgive. Maybe there is only one person on your list, but in the act of forgiving you will be changed and blessed.

"THINGS" THAT STEAL JOY

It is easy for us to get wrapped up in "things," not only the tangible things that we can see, but also the intangibles such as reputation, fame, achievement. Paul wrote about things that he thought were especially important before he received Christ. Some of those "things" were intangible, such as religious achievements, a feeling of self-satisfaction, morality. We today can be snared both by tangibles and intangibles, and as a result lose our joy.

But even the tangible things are not in themselves sinful. God made things, and the Bible declares that these things are good. God knows that we need certain things in order to live. In fact, He "giveth us richly all things to enjoy" (1 Timothy 6:17). But Jesus warns us that our lives do not consist in the abundance of the things that we possess. Quantity is no assurance of quality. Many people who have the things money can buy have lost the things that money cannot buy.

Today's Verse: "And He said unto them, 'Take heed, and beware of covetousness: for a man's life consisteth not in the abundance of the things which he possesseth' " (Luke 12:15).

Also read: Matthew 6:31-34; 1 Timothy 6:17; Philippians 3:4-9.

Action assignment: Make Matthew 6:33 your prayer this day. Substitute the word *rightness* for the word *righteousness,* and ask God to show you how you can make some "right" things happen.

A CHRISTIAN WIFE

It is the character and conduct of the wife that will win the lost husband—not arguments, but such attitudes as submission, understanding, love, kindness, and patience. These qualities are not manufactured; they are the fruit of the Spirit that comes when we are submitted to Christ and to one another. A Christian wife with purity and reverence will reveal in her life the character of God and influence her husband to trust Christ.

One of the greatest examples of a godly wife and mother in church history is Monica, the mother of St. Augustine. God used Monica's witnesses and prayers to win both her son and her husband to Christ, though her husband was not converted until shortly before his death. Augustine wrote in his *Confessions,* "She served him as her lord; and did her diligence to win him unto Thee . . . preaching Thee unto him by her conversation [behavior]; by which Thou ornamentest her, making her reverently amiable unto her husband."

The Bible says: "Wives, in the same way be submissive to your husbands so that, if any of them do not believe the Word, they may be won over without talk by the behavior of their wives, when they see the purity and reverence of your lives" (1 Peter 3:1-2).

Also read: all of 1 Peter 3; Proverbs 31:30-31.

Action assignment: Without rereading today's reading, see if you can write down the five qualities of a godly wife that are mentioned. Add other qualities that occur to you.

July

Be Renewed:

"Walk worthy
of the Lord unto all
pleasing, being fruitful in
every good work, and increasing
in the knowledge of God."

Colossians 1:10

1

WAITING EXPECTANTLY

Christians are waiting for Jesus Christ, and He may return at any time. We are not waiting for any "signs"; we are waiting for the Saviour. We are waiting for the redemption of the body and the hope of righteousness. When Jesus Christ returns, we will receive new bodies and be like Him. He will take us to the home He has prepared, and He will reward us for the service we have given in His name.

A local church that truly lives in the expectation of seeing Christ at any time will be a vibrant, victorious group of people. Expecting the Lord's return is a great motivation for soul-winning. If believers have these spiritual characteristics, our churches will become what God wants them to become. The result will be the winning of the lost and the glorifying of the Lord.

What every church should be is what every Christian should be: *elect* (born again), *exemplary* (imitating the right people), *enthusiastic*, (sharing the Gospel with others), and *expectant* (daily looking for Christ to return).

Perhaps it is time for an inventory.

Memorize: "Beloved, now are we the sons of God, and it doth not yet appear what we shall be: but we know that, when He shall appear, we shall be like Him; for we shall see Him as He is. And every man that hath this hope in him purifieth himself, even as He is pure" (1 John 3:2-3).

Dig deeper: Romans 8:23-25; 14:10-12; Philippians 3:20-21, 1 John 3:1-2; 14:1-6.

Action assignment: Find a familiar hymn in your hymnal about the Lord's return and sing it. John Peterson's "Marvelous Message We Bring" is an excellent choice. Thank God for the promise of Christ's return. Share with someone the gist of what you just read.

A SUBMISSIVE MIND

Timothy knew the meaning of sacrifice and service, but God rewarded him for his faithfulness. To begin with, Timothy had the joy of helping others. There were hardships and difficulties, but there were also victories and blessings. Because Timothy was faithful over a few things, God rewarded him with many things, and he entered into the joy of the submissive mind. He had the joy of serving with the great Apostle Paul and assisting him in some of his most difficult assignments.

But perhaps the greatest reward God gave to Timothy was to choose him to be Paul's replacement when the great apostle was called home. What an honor! Timothy was not only Paul's spiritual son and servant, but he became Paul's substitute—something young Timothy never dreamed of when he was busy serving Christ.

The submissive mind is not the product of an hour's sermon or a week's seminar or even a year's service. The submissive mind grows in us as, like Timothy, we yield to the Lord and seek to serve others.

Verse for today: "God resisteth the proud, but giveth grace unto the humble. Submit yourselves therefore to God" (James 4:6-7).

Also consider: 1 Peter 2:13-17; James 4:10.

Action assignment: After reading Philippians 2:5-8, thank God for your Saviour's submissiveness and His supreme example of humbleness. Think about some definite action you can take today that will involve your humbly serving another.

3

LEARNING HOW TO WALK

We who are parents know that our children (especially teenagers) do not like to hear us say, "Now, back when I was a kid. . . ." But this is an important part of training a family. It is a wonderful thing when a "spiritual father" can encourage and help his "children" out of his own experience with the Lord. "Come, ye children, hearken unto me: I will teach you the fear of the Lord" (Psalm 34:11).

What was the purpose for the Apostle Paul's fatherly ministry to believers? His aim was that his "children" might "walk worthy of God" (1 Thessalonians 2:12). Just as a father wants to be proud of his children, so the Lord wants to get glory through the lives of His children. Paul ministered to them in such a personal way because he was teaching them how to walk.

Every child must learn how to walk. He must have good models to follow. Paul admonished his children to walk "worthy of the Lord." We are to walk worthy of the calling we have in Christ Jesus. God has called us; we are saved by grace. We are a part of His kingdom and glory. One day we shall enter the eternal kingdom and share His glory. This assurance ought to govern our lives and make us want to please the Lord.

From the Bible: "That ye might walk worthy of the Lord unto all pleasing, being fruitful in every good work, and increasing in the knowledge of God" (Colossians 1:10).

Look up: Ephesians 4:1-3; Philippians 1:27; 2 John 4.

Action assignment: Write down things that will be counted as walking worthy of the Lord, things that you feel you should do today.

_____

_____

_____

Take time to talk with the Lord about these matters. Ask Him to enable you to let the Holy Spirit govern you in your walk today.

A TIME FOR CONCERN

The only nation on earth that is in a special covenant relationship with God is the nation of Israel. While many of the founding fathers of the United States of America were God-fearing men, the people of the United States can't claim special privileges from God because of their citizenship. It's true that the Puritan forefathers felt called to build God's kingdom on American soil, but we have no biblical basis for their vision.

What do we have? The promises of God for those of His people who will obey 2 Chronicles 7:14 and intercede for their country. God works in response to believing prayer, and believing prayer must be based on the Word of God.

Edward Everett Hale, author of *The Man without a Country,* wrote: "I am only one, but still I am one. I cannot do everything, but still I can do something. And because I cannot do everything, I will not refuse to do the something that I can do."

That's a good motto for the "company of the concerned." But add to it the great words of Paul: "I can do all things through Christ who strengthens me . . . for it is God who works in you both to will and to do for His good pleasure" (Phil. 4:13; 2:13).

It's time to be concerned.

Today's verse: "If My people who are called by My name will humble themselves, and pray and seek My face, and turn from their wicked ways, then I will hear from heaven, and will forgive their sin and heal their land" (2 Chron. 7:14).

Read: 2 Chronicles 7

Action assignment: Ask God to speak to you through some portion of 2 Chronicles 7. Read it over until He does. Take at least five minutes to pray specifically for your country and its leaders.

5

THE DISCIPLINE OF "WORKING OUT"

Chastening is a Greek word that means "child training, instruction, discipline." A Greek boy was expected to "work out" in the gymnasium until he reached his maturity. It was part of his preparation for adult life. Trials of the Christian life are viewed in Hebrews 12:5-13 as spiritual discipline that could help a believer mature. Instead of trying to escape the difficulties of life, we should rather be exercised by them so that we might grow.

When we are suffering, it is easy to think that God does not love us. But the writer of Hebrews gives proof that chastening comes from the Father's heart of love.

The words "son," "children," and "sons" are used six times in Hebrews 12:5-8. They refer to *adult sons* and not little children. A parent who would repeatedly chasten an *infant* child would be considered a monster. God deals with us as *adult* sons because we have been adopted and given adult standing in His family. The fact that the Father chastens us is proof that we are maturing, and it is the means by which we can mature even more.

Verse for today: "My son, despise not the chastening of the Lord; neither be weary of His correction" (Proverbs 3:11).

Also consider: Proverbs 3:12; Hebrews 12:5-13; Romans 8:18.

Action assignment: As trials come, thank God for them; remind yourself of at least two reasons why God has allowed them in your life.

"I WILL NEVER LEAVE YOU"

God has given us "all spiritual blessings . . . in Christ" (Eph. 1:3), and we must step out by faith and claim them. He has set before His church an open door that nobody can close (Rev. 3:8), and we must walk through that door by faith and claim new territory for the Lord. *It is impossible to stand still in Christian life and service; for when you stand still, you immediately start going backward.* "Let us go on!" is God's challenge to His church (Heb. 6:1), and that means moving ahead into new territory.

The writer of Hebrews 13:5 quotes Joshua 1:5 and applies it to Christians today: "I will never leave you nor forsake you."

This means that God's people can move forward in God's will and be assured of God's presence. "If God is for us, who can be against us?" (Rom. 8:31). Before Joshua began his conquest of Jericho, the Lord appeared to him and assured him of His presence (Josh. 5:13–15). That was all Joshua needed to be guaranteed of victory.

When my wife and I were in our first pastorate, God led the church to build a new sanctuary. The congregation was neither large nor wealthy, and a couple of financial experts told us it couldn't be done; but the Lord saw us through. He used 1 Chronicles 28:20 in a special way to strengthen and assure me throughout that difficult project. I can assure you from experience that the promise of God's presence really works!

A promise: "Have I not commanded you? Be strong and courageous. Do not be terrified; do not be discouraged, for the LORD your God will be with you wherever you go" (Josh. 1:9, NIV).

Read: Joshua 5:13–6:20; 1 Chronicles, as mentioned above.

Action assignment: Dedicate the actions of the day to God and the word of His grace, resulting in a satisfactory profit in spiritual growth (see Acts 20:32). A smile, a kind look, considerate responses, prayerful reactions—all help toward maturity and lead into new territory. Go another step: Read 2 Corinthians 4.

7

YOU ARE WRITING A GOSPEL

"We have some neighbors who believe a false gospel," a church member told his pastor. "Do you have some literature I can give them?"

The pastor opened his Bible to 2 Corinthians 3:2, "You are our letter, written in our hearts, known and read by all men" (NASB). He said, "The best literature in the world is no substitute for your own life. Let them see Christ in your behavior and this will open up opportunities to share Christ's Gospel with them."

The greatest weapon against the devil is a godly life. And a local church that practices the truth, that "behaves what it believes," is going to defeat the enemy. This is the first essential for victory in this battle.

> *You are writing a gospel,*
> *A chapter each day,*
> *By the deeds that you do*
> *And the words that you say.*
> *Men read what you write,*
> *Whether faithful or true:*
> *Just what is the gospel*
> *According to you?*
> (source unknown)

Verse for today: "Whatever happens, conduct yourselves in a manner worthy of the Gospel of Christ" (Philippians 1:27, NIV).

Also read: Ephesians 4:1; Colossians 1:10; Philippians 3:20.

Action assignment: The old English word *conversation* means *walk* and not *talk*. Keep this in mind if you use the *King James Version* of the Bible in your study. The world around us knows only the gospel that it sees in our lives. Ask God to give you a consistent testimony to the unbelievers in your world.

CHERISH GOD'S BOOK

Today's thought: The most important book to the Christian is the Bible.

Paul was thankful that the saints in Thessalonica had the right spiritual attitudes toward the Word of God. This helped them endure in the hour of suffering. They did not receive it as the word of men; they received it as the Word of God. We must never treat the Bible just like any other book, for the Bible is different in origin, character, and content. The Bible is the Word of God. It was inspired by the Spirit of God and written by men of God who were used by the Spirit. God's Word is holy, pure, and perfect. The Bible was written at great cost, not only to the writers, but to Jesus Christ who became Man that the Word of God might be given to us.

It may be a personal prejudice, but I dislike seeing a Bible on the floor or at the bottom of a stack of books. If I am carrying several books with my Bible, I try to remember to put the Bible on top. If we appreciate the Bible as the inspired Word of God, we will reveal this appreciation in our treatment of the Bible.

From God's Word: "All Scripture is given by inspiration of God, and is profitable for doctrine, for reproof, for correction, for instruction in righteousness" (2 Timothy 3:16).

Check out: 1 Peter 1:23, 25; Psalm 19:7; 119:11, 89; Job 23:12; 2 Peter 1:21; Hebrews 5:11-14; Matthew 4:4.

Action assignment: Think for a moment what your life would be like if you did not have God's Word. Ask God to enable you to give your Bible its rightful place in your life.

9

YOUR HEAVENLY SANCTUARY

The Christian is a citizen of two worlds, the earthly and the heavenly. He must render to Caesar the things that are Caesar's and to God the things that are God's. Because he is a citizen of two worlds, the Christian must learn how to walk by faith in a world that is governed by sight. Practical man says, "Seeing is believing!" But the man of faith replies, "Believing is seeing!"

This principle of faith must apply to our relationship to the heavenly sanctuary. We have never seen this sanctuary. Yet we believe what the Bible tells us about it. We realize that God is not worshiped today in temples made with hands. There is no special place on earth where God dwells. We may call a local church building a "house of God," but we know that God does not live there. The building is dedicated to God and His service, but it is not His dwelling place.

Hebrews 9 presents a detailed contrast between the Old Covenant sanctuary (the tabernacle) and the New Covenant heavenly sanctuary where Jesus Christ now ministers. This contrast makes it clear that the New Covenant sanctuary is superior.

The Bible says: "For Christ is not entered into the holy places made with hands . . . but into heaven itself, now to appear in the presence of God for us" (Hebrews 9:24).

Also read: Isaiah 57:15; Acts 7:46-50; John 4:19-24; Hebrews 4:15.

Action assignment: Spend a few minutes now worshiping at your heavenly sanctuary. Thank God that Jesus Christ, your High Priest, is ministering for you in the presence of God today.

WHO CONTROLS YOUR THINKING?

The world wants to control your mind, but God wants to transform your mind. The word *transform* is the same as *transfigure* in Matthew 17:2. It has come into the English language as the word *metamorphosis*, which describes a change from within. The world wants to change your mind, so it exerts pressure from without. But the Holy Spirit changes your mind by releasing power from within. If the world controls your thinking, you are a conformer; if God controls your thinking, you are a transformer.

God transforms our minds and makes us spiritually minded by His living Word. As you spend time meditating on God's Word, memorizing it, and making it a part of your inner self, God's Spirit will gradually make your mind more spiritual.

Verse for today: "Do not conform any longer to the pattern of this world, but be transformed by the renewing of your mind. Then you will be able to test and approve what God's will is— His good, pleasing and perfect will" (Romans 12:2, NIV).

More to consider: Ephesians 4:17-24; Colossians 3:1-11; Matthew 17:2; 1 Corinthians 2:16; Philippians 2:5.

Action assignment: Consider the change a butterfly undergoes —from one stage to another. It changes through a series of inner reformations. On the outside, you may look the same as before your spiritual rebirth; on the inside, however, wonderful changes have been taking place. Mentally list some of those changes— even if your conversion was years ago.

To keep spiritually sharp, try to memorize at least one new verse a week. You may wish to use index cards with the verses on the side and the references on the other. Thank God for His transforming power that helps you not only memorize His Word, but also live it.

11

A SUBMISSIVE WIFE

Any husband is proud of a wife who is attractive; but that beauty must come from the heart, not the store. We are not *of* this world, but must not look as though we came from *out of* this world!

Peter did not forbid the wearing of jewelry any more than the wearing of apparel. The word "wearing" in 1 Peter 3:3 means "the putting around," and refers to a gaudy display of jewelry. It is possible to wear jewelry and still honor God, and we must not judge one another in this matter.

Peter closed this section on godly wives by pointing to Sarah as an example of a godly, submissive wife. Christian wives today would probably embarrass their husbands if they called them "lord," but their attitudes ought to be such that they could call them "lord" and people would believe it. The believing wife who submits to Christ and to her husband, and who cultivates a "meek and quiet spirit" (v. 4) will never have to be afraid. God will watch over her even when her unsaved mate creates problems for her.

Scripture for today: "Wives, be in subjection to your own husbands; that, if any obey not the Word, they also may without the Word be won by the conversation of the wives; while they behold your chaste conversation coupled with fear. Whose adorning let it not be that outward adorning of plaiting the hair, and of wearing of gold, or of putting on of apparel" (1 Peter 3:1-3).

Also read: Genesis 18, for background.

Action assignment: Can you list the names of five submissive women mentioned in the Bible?

BEAUTIFUL FRUIT

What is the "fruit" God wants to see from our lives? He is not interested simply in "church activities," but in the kind of spiritual fruit that is produced when we are in fellowship with Christ. Too many Christians try to "produce results" in their own efforts instead of abiding in Christ and allowing His life to produce the fruit.

The fruit tree does not make a great deal of noise when it produces its crop; it merely allows the life within to work in a natural way, and fruit is the result. "He that abideth in Me, and I in him, the same bringeth forth much fruit: for without Me ye can do nothing" (John 15:5).

The difference between spiritual fruit and human "religious activity" is that the fruit brings glory to Jesus Christ. Whenever we do anything in our own strength, we have a tendency to boast about it. True spiritual fruit is so beautiful and wonderful that no man can claim credit for it; the glory must go to God alone.

Verse for today: "Abide in Me, and I in you. As the branch cannot bear fruit of itself, except it abide in the vine; no more can ye, except ye abide in Me" (John 15:4).

Also read: Romans 1:13; 6:22; Hebrews 13:15.

Action assignment: Christian character that glorifies God is an evidence of the "fruit of the Spirit." Study Galatians 5:22-23. As you daily fellowship with Christ and abide in Him, you will also glorify Him. Thank Him for this great truth.

13

TRUE LEADERSHIP

When my wife and I have ministered in England, we have always tried to arrange a stay in London. We especially enjoy shopping at Selfridge's and Harrod's, London's two leading department stores. H. Gordon Selfridge, who built the great store that bears his name, always claimed that he was a success because he was a *leader* and not a *boss.*

The leader says, "Let's go!" while the boss says, "Go!" The boss *knows* how it's done, but the leader *shows* how it's done. The boss inspires fear; the leader inspires enthusiasm based on respect and good will. The boss fixes the *blame* for the breakdown, while the true leader fixes the breakdown.

This philosophy of management certainly agrees with the Apostle Paul's philosophy of leadership. As a spiritually mature person, he did not use authority to *demand* respect, but to *command* respect. The life that he lived and the work that he did were his credentials, for it was evident that the hand of God was upon his life. Paul could dare to write, "From henceforth let no man trouble me: for I bear in my body the marks of the Lord Jesus" (Galatians 6:17).

Verse for today: "I have set you an example that you should do as I have done for you" (John 13:15, NIV).

Also read: 1 Corinthians 9:24-27; Philippians 3:17; 4:8-9; 1 Timothy 4:12; Colossians 1:15-20, 28-29.

Action assignment: What makes a good leader? List three or more characteristics of a few people you consider to be good leaders. What traits do they have in common? Compare their leadership styles to that of the Lord Jesus and the Apostle Paul.

No matter who you are, you are influencing those around you. Ask God to help you set the best example you can—influencing others so they *want* to become Christians.

USE THE TOOLS YOU HAVE

Only one verse (4:31) is devoted to Shamgar in the Book of Judges. What was significant about Shamgar was the weapon that he used. An ox goad was a strong pole about eight feet long. At one end was a sharp metal point for prodding the oxen and at the other end a spade for cleaning the dirt off the plow. It was the closest thing Shamgar could find to a spear because the enemy had confiscated the weapons of the Israelites (5:8; see 1 Sam. 13:19–22).

Here was a man who obeyed God and defeated the enemy even though his resources were limited. Instead of complaining about not possessing a sword or spear, Shamgar gave what he had to the Lord, and the Lord used it. To stand his ground against the enemy, having only a farmer's tool instead of a soldier's full military equipment, marks Shamgar out as a brave man with steadfast courage.

Charles Spurgeon once gave a lecture at his Pastor's College entitled "To Workers with Slender Apparatus." Shamgar didn't hear that lecture, but I'm sure he could have given it! And I suspect he would have closed his lecture by saying, "Give whatever tools you have to the Lord, stand your ground courageously, and trust God to use what's in your hand to accomplish great things for His glory."

Don't forget: "Whatever you do, work at it with all your heart, as working for the Lord, not for men, since you know that you will receive an inheritance from the Lord as a reward. It is the Lord Christ you are serving" (Col. 3:23–24, NIV).

Read: Judges 3

Action assignment: What are some of the tools you can use to serve the Lord? A pen, to write a letter? Or better, a computer? Your kitchen? Your hands? Think about a way you can use one or more of these tools to reach out in love to someone.

15

ON YOUR MARK, GET SET, GO!

No chastening is pleasant either to the father or his son at the time, but the benefits are profitable. Few children believe it when their parents say, "This hurts me more than it hurts you." But it is true just the same. The Father does not enjoy having to discipline His children, but the benefits "afterward" make the chastening an evidence of His love.

What are some of the benefits? For one thing, there is "the peaceable fruit of righteousness" (Hebrews 12:11). Instead of continuing to sin, the child strives to do what is right. There is also peace instead of war—the *peaceable* fruit of righteousness. The rebellion has ceased and the child is in a loving fellowship with the Father. Chastening also encourages a child to exercise in spiritual matters—the Word of God, prayer, meditation, witnessing. All lead to a new joy. Of course, the important thing is how God's child responds to chastening. He can despise it or faint under it, both of which are wrong. He should show reverence to the Father by submitting to His will, using the experience to exercise himself spiritually.

Remember this: "No discipline seems pleasant at the time, but painful. Later on, however, it produces a harvest of righteousness and peace for those who have been trained by it" (Hebrews 12:11, NIV).

Also consider: Isaiah 35:3; Proverbs 4:26; Hebrews 12:5, 12-13; 1 Timothy 4:7-8.

Action assignment: Think of four areas in which chastening can encourage you to exercise yourself spiritually. Ask God for strength during "training."

THE SECURE MIND

Worry is actually wrong thinking (the mind) and wrong feeling (the heart) about circumstances, people, and things. So, if we have a single mind, a submissive mind, and a spiritual mind, we should not have too much trouble with worry. All we need is something to *guard* the heart and mind so that worry will not enter. Paul describes *the secure mind:* "And the peace of God, which passeth all understanding, shall keep your hearts and minds through Christ Jesus" (Philippians 4:7). That word *keep* is a military term; it means "stand guard, garrison." (Paul was chained to a soldier, you will remember.)

God gives us regular "examinations" in our daily lives to help us develop our spiritual attitudes. Learning and living go together, and He will give us the grace we need for every demand. As we practice exercising the right kind of attitudes, we will find deep joy welling up in our hearts—joy in spite of circumstances, people, and things—and joy that defeats worry and fills us with the peace of God.

Verse for today: "But the fruit of the Spirit is love, joy, peace, longsuffering, gentleness, goodness, faith, meekness, temperance: against such there is no law" (Galatians 5:22-23).

Also read: Philippians 4.

Action assignment: List the spiritual resources the believer has in Christ as found in Philippians 4. Underline the ones in which you need more development. Then thank God that He makes available every provision you need to eliminate worry from your life.

17

JESUS, OUR EXAMPLE

Jesus is the Christian's example, especially in the way He responded to suffering. He proved that a person could be in the will of God, be greatly loved by God, and still suffer unjustly. There is a shallow brand of popular theology today that claims Christians will *not* suffer if they are in the will of God. Those who promote such ideas have not meditated much on the Cross.

Our Lord's humility and submission were not an evidence of weakness but of power. Jesus could have summoned the armies of heaven to rescue Him! His words to Pilate in John 18:33-38 are proof that He was in complete command of the situation. It was Pilate who was on trial, not Jesus! Jesus had committed Himself to the Father, and the Father always judges righteously.

We are not saved by following Christ's example, because each of us would stumble over 1 Peter 2:22, which records that Jesus "did no sin." Sinners need a Saviour, not an example. Christ becomes our example only after we have received Him as Saviour. Then He is our example in many respects, including suffering. We will want to "follow closely upon His steps" (a literal translation of the final words in 1 Peter 2:21, below).

Verse for today: "For even hereunto were ye called: because Christ also suffered for us, leaving us an example, that ye should follow His steps" (1 Peter 2:21).

Also read: Matthew 11:29; 20:27-28; John 10:4; 13:13.

Action assignment: List as many ways as possible that you can follow Jesus. Ask God to help you grow more and more like His Son.

HOW GREAT A DEBT

Paul and his associates had received a special offering from the Gentile churches in Greece for the suffering Jewish saints in Jerusalem. It was an expression of unfeigned love on the part of the Gentiles toward their Jewish brethren. It also meant practical relief at a time when the poor Jewish believers needed it the most. And it was a bond that brought Jews and Gentiles in the church closer together.

Paul considered this offering the paying of a debt. The Gentiles, having received spiritual wealth from the Jews, now were returning material wealth, thereby paying their debt. It was the Jews who had given the Gentiles the Word of God and the Son of God.

Today we Christians also ought to feel an obligation to pay our debt by praying for Israel, sharing the Gospel, and helping in a material way. Anti-Semitism has no place in the life of a dedicated Christian.

Verse for today: "I am obligated both to Greeks and non-Greeks, both to the wise and the foolish" (Romans 1:14, NIV).

Also read: 2 Corinthians 8 and 9; Romans 8:12; 11:33-36; 13:8.

Action assignment: One version of the Lord's Prayer says, "Forgive us our debts as we forgive our debtors." Who are your debtors? List them:_____

_____.

What are your debts—spiritually speaking? List the 3 to 5 that readily come to mind:

1. _____ 2. _____

3. _____ 4. _____ 5. _____

Ask God's help in finding tangible ways to pay up your "debt" to Him as well as ways to show your love to Christians and non-Christians alike.

19

SLIP-SLIDING AWAY?

The sin of Israel was apostasy—"departing from the living God." Does "apostasy" mean abandoning one's faith and therefore being condemned forever? No. The children of Israel departed from the living God by refusing God's will for their lives and stubbornly wanting to go their own way back to Egypt. God did not permit them to return to Egypt. Rather, He disciplined them in the wilderness.

True believers have an eternal salvation because they trust a living Saviour who constantly intercedes for them. But this confidence is no excuse for sin. God disciplines His children. Believers who doubt God's Word and rebel against Him do not miss heaven, but they do miss out on the blessings of their inheritance today—and they must suffer the chastening of God.

Verse for today: "And surely I will be with you always, to the very end of the age" (Matthew 28:20, NIV).

More from God's Word: Psalms 95 and 139; Matthew 28:17-20; 1 Timothy 4:1-5; Hebrews 4:12-13.

Action assignment: Name three things you look forward to in heaven. Look for ways of cultivating these in your activities and experiences today. For example, if you look forward to worshiping God in heaven, worship Him today. If you look forward to living in peace and understanding with others, work for that now. Cultivating your hopes about heaven can help you not to depart from God. Thank God for His faithfulness to you.

STILL IN CIRCULATION

"I just *love* that hat!"

"I really *love* old-fashioned peanut butter!"

Words, like coins, can be in circulation for such a long time that they start wearing out. Unfortunately, *love* is one word that is fast losing its value. *Christian* love, however, has eternal value.

In describing the life that is real, the Apostle John uses three words repeatedly: *love, life,* and *light.* He explains that love, life, and light belong together.

Christian love is affected by light *and* darkness. A Christian who is walking in the light (which simply means he is obeying God) is going to love his brother Christian. Moreover, Christian love is a matter of life *or* death; to live in hatred is to live in spiritual death. Finally, Christian love is a matter of truth *or* error because if we know God's love toward us, we show God's love toward others. So some things never change!

Verse for today: "Dear friends, let us love one another, for love comes from God. Everyone who loves has been born of God and knows God" (1 John 4:7, NIV).

Also read: 1 John 2:7-11; 3:10-24; 4:8-21; James 2:8; Ephesians 5:1-2.

Action assignment: Life, love, and light must not be separated. Have you ever tried to separate them? For example, have you said you were walking in the light while at the same time you were detesting someone?

How does Christian love make a difference in your lifestyle? Think of two people who do not know that you are a Christian, and prayerfully consider what you can do today to show that you love them. Ask God to make His life, love, and light an integrated reality in your life day by day.

THE QUEST FOR THINGS

When five missionaries were martyred by the Auca Indians in Ecuador, some newspapers and magazines considered the tragedy to be a great waste of life. While it did bring sorrow and grief to friends and loved ones, subsequent events proved that their deaths were not a waste either for them or for the world. The words of Jim Elliot were true: "He is no fool who gives what he cannot keep to gain what he cannot lose."

The quest for "things" is robbing people of joy, and this includes Christian people. We want to possess things, and then we discover that things possess us. The only way to victory and joy is to have a spiritual mind and to look at things from God's point of view. Like Paul, we must be *accountants* with the right *values*, *athletes* with the right *vigor*, and *aliens* with the right *vision*. "I count ... I press ... I look" are the verbs that described Paul—a man with a spiritual mind.

Verse for today: "For to me to live is Christ, and to die is gain" (Philippians 1:21).

Also read: Matthew 6:19-21; Hebrews 13:5.

Action assignment: Read Philippians 3 and especially note verses 8, 14 and 20. Take the words "I count ... I press ... I look" and write out Paul's philosophy of life. Ask God to make you an imitator of Paul because he had the right value system.

CHRIST ABOVE ALL!

"The Word of God" is one of the familiar names of our Lord in Scripture (John 1:1-14). Just as we reveal our minds and hearts to others by our words, so the Father reveals Himself to us through His Son, the incarnate Word (John 14:7-11). A word is made up of letters, and Jesus Christ is "Alpha and Omega" (Revelation 22:13). He is the "divine alphabet" of God's revelation to us.

The Word of God is "living and powerful" (Hebrews 4:12); what's more, it fulfills His purposes on earth (Revelation 17:17). Jehovah Himself says, "I am watching to see that My Word is fulfilled" (Jeremiah 1:12, NIV). Just as the Word was the Father's agent in creation (John 1:1-3), so the Word is His agent for judgment and consummation.

Christ's most important name is "King of kings, and Lord of lords" (Revelation 19:16). This is His victorious name, and it brings to mind references such as Daniel 2:47. Paul used this same title for our Lord Jesus Christ in 1 Timothy 6:15. The title speaks of Christ's sovereignty, for all kings and lords must submit to Him. No matter who was on the throne of the Roman Empire, Jesus Christ was his King and Lord!

Scripture to remember: "Pursue righteousness, godliness, faith, love, perseverance, and gentleness.... Keep the commandment without stain or reproach, until the appearing of our Lord Jesus Christ, which He will bring about at the proper time—He who is the blessed and only Sovereign, the King of kings and Lord of lords" (1 Timothy 6:11, 14-15, NASB).

Additional Scripture: Go back to today's reading and look up the verses listed.

Action assignment: Make your prayer one of worship and adoration. Praise God for His attributes. List these attributes before you pray.

23

LOVE YOUR ENEMIES

We should not only love God's people; we should also *love our enemies.* The recipients of Peter's first letter were experiencing a certain amount of personal persecution because they were doing the will of God. Peter warned them that *official* persecution was just around the corner, so they had better prepare. The church today had better prepare too, because difficult times are ahead.

As Christians, we can live on one of three levels. We can return evil for good, which is the satanic level. We can return good for good and evil for evil, which is the human level. Or, we can return good for evil, which is the divine level. Jesus is the perfect example of this last approach. As God's loving children, we must not give "an eye for an eye, and a tooth for a tooth," which is the basis for *justice.* We must operate on the basis of *mercy,* for that is the way God deals with us.

Jesus tells us: "Love your enemies and pray for those who persecute you, that you may be sons of your Father in heaven" (Matthew 5:44-45, NIV).

Also read: Matthew 5:38-48; 1 Peter 2:21-23; 3:9.

Action assignment: Surprise someone on your "enemy list" by doing a kind deed. Ask God to help you live by Jesus' command.

WHEN WE GIVE ENTHUSIASTICALLY

It is possible to give generously but not give enthusiastically. "The preacher says I should give until it hurts," says a miserly church member, "but for me, it hurts just to think about giving!" The Macedonian churches needed no prompting or reminding, as did the church at Corinth. They were more than willing to share in the collection. In fact, *they begged to be included!* How many times have you heard a Christian *beg* for somebody to take an offering?

Their giving was voluntary and spontaneous. It was of grace, not pressure. They gave because they wanted to give and because they had experienced the grace of God. Grace not only frees us from our sins, but it frees us from ourselves. The grace of God will open your heart *and your hand.* Then your giving is not the result of cold calculation, but of warmhearted jubilation!

Believe it or not: "The Macedonian churches . . . gave as much as they were able, and even beyond their ability. Entirely on their own, they urgently pleaded with us for the privilege of sharing in this service to the saints" (2 Corinthians 8:1, 3-4, NIV).

For further thought: 1 Samuel 15:22; Mark 12:33; 2 Corinthians 9:6-7.

Action assignment: Write out reasons you think the Macedonian churches were so eager to give their money—and themselves. Talk to God about your attitude toward giving.

WORRY—A JOY THIEF

How many people have been robbed of peace and fulfillment because of worry! In fact, worry even has *physical* consequences, and, while medicine can remove the symptoms, it cannot remove the cause. Worry is an "inside job." You can purchase "sleep" at the drugstore, but you cannot purchase "rest."

If Paul had wanted to worry, he had plenty of occasion. He was a political prisoner facing possible execution. His friends in Rome were divided in their attitudes toward his case. He had no mission board supporting him and no Legal Aid Society defending him. But in spite of all these difficulties, *Paul did not worry!* Instead, he wrote a letter filled with joy and told us how to stop worrying.

How do we capture this thief and keep it from taking away the joy that is rightfully ours in Christ? The answer is: *we must cultivate the right kind of mind.* If outlook determines outcome, then the attitude of mind that we cultivate will determine our joy or lack of it.

Verse for today: "Are not five sparrows sold for two farthings, and not one of them is forgotten before God? But even the very hairs of your head are all numbered. Fear not therefore: ye are of more value than many sparrows" (Luke 12:6-7).

Also consider: Psalm 56:3-4; Romans 8:15.

Action assignment: Fear and worry are akin to each other. The best antidote to fear is faith. Make a list of the things, people, and circumstances which cause you to worry. Then commit each one to God in prayer for His will to be done. Make faith a fact that eliminates worry and fear.

SALVATION OR JUDGMENT?

Malachi 4:5 promises that Elijah himself will come, and that his coming is related to the "Day of the Lord" that will burn the wicked like stubble (v. 1). Inasmuch as "the great and terrible Day of the Lord" did not occur in New Testament times, we have to believe that John the Baptist was not the promised Elijah, even though he ministered like Elijah. Therefore, this prophecy is yet to be fulfilled. It may well be that Elijah will return to earth as one of the two witnesses of Revelation 11:3–12, for the signs that these two men will perform remind us of the miracles of Elijah.

It seems odd that the Old Testament should end with the word "*curse.*" When we get near the end of the New Testament, we read, "And there shall be no more curse" (Rev. 22:3). All of creation is eagerly awaiting the return of the Savior, expecting Him to deliver creation from the bondage of sin (Rom. 8:18–23). We, too, should be expecting Him and, while we're waiting, witness of Him to others. For when the Sun of righteousness arises, it will mean either burning or blessing (Mal. 4:1–2): blessing to those who have trusted Him, burning to those who have rejected Him.

Nobody can afford to argue with God the way the Israelites did when they heard Malachi, because God will always have the last word. For you, will that last word be salvation or judgment?

Today's verse: "'Surely the day is coming; it will burn like a furnace. All the arrogant and every evildoer will be stubble, and that day that is coming will set them on fire,' says the LORD Almighty. 'Not a root or a branch will be left to them. But for you who revere My name, the sun of righteousness will rise with healing in its wings. And you will go out and leap like calves released from the stall'" (Mal. 4:1–2, NIV).

Read: Malachi 4

Action assignment: Review the admonition of Titus 2:11–15, and if you are a believer, offer God a word of praise for His complete salvation. If you lack this personal knowledge of Christ, consider His redemptive sufficiency and surrender to His authority, before God's judgment descends.

WHY WE WORSHIP JESUS

We worship Jesus Christ because of who He is. But there is a second reason why we worship Him.

To begin with, Jesus is in heaven. He is not in the manger, in Jerusalem, on the cross, or in the tomb. He is ascended and exalted in heaven. What an encouragement this is to suffering Christians, to know that their Saviour has defeated every enemy and is now controlling events from glory! He too suffered, but God turned His suffering into glory.

But where is Christ in heaven? He is *in the midst.* The Lamb is the center of all that transpires in heaven. All creation centers in Him (the four living creatures), as do all of God's people (the elders). The angels around the throne encircle the Saviour and praise Him.

He is also *at the throne.* Some sentimental Christian poetry and hymnody dethrones our Saviour and emphasizes only His earthly life. These poems and songs glamorize "the gentle carpenter" or "the humble teacher," but they fail to exalt the risen Lord! We do not worship a babe in a manger or a corpse on a cross. We worship the living, reigning Lamb of God who is in the midst of all in heaven.

Scripture for today: "Since then we have a great High Priest who has passed through the heavens, Jesus the Son of God, let us hold fast our confession. For we do not have a high priest who cannot sympathize with our weaknesses, but one who has been tempted in all things as we are, yet without sin" (Hebrews 4:14-15, NASB).

Additional Scripture: Read all of Revelation 5.

Action assignment: Meditate on the fact that Jesus Christ is in heaven as your personal Mediator, pleading your case (1 Timothy 2:5).

WHY? WHY? WHY?

One of the modern "Christian myths" that ought to be silenced says that when you trust Jesus Christ, you get rid of all your problems.

You don't.

It's true that your basic *spiritual* problem—your relationship with God—has been solved; but with that solution comes a whole new set of problems that you didn't face when you were an unbeliever, like: "Why do good people suffer and evil people prosper?" or "Why isn't God answering prayer?" or "When I'm doing my best for the Lord, why do I experience the worst from others?"

Christians who claim to be without problems are either not telling the truth or not growing and experiencing real life. Perhaps they're just not thinking at all. They're living in a religious dream world that has blocked out reality and stifled honest feelings. Like Job's uncomfortable comforters, they mistake shallow optimism for the peace of God and "the good life" for the blessing of God. You never hear them ask what David and Jesus asked: "My God, My God, why have You forsaken Me?" (Ps. 22:1; Matt. 27:46)

Habakkuk wasn't that kind of believer. As he surveyed the land of Judah, and then watched the international scene, he found himself struggling with some serious problems. But he did the right thing: he took his problems to the Lord.

Today's Verse: "The LORD God is my strength, and He will make my feet like hinds' feet, and He will make me to walk upon mine high places. To the chief singer on my stringed instruments" (Hab. 3:19, KJV).

Read: Habakkuk 1:1–4; 3:16–19

Action assignment: Sing a song such as "What a Friend We Have in Jesus" or "Take Your Burdens to the Lord."

JOY DESPITE CIRCUMSTANCES

Most of us must confess that when things are "going our way" we feel a lot happier and are much easier to live with. "Dad must have had an easy day at the office," little Peggy said to her visiting girlfriend. "He didn't squeal the tires when he pulled into the driveway, and he didn't slam the door when he came into the house. And he even gave Mother a kiss!"

But have you ever stopped to consider how few of the circumstances of life are really under our control? We have no control over the weather or over the traffic on the expressway or over the things other people say and do. The person whose happiness depends on ideal circumstances is going to be miserable much of the time! The poet Byron wrote, "Men are the sport of circumstances." And yet, the Apostle Paul in the worst of circumstances wrote the Philippian letter and saturated it with joy.

Jesus Christ was "a Man of sorrows and acquainted with grief." Yet He possessed a deep joy that was beyond anything the world could offer. As He faced the cruel death of Calvary, Jesus said to His followers, "These things have I spoken unto you, that My joy might remain in you, and that your joy might be full" (John 15:11).

Verse for today: "And my soul shall be joyful in the Lord: it shall rejoice in His salvation" (Psalm 35:9).

Consider: Isaiah 61:10; Psalm 16:11; Romans 14:17; 1 Peter 4:13-14.

Action assignment: How is your joy? Illness, death, and financial problems are among the facts of everyday life. But God's Word is laced throughout with promises of joy for those who keep their minds on Him. Trust God to lead you into His joy.

REMOVE THOSE WEIGHTS!

Athletes used to wear training weights to help them prepare for contests. One modern example is a baseball player who swings a bat that has a heavy metal collar before he steps to the plate. No athlete would actually *participate* wearing the weights, however, because they would slow him down. Too much weight would tax one's endurance.

What are the "weights" (Hebrews 12:1) that we should remove so that we might win the race? All the things that hinder our progress. They might even be "good things" in the eyes of others. A winning athlete does not choose between the good and the bad; he chooses between the better and the best. We should also get rid of "the sin that so easily entangles (Hebrews 12:1, NIV). While he does not name any specific sin, the writer of Hebrews was probably referring to the sin of unbelief. It was unbelief that kept Israel out of the Promised Land, and it is unbelief that hinders us from entering into our spiritual inheritance in Christ. The phrase "by faith" (or "through faith") is used 21 times in Hebrews 11, indicating that it is faith in Christ that enables us to endure.

The Bible commands: "Wherefore . . . let us lay aside every weight, and the sin which doth so easily beset us, and let us run with patience the race that is set before us" (Hebrews 12:1).

Also read: 1 Corinthians 9:24-27; Hebrews 11:6; 12:2-3; James 5:11.

Action assignment: What "weights" hinder your progress? Ask God to help you lay them aside today.

31

A HISTORY LESSON

The Jews wanted Jesus to give them a sign to prove He was the Messiah. Jesus answered (Matthew 12:38-41) that they would be given only the sign of Jonah—that He would spend three days and nights in the grave as Jonah had in the great fish.

Jesus is far greater than Jonah, however. Jesus is greater in His person, for Jonah was a mere man. Jesus was greater in His obedience, for Jonah disobeyed God and was chastened. Jesus actually died, while Jonah's "grave" was in the belly of the fish. Jesus rose from the dead under His own power. Jonah ministered only to one city, while Jesus gave His life for the whole world.

Certainly Jesus was greater in His love, for Jonah did not love the people of Nineveh; he wanted them to die. Jonah's message saved Nineveh from judgment; he was a messenger of the wrath of God. Jesus' message was that of grace and salvation. When we trust Christ, we are not only saved from judgment, but we receive eternal, abundant life.

Verse for today: "For whosoever shall do the will of My Father which is in heaven, the same is My brother, and sister, and mother" (Matthew 12:50).

Also read: Jonah 2; Luke 24:13-35; Matthew 28:11-15.

Action assignment: God will not forgive the rejection of His Son. The Jewish religious leaders rejected Jesus and failed to honor Him as God. Think about several ways in which you honor Jesus as God's Son. Are there any ways in which you dishonor Him? For instance, if you hear others take His name in vain, what do you do? Pray about wisdom concerning more ways to honor Jesus.

August

Be Renewed:

"Whosoever will be great among you, let him be your minister; and whosoever will be chief among you, let him be your servant."

Matthew 20:26-27

PRIORITIES THAT COUNT

Like the Pharisees of old, we Christians have a way of majoring in the minors—dividing over matters insignificant to vital Christian faith. I have heard of churches splitting over such petty matters as the location of the piano and the serving of meals on Sundays.

What must be first in our lives? Not the externals, but the eternals: righteousness, peace, and joy. Where do they come from? The Holy Spirit of God. If each believer would yield to the Spirit and major in a godly life, Christians would not be fighting with each other over minor matters. If we fail to keep our spiritual priorities in order, how can we expect to see the harmony so essential for healthy church life?

Verse for today: "Woe to you, teachers of the Law and Pharisees, you hypocrites! You give a tenth of your spices—mint, dill and cummin. But you have neglected the more important matters of the law—justice, mercy and faithfulness. You should have practiced the latter, without neglecting the former" (Matthew 23:23, NIV).

More to read: Matthew 23:13-32; Romans 14; 1 Corinthians 8:9-13.

Action assignment: A normal body temperature is 98.6 degrees Fahrenheit. If you gave your church a "body temperature reading," would it be abnormally low, high, or normal?

A low reading might indicate lethargy. A high reading might indicate heated argumentation, disharmony, and strife. What factor(s) might be contributing to a less-than-ideal situation in your church? List as many as you can think of:_____

_____

_____

Commit these to God in prayer, asking Him to show you how you can be an instrument of His righteousness, peace, and joy.

WHEN GOD DISCIPLINES

It wasn't the sailors who cast Jonah into the stormy sea; it was God. "*You* hurled me into the deep . . . all *Your* waves and breakers swept over me" (Jonah 2:3, NIV, italics mine). When Jonah said those words, he was acknowledging that God was disciplining him and that he deserved it.

How we respond to discipline determines how much benefit we receive from it. According to Hebrews 12:5–11, we have several options: we can despise God's discipline and fight (v. 5); we can be discouraged and faint (v. 5); we can resist discipline and invite stronger discipline, possibly even death (v. 9); or we can submit to the Father and mature in faith and love (v. 7). Discipline is to the believer what exercise and training are to the athlete (v. 11); it enables us to run the race with endurance and reach the assigned goal (vv. 1–2).

The fact that God chastened His servant is proof that Jonah was truly a child of God, for God disciplines only His own children. "But if you are without chastening, of which all have become partakers, then you are illegitimate and not sons" (v. 8). And the Father chastens us in love so that "afterward" we might enjoy "the peaceable fruit of righteousness" (v. 11).

Remember: "No discipline seems pleasant at the time, but painful. Later on, however, it produces a harvest of righteousness and peace for those who have been trained by it" (Heb. 12:11, NIV).

Read: Jonah 2

Action assignment: Ask yourself how you respond to God's discipline. Do you need to improve your attitude in regard to discipline? Talk to God about it.

3

WHAT ABOUT THE TRIBULATION?

I realize that godly men differ in their interpretations of prophecy, particularly the matter of the church escaping or entering the time of Tribulation. My own position is that the church will be taken to heaven before the Tribulation, and then will return to the earth with the Lord to bring the Tribulation to a close. I see 1 Thessalonians emphasizing the rapture of the church and 2 Thessalonians the revelation of the Lord with the church when He comes to judge.

Paul did not write these letters to stir up a debate. His desire was that these letters bless our lives and our churches. The doctrine of the Lord's return is not a toy to play with or a weapon to fight with, but a tool with which to build. Believers may disagree on some of the fine points of Bible prophecy, but we all believe that Jesus Christ is coming again to reward believers and judge the lost. And we must all live in the light of His coming.

From God's Word: "This same Jesus, who is taken up from you into heaven, shall so come in like manner as ye have seen Him go into heaven" (Acts 1:11).

Action assignment: Take time to read 1 Thessalonians 4:13–5:6 and 2 Thessalonians 2. See if you agree that the first portion speaks of the rapture of the church and that the second portion teaches that the Lord is coming with His church to judge those on earth.

Think for a minute about these two events and your role in them. Close with prayer.

"A GREATER THAN JONAH"

"The men of Nineveh will rise in judgment with this generation and condemn it; because they repented at the preaching of Jonah; and, indeed a greater than Jonah is here" (Matt. 12:41).

How is Jesus greater than Jonah? Certainly Jesus is greater than Jonah in His person, for though both were Jews and both were prophets, Jesus is the very Son of God. He is greater in His message, for Jonah preached a message of judgment, but Jesus preached a message of grace and salvation (John 3:16–17). Jonah almost died for his own sins, but Jesus willingly died for the sins of the world (1 John 2:2).

Jonah's ministry was to but one city, but Jesus is "the Savior of the world" (John 4:42; 1 John 4:14). Jonah's obedience was not from the heart, but Jesus always did whatever pleased His Father (John 8:29). Jonah didn't love the people he came to save, but Jesus had compassion for sinners and proved His love by dying for them on the cross (Rom. 5:6–8). On the cross, outside the city, Jesus asked God to forgive those who killed Him (Luke 23:34), but Jonah waited outside the city to see if God would kill those he would not forgive.

God asked Jonah: "Should I not be concerned about that great city?" *How are you and I today answering God's question?* Do we agree with God that people without Christ are lost? How do we show this compassion? Do we have a concern for those in our cities where there is so much sin and so little witness? Do we pray that the gospel will go to people in every part of the world, and are we helping to send it there?

A command: "He told them, 'The harvest is plentiful, but the workers are few. Ask the Lord of the harvest, therefore, to send out workers into his harvest field' " (Luke 10:2, NIV).

Read: Jonah 4

Action assignment: Reread the last paragraph of today's reading. What are your answers to the questions? Ask the Lord to give you a greater burden for reaching the lost.

5

A CHRISTIAN HOME

In a Christian home, we must minister to each other. A Christian husband must minister to his wife and help "beautify her" in the Lord. A Christian wife must encourage her husband and help him grow strong in the Lord. Spouses must take time to be with each other. Christian workers and church officers who get too busy running around solving other people's problems may end up creating problems of their own at home. One survey revealed that the average husband and wife had thirty-seven minutes a week together in actual communication! Is it any wonder that marriages fall apart after the children grow up and leave home? The husband and wife are left alone—to live with strangers!

Parents and children must share burdens and blessings and seek to maintain an atmosphere of spiritual excitement and growth in the home. If there are unsaved people in the home, they will be won to Christ more by what they see in our lives and relationships than by what they hear in our witness.

Remember this: "Carry each other's burdens, and in this way you will fulfill the law of Christ" (Galatians 6:2, NIV).

Also: Ephesians 5:21–6:4.

Action assignment: Name five things parents and children can do to make a happy home. Talk to God about how you can help make your home happier.

BE ON THE WINNING SIDE

When congregations at Christmastime sing "Peace on earth and mercy mild," they are expressing only one aspect of the Christmas story. Our Lord's birth at Bethlehem involved *war* as well as peace. It was part of an agelong conflict between God and Satan, a war that was declared in Genesis 3:15. You and I are not merely spectators—we must be participants. This is one war in which it is impossible to be neutral. We are either with Him or against Him.

Either we are with Him, helping to gather the spoils, or we are against Him, helping Satan to scatter the spoils. There is no middle ground. If we are with Him, then we are on the winning side. If we are against Him, we are on the losing side. And one of these days, He shall return to earth to finish the war. Satan will be cast into hell, sinners will be judged, and Jesus Christ will usher in the new heaven and the new earth.

Verse for today: "He that is not with Me is against Me: and he that gathereth not with Me scattereth" (Luke 11:23).

Consider: Joshua 24:15; Acts 26:18; Revelation 20:10-15.

Action assignment: Realizing that there is a spiritual war going on, can you spot any areas in your life where you are attempting to be neutral? If so, ask God to forgive you and claim victory through Christ. Thank God for the privilege of being on His (the winning) side.

7

A GRACIOUS INVITATION

"Let us draw near . . . Let us hold fast . . . Let us consider one another." This threefold invitation from Hebrews 10:19-25 hinges on our boldness to enter into the holiest. And this boldness ("freedom of speech") rests on the finished work of the Saviour. On the Day of Atonement, the high priest could not enter the holy of holies unless he had the blood of the sacrifice. But our entrance into God's presence is not because of an animal's blood, but because of Christ's shed blood.

This open way into God's presence is new and not part of the Old Covenant that grows old and is ready to vanish (Hebrews 8:13). It is "living" because Christ "ever liveth to make intercession" for us (Hebrews 7:25). Christ is the new and living way! We come to God through Him, our High Priest over the house of God. When His flesh was torn on the cross, and His life sacrificed, God tore the veil in the temple. This symbolized the new and living way now opened for all who believe.

On the basis of these assurances—that we have boldness to enter because we have a living High Priest—we have an "open invitation" to enter the presence of God. The Old Covenant high priest *visited* the holy of holies once a year, but we are invited to *dwell in the presence of God* every moment of each day. What a tremendous privilege!

Scripture says: "Come unto Me, all ye that labor and are heavy laden, and I will give you rest" (Matthew 11:28).

Look up: Hebrews 7:25; 8:13; 9:7; James 4:8.

Action assignment: Personalize Hebrews 10:19-25 by making it your prayer today. Accept God's invitation with all your heart.

TWO KINDS OF LOVE

Peter used two different words for love: *philadelphia,* which is "brotherly love," and *agape* (1 Peter 1:22), which is Godlike sacrificial love. It is important that we share both kinds of love. We share brotherly love because we have the common ground of being brothers and sisters in Christ; we share *agape* love because we belong to God and therefore can overlook differences.

By nature, all of us are selfish. So it took a miracle of God to give us this love. Because we "obeyed the truth through the Spirit," God purified our souls and poured His love into our hearts. Love for the brethren is an evidence that we truly have been born of God. Now we are "obedient children" who no longer want to live in the selfish desires of the old life.

It is tragic when people try to "manufacture" love, because the product is obviously cheap and artificial. The love that we share with each other, and with a lost world, must be generated by the Spirit of God. It is a *constant* power in our lives, and not something that we turn on and off like a radio.

Today's Scripture: "Seeing you have purified your souls in obeying the truth through the Spirit unto unfeigned love of the brethren, see that ye love one another with a pure heart fervently" (1 Peter 1:22).

Also read: John 13:35; Romans 5:5; 1 John 4:7-21.

Action assignment: Ask God to show you someone who especially needs love, and do something out of love for that person.

9

NEW BEGINNING

Unfaithfulness to the Lord is a serious sin, just as unfaithfulness to one's mate is a serious sin. The man who says he's 90 percent faithful to his wife isn't faithful at all. As Israel was tempted to forsake God for idols, the church is tempted to turn to the world system that hates God and wants nothing to do with God.

The key word is "return" (Hos. 3:5), a word that's used twenty-two times in Hosea's prophecy. When Israel repents and returns to the Lord, then the Lord will return to bless Israel (2:7–8). God has returned to His place and left Israel to herself (5:15) until she seeks Him and says, "Come, and let us return to the LORD" (6:1).

This is Hosea's message: "O Israel, return to the LORD your God . . . Take words with you, and return to the LORD. Say to Him, 'Take away all iniquity; receive us graciously'" (14:1–2).

That prayer is good for any sinner. To summarize:

God is gracious, and no matter what "name" our birth has given to us, He can change it and give us a new beginning.
God is holy and He must deal with sin. To live for the world is to break God's heart and commit "spiritual adultery."
God is love and promises to forgive and restore all who repent and return to Him. He promises to bless all who trust Him.

A Bible reminder: "Seek the LORD while He may be found; call on Him while He is near. Let the wicked forsake his way and the evil man his thoughts. Let him turn to the LORD, and He will have mercy on him, and to our God, for He will freely pardon" (Isa. 55:6–7, NIV).

Read: Hosea 14

Action assignment: Think about your relationship to the world and to God. Search out and read the Scripture referenced in the last paragraph of today's reading. Determine if you need a new attitude toward the world.

COMPLETELY SETTLED

Believers are complete in Christ (Colossians 2:10). We have a perfect standing before God because of the finished work of Jesus Christ. We know *personally* that we have this perfect standing before God because of the witness of the Holy Spirit through the Word. The witness of the Spirit is based on the work of the Son. The Old Covenant worshiper could not say that he had no more "consciousness of sins" (Hebrews 10:2, NASB). But the New Covenant believer *can* say that his sins and iniquities are remembered *no more*. There is "no more offering for sin" (10:18) and no more remembrance of sin!

A fine Christian psychiatrist explained, "The trouble with psychiatry is that it can only deal with symptoms. A psychiatrist can remove a patient's *feelings* of guilt, but he cannot remove the guilt. It's like a trucker loosening a fender on his truck so he won't hear the motor knock. A patient can end up feeling better, but have *two* problems instead of one!"

When a sinner trusts Christ, his sins are all forgiven, the guilt is gone, and the matter is completely settled forever.

The Bible says: "I, even I, am He that blotteth out thy transgressions for mine own sake, and will not remember thy sins" (Isaiah 43:25).

For further study: 1 John 2:12; Romans 8:1-4; Hebrews 10:15-18.

Action assignment: Repeat the words of this hymn by Cecil F. Alexander as a prayer:

> "Complete in Thee! no work of mine
> May take, dear Lord, the place of Thine;
> Thy blood hath pardon bought for me,
> And I am now complete in Thee."

Take time to commit this stanza to memory.

11

ELECTION AND YOU

A seminary professor once told me, "Try to explain election, and you may lose your mind. But explain it away—and you may lose your soul!"

We will never on earth understand the total concept of divine election, but let's notice some obvious facts about it:

1. *Salvation begins with God.* God planned salvation before He created man.

2. *Salvation involves God's love.* His love made Calvary a reality.

3. *Salvation involves faith.* We are saved by believing God's Word.

4. *Salvation involves the Trinity.* As far as God the Father is concerned, I was saved when He chose me in Christ before the world began. As far as God the Son is concerned, I was saved when He died for me on the cross. As far as God the Holy Spirit is concerned, I was saved one Saturday night in May 1945, when I heard the Word and trusted Jesus Christ. At that moment, the entire plan fell together and I became a child of God. If you had asked me that night if I was one of the elect, I would have been speechless. At that time I knew nothing about election. But the Holy Spirit witnessed in my heart that I was a child of God.

5. *Salvation changes the life.* Those whom God chooses, He changes. This does not mean they are perfect, but they are possessors of a new life that cannot be hidden.

From God's Word: "For by grace are ye saved through faith; and that not of yourselves: it is the gift of God: not of works, lest any man should boast" (Ephesians 2:8-9).

Find and read: John 15:16; Ephesians 1:4; 2 Thessalonians 2:13; Romans 5:8.

Action assignment: Find the song, "I'm a Child of the King," and make it your song for today. Thank God for His love that has reached you and made you His.

BEING A GOOD NEIGHBOR

The ingredients that make up the familiar story of the Good Samaritan are found on the pages of daily newspapers. There is really nothing new under the sun. In this story, Christ talked about violence—and we certainly have plenty of that today. He talked about crime, racial discrimination, and hatred. In this parable we see neglect and unconcern, but we also see love and mercy. The person who says the Bible is not relevant to our modern world has never read this parable.

We know what the parable *says*, but what does it *mean*? Some ancient scholars tried to make everything in this story symbolize something, but this approach took them on a detour. The story was given because a lawyer (an expert in Jewish law) asked Jesus, "And who is my neighbor?" He was really trying to rescue himself from losing an argument, but Jesus used his question as an opportunity to teach an important truth: namely, *you cannot separate your relationship with God from your relationship with your fellowman.*

One act of ministry, motivated by Christian compassion, not only pleases the Lord and helps the needy—it also blesses the one ministering. The results go on forever.

Verse for today: "For all the law is fulfilled in one word, even in this; thou shalt love thy neighbor as thyself" (Galatians 5:14).

Consider: Matthew 19:19; Luke 16:15.

Action assignment: Read the parable of the Good Samaritan in Luke 10:25-37. Today, determine in what way you can act upon Jesus' command, "Go, and do thou likewise."

13

REJOICE IN THE WORD

The secret of Christian joy is to believe what God says in His Word and act upon it. Faith that isn't based on the Word is not faith at all; it is presumption or superstition. Joy that isn't the result of faith is not joy at all; it is only a "good feeling" that will soon disappear. Faith based on the Word will produce joy that will weather the storms of life.

It isn't enough for us to *read* the Word or *receive* the Word as others expound it; we must also *rejoice* in the Word. "I rejoice at Your word as one who finds great treasure" (Ps. 119:162). In Bible days, people sometimes hid their wealth in jars buried in the ground (Matt. 13:44; Jer. 41:8). If a farmer plowing his field suddenly discovered a jar filled with gold, he would certainly rejoice. There are great treasures buried in God's Word, and you and I must diligently "dig" for them as we read, meditate, and pray; and when we find these treasures, we should rejoice and give thanks.

If we read and study the Word of God only from a sense of duty, then its treasures may never be revealed to us. It is the believer who rejoices in the Word, who delights to read and study it day by day, who will find God's hidden treasures. "Blessed is the man who fears the LORD, who finds great delight in his commands" (Ps. 112:1, NIV). "But his delight is in the law of the LORD, and in His law he meditates day and night" (Ps. 1:2).

Do you delight in God's Word? Would you rather have God's Word than food (Ps. 119:103; Luke 10:38–42), or sleep (Ps. 119:55, 62, 147–148), or wealth (vv. 14, 72, 137, 162)?

True of you? "Oh, how I love Your law! I meditate on it all day long. . . . Your word is a lamp to my feet and a light for my path" (Psalm 119:97, 105, NIV).

Read: Nehemiah 8

Action assignment: Look up and read the Scripture referenced in the last paragraph of today's reading. Commit one or two to memory. What promise of God gives you greatest reason to rejoice?

GOOD NEWS!

When he was a Jewish rabbi, Paul was separated as a Pharisee to the laws and traditions of the Jews. But when he yielded to Christ, he was separated to the Gospel and its ministry. *Gospel* means "the Good News." It is the message that Christ died for our sins, was buried, and rose again, and now is able to save all who trust Him.

The Gospel is not a new message; it was promised in the Old Testament, beginning in Genesis 3:15. The Prophet Isaiah certainly preached the Gospel, too. The salvation we enjoy today was promised by the prophets, though they did not fully understand all that they were preaching and writing.

Jesus Christ is the center of the Gospel message. Paul identifies Him as a man, a Jew, and the Son of God. He was born of a virgin into the family of David, which gave Him the right to David's throne. He died for the sins of the world, and then was raised from the dead. It is this miraculous event of substitutionary death and victorious resurrection that constitutes the Gospel; and it was this Gospel that Paul preached.

The Bible says: "For I am not ashamed of the Gospel of Christ: for it is the power of God unto salvation to every one that believeth; to the Jew first, and also to the Greek" (Romans 1:16).

Look up: 1 Corinthians 15:1-4; Isaiah 1:18; 55:1-13.

Action assignment: Ask the Spirit of God to help you choose one verse from today's reading. Repeat it often during the day.

15

DISCIPLINED PRAYING

The Apostle Paul labored in prayer to the point of exhaustion for the Christians at Colosse. So much of our praying is calm and comfortable, yet Paul exerted his spiritual muscles the way a Greek runner would exert himself in the Olympic games.

This does not mean that our prayers are more effective if we exert all kinds of fleshly energy. Nor does it mean that we must "wrestle with God" and wear Him out before He will meet our needs. Paul described a *spiritual* striving: it was *God's* power at work in his life. True prayer is directed to the Father, through the Son, in the power of the Holy Spirit. When the Spirit is at work in our lives, then we can pray mightily in the will of God.

How does the Spirit assist us in our praying? For one thing, the Spirit teaches us the Word and shows us the will of God. Prayer is not our trying to change God's mind. It is learning what is the mind of God and asking accordingly. The Holy Spirit constantly intercedes for us even though we do not hear His voice. He knows the Father's will and He helps us pray in that will.

Verse for today: "And this is the confidence that we have in Him, that, if we ask anything according to His will, He heareth us; and if we know that He hears us, whatsoever we ask, we know that we have the petitions that we desired of Him" (1 John 5:14-15).

Also read: Matthew 6:9-13; John 14:13-14; 16:13-15; Romans 8:26-27.

Action assignment: Praying is one of the Christian's greatest privileges. Make yourself available to God, His Word, and His Spirit as you learn to exercise the privilege of disciplined praying.

HOW TO BRING UNITY

The only way to enter God's spiritual family is by a spiritual birth, through faith in Jesus Christ. Just as there are two parents in physical birth, so there are two parents in spiritual birth: the Spirit of God and the Word of God. The new birth gives to us a new nature as well as a new and living hope.

Our first birth was a birth of "flesh," and the flesh is corruptible. Whatever is born of flesh is destined to die and decay. This explains why mankind cannot hold civilization together: it is all based on human flesh and is destined to fall apart. Like the beautiful flowers of spring, man's works look successful for a time, but then they start to decay and die. All the way from the Tower of Babel in Genesis 11 to "Babylon the Great" in Revelation 17 and 18, man's great attempts at unity are destined to fail.

If we try to build unity in the church on the basis of our first birth, we will fail; but if we build unity on the basis of the new birth, it will succeed. Each believer has the same Holy Spirit dwelling within. We call upon the same Father and share His divine nature. We trust the same Word, and that Word will never decay or disappear. We have trusted the same Gospel and have been born of the same Spirit. The *externals* of the flesh that could divide us mean nothing when compared with the *internals* of the Spirit that unite us.

Scripture for unity: "Neither pray I for these alone, but for them also which shall believe on Me through their Word; that they all may be one, as Thou, Father, art in Me, and I in Thee, that they also may be one in Us: that the world may believe that Thou hast sent Me" (John 17:20-21).

Other Scripture: John 3:1-16; Romans 8:6-9; 1 Peter 1:23.

Action assignment: Ask God to enable you to focus on the internals of the Spirit that unite us rather than externals of the flesh that divide.

17

DEMOLISHING STRONGHOLDS

Many believers today do not realize how deeply the church is involved in spiritual warfare. Those who do understand the seriousness of the battle do not always know how to fight the enemy. They try to use human methods to defeat demonic forces, but these methods are doomed to fail. When Joshua and his army marched around Jericho for a week, the spectators thought they were mad. Because the Israelites trusted God and obeyed orders, they brought down the high walls and conquered the foe.

When I was pastoring in Chicago, I met each week with three pastor friends to engage in "warfare praying." We claimed God's promise to cast down the wrong thinking that was keeping people from surrendering to God. What a joy it was to see God do great things in the lives of many people for whom we interceded. Usually once the walls in the mind have been torn down, the door to the heart can be opened.

Verse for today: "Put on the full armor of God so that you can take your stand against the devil's schemes" (Ephesians 6:11, NIV).

Also read: Joshua 6:1-20; Psalm 24:8; Proverbs 21:30-31; 2 Corinthians 10:3-5; Ephesians 6:12-17.

Action assignment: Today when you read the paper or listen to the news on radio or TV, take careful note of the negative news items. Jot down two or three items to pray about, interceding for the individuals involved. Ask God to bring peace and justice to the situations on which you focus.

RETURN GOOD FOR EVIL

A friend of mine once heard a preacher criticize him over the radio and tell things that were not only unkind, but also untrue. My friend became very angry and was planning to fight back, when a godly preacher said, "Don't do it. If you defend yourself, then the Lord can't defend you. Leave it in His hands." My friend followed that wise counsel, and the Lord vindicated him.

As children of God, we must live on the highest level—returning good for evil. Anyone can return good for good and evil for evil. The only way to overcome evil is with good. If we return evil for evil, we only add fuel to the fire. And even if our enemy is not converted, we have still experienced the love of God in our own hearts and have grown in grace.

Verse for today: "Therefore if thine enemy hunger, feed him; if he thirst, give him drink: for in so doing thou shalt heap coals of fire on his head. Be not overcome of evil, but overcome evil with good" (Romans 12:20-21).

Consider: Deuteronomy 32:35; Proverbs 25:21-22; Matthew 5:44-48.

Action assignment: Study 1 Peter 2:20-25. Surely we need to pray and ask God for love as we try to show love to our enemies (or even those who simply dislike us). Will they take advantage of us? Will they hate us even more when we are kind? Only the Lord knows. Our task is to obey the Lord and leave the results with Him. Pray for God to give you His strength and wisdom as you learn definite ways in which you can overcome evil with good.

19

WALKING IN FEAR OF THE LORD

"The fear of our God" is not the servile dread of a slave toward a master but the loving respect of a child toward a parent. To fear the Lord means to seek to glorify God in everything we do. It means listening to His Word, honoring it, and obeying it. "The remarkable thing about fearing God," wrote Oswald Chambers, "is that when you fear God, you fear nothing else, whereas if you do not fear God, you fear everything else." Because Nehemiah's life was motivated by the fear of the Lord (Neh. 5:15), he did not fear what the enemy might do (vv. 14, 19). The fear of the Lord moved Nehemiah to be a faithful servant of the Lord.

To walk in the fear of God, of course, means to walk by faith, trusting God to deal with your enemies and one day balance the accounts. It means claiming Matthew 6:33 and having the right priorities in life. "The fear of the Lord leads to life, and he who has it will abide in satisfaction; he will not be visited with evil" (Prov. 19:23).

Christ says: "Seek first His kingdom and His righteousness, and all these things will be given to you as well" (Matt. 6:33, NIV).

Read: Nehemiah 5

Action assignment: Write your own definition of fear of the Lord. Get your hymnbook and sing all four stanzas of "Holy, Holy, Holy."

CONFESS IMMEDIATELY

"I went out and sinned," a student told his campus chaplain, "because I knew I could come back and ask God to forgive me."

"On what basis can God forgive you?" the chaplain asked, pointing to 1 John 1:9.

"God is faithful and just," the boy replied.

"Those two words should have kept you *out* of sin," the chaplain said. "Do you know what it cost God to forgive your sins?"

The boy hung his head. "Jesus had to die for me."

Then the chaplain zeroed in. "That's right—forgiveness isn't some cheap sideshow trick God performs. God is faithful to His promise, and God is just, because Christ died for your sins and paid the penalty for you. Now, the next time you plan to sin, remember that you are going to sin against a faithful, loving God!"

Cleansing has two sides to it: the judicial and the personal. The blood of Jesus Christ, shed on the cross, delivers us from the guilt of sin and gives us right standing ("justification") before God. God is able to forgive because Jesus' death has satisfied His holy law.

But God is also interested in cleansing the sinner inwardly. When our confession is sincere, God does a cleansing work in the heart by His Spirit and through His Word.

King David covered his sins instead of confessing them. For perhaps a whole year he lived in deceit and defeat.

When should we confess our sin? As soon as we discover it! By walking in the light, we are able to see the "dirt" in our lives and deal with it immediately.

Today's Scripture: "He that covereth his sins shall not prosper; but whoso confesseth and forsaketh them shall have mercy" (Proverbs 28:13).

Also read: 2 Chronicles 7:14; Psalm 51.

Action assignment: Confess to God any known sin in your life and ask Him to reveal other sins to you. Turn from your sin and thank God for His forgiveness.

GOD'S PEOPLE AROUND US

In my pastoral work I often found that suffering people can become very self-centered; they think they are the only ones going through the furnace. Everyone goes through normal human suffering such as sickness, pain, and bereavement. But what about the suffering we endure *because we are Christians?*

Perhaps your family has disowned you because of your faith; perhaps you have been bypassed for a promotion at work because you are a Christian. These experiences hurt, but they are not ours alone. Other Christians are going through the same trials—and many in other parts of the world face much greater difficulty.

Paul encouraged suffering Christians by assuring them that their experiences were not new or isolated. Others had suffered before them and were even then suffering with them. The churches in Judea had not been exterminated by suffering; if anything, they had been purified and increased.

Here is one of the great values of the local church: we stand together in times of difficulty and encourage one another. A lonely saint is very vulnerable to the attacks of Satan. We need each other in the battles of life.

God urges: "Let us consider how to stimulate one another to love and good deeds, not forsaking our own assembling together, as is the habit of some, but encouraging one another" (Hebrews 10:24-25, NASB).

Also consider: John 13:34; Romans 12:10; Acts 2:42.

Action assignment: Think of three people you could turn to for support during a period of suffering. Thank God for them, and ask Him to help you be an encouragement to someone today or this week.

RECEIVE ONE ANOTHER

It is not our responsibility to decide the requirements for Christian fellowship in a church; only the Lord can do this. To set up man-made restrictions on the basis of personal prejudices (or even convictions) is to go beyond the Word of God. Because God has received us, we must receive one another. We must not argue over these matters, nor must we judge or despise one another.

In every church there are weak and strong believers. The strong understand spiritual truth and practice it, but the weak have not yet grown into that level of maturity and liberty. The weak must not condemn the strong and call them unspiritual. The strong must not despise the weak and call them immature. God has received both the weak and the strong; therefore, they should receive one another.

Verse for today: "Wherefore receive ye one another, as Christ also received us to the glory of God" (Romans 15:7).

Consider: Psalm 133; Acts 15; Romans 14:1-12.

Action assignment: Can you agree with St. Augustine's statement, "In essentials, unity; in nonessentials, liberty; in all things, charity"? If fellowship in the body of Christ is a lack in your life, think through the self-made restrictions you might be imposing on others. List them and then pray for God to give you love and understanding in these areas. Then practice "receiving" a specific person who differs from you.

"WHO AM I?"

If anyone else asked, "Whom do men say that I am?" we would think him either mad or arrogant. But in the case of Jesus, a right confession of His Person is basic to salvation. His Person and His work go together and must never be separated. It is amazing to see how confused the public was about Jesus. Perhaps, like Herod, the people thought Jesus was John raised from the dead.

It had been prophesied that Elijah would come again, and some thought that this prediction was fulfilled in Christ. However, Jesus did not minister as did Elijah; it was John the Baptist who came "in the spirit and power of Elias" (Luke 1:17).

One thing is clear: we can never make a true decision about Jesus Christ by taking a poll. The important thing is not what others say, but what you and I say. The decisions of the crowd, wrong or right, can never substitute for personal decisions.

Peter had the correct response: "Thou art the Christ [the Messiah]" (Mark 8:29). This confession was Peter's response to the revelation God the Father had given him. This revelation was not the result of Peter's own investigation. It came as the gracious act of God. God had hidden these things from the proud Pharisees and Sadducees and revealed them to "babes," the humble disciples.

Verse for today: "Jesus ... asked His disciples saying, 'Whom do men say that I the Son of man am?'" (Matthew 16:13).

Also read: Romans 10:9-10; 1 John 2:18-23; 4:1-3; John 10:19-21; Malachi 4:5; Luke 1:13-17; Matthew 11:25-27.

Action assignment: You know that Jesus is the Christ, the Son of the living God. But you probably have a friend who does not believe. Pray for this friend, believing that he or she will come to know Jesus as the Son of God, and will begin a personal relationship with Him.

A NURTURING ATTITUDE

Young Christians need the kind of fellowship that will protect them and encourage them to grow. But we cannot treat them as "babies" all their lives! More mature Christians must exercise love and patience and be careful not to cause them to stumble. Younger Christians must mature in the faith and thus help other believers grow.

The weak must learn from the strong, and the strong must love the weak. The wonderful result will be peace and maturity to the glory of God.

Verse for today: "But grow in the grace and knowledge of our Lord and Saviour Jesus Christ. To Him be glory both now and forever! Amen" (2 Peter 3:18, NIV).

More to read: Titus 2:1-8; Ephesians 4:1-3.

Action assignment: Describe one mature Christian and one young-in-the-faith Christian you know, using descriptive words like loving, etc.:

A mature Christian I know is:	A young Christian I know is:
_____	_____
_____	_____
_____	_____

Take special note of their strong and weak points (as far as you have been able to discern them).

How do *you* line up—as mature or immature in the faith—according to your own evaluation of the other two? Are you surprised about yourself? Now commit the three of you to the Lord, asking Him to help you encourage the weak and strong alike.

25

A WORTHY HABIT

When we live in an atmosphere of humility and honesty, we take some risks and expect some dangers. Unless humility and honesty result in forgiveness, relationships cannot be mended and strengthened. Peter recognized the risks involved and asked Jesus how many times he should forgive a brother's sin against him (Matthew 18:22-23).

Our Lord's reply, "Until seventy times seven" (490 times), must have startled Peter. Who could keep count for that many offenses? But that was exactly the point Jesus was making: Love "keeps no record of wrongs" (1 Corinthians 13:5, NIV). By the time we have forgiven a brother that many times, we are in the habit of forgiving.

But Jesus was not advising careless or shallow forgiveness. Christian love is not blind. If a brother is guilty of a repeated sin, no doubt he would find strength and power to conquer that sin through the encouragement of his loving and forgiving brethren. If we condemn a brother, we bring out the worst in him. But if we create an atmosphere of love and forgiveness, we can help God bring out the best in him.

Verse for today: "Forbearing one another, and forgiving one another, if any man have a quarrel against any: even as Christ forgave you, so also do ye" (Colossians 3:13).

Also read: Matthew 18:15-23; Ephesians 3:17-19; Philippians 1:9-10.

Action assignment: Make two lists today. On the first one, put down every recent occasion in which you exercised forgiveness. On the second list, put down the recent times you were not forgiving. Then ask God to increase your ability to forgive others, "even as Christ forgave you."

COMFORTABLE OR CONFORMABLE?

In one of my radio messages I made the statement, "God does not expect us to be comfortable—but He does expect us to be conformable." No sooner had the program ended than my office phone rang and an anonymous listener wanted to argue with me about that statement.

"Conformable to what?" the voice thundered. "Haven't you read Romans 12:2—'Be not conformed to this world'?"

"Sure I've read Romans 12:2," I replied. "Have you read Romans 8:29? God has predestined us 'to be conformed to the image of His Son.'"

After a long pause (I was glad he was paying the phone bill), he grunted and said, "OK."

Comfortable or conformable: that is the question. If we are looking for comfortable lives, we will protect our plans and desires, save our lives, and never be planted. But if we yield our lives and let God plant us, we will never be alone but will have the joy of being fruitful to the glory of God.

Verse for today: "He that findeth his life shall lose it: and he that loseth his life for My sake shall find it" (Matthew 10:39).

Consider: John 17:21-26; Romans 8:28-29; 12:2.

Action assignment: "And be not conformed to this world" is the goal of those who wish to be conformed to the image of Christ. Examine your lifestyle. If you find a comfortable rut that opposes your becoming conformed to Christ's image, reject that rut. Through prayer and purposeful action you can get out of "comfortable" ruts.

TROPHIES AHEAD?

In times of trouble and testing, it is important that we take the long view of things. Paul lived in the future tense as well as in the present. His actions were governed by what God would do in the future. He knew that Jesus Christ would return and reward him for his faithful ministry: and on that day, the saints he had won to Christ would bring glory to God and joy to Paul's heart. As the familiar song says, "It will be worth it all, when we see Jesus."

The fact that we shall one day stand at the Judgment Seat of Christ ought to motivate us to be faithful in spite of difficulties. At the Judgment Seat of Christ, our works will be judged and rewards will be given. Paul said that *the saints themselves* would be his crown when he met them at the Judgment Seat. This joy of greeting believers in heaven also brings with it a solemn warning: we will lose joy if we go to heaven empty-handed. The Christian who has not sincerely tried to win others to Christ will not experience this glory and joy when Jesus Christ returns. We must witness for God so that when we get to heaven, He will have trophies to present for His glory.

Remember: "They that be wise shall shine as the brightness of the firmament; and they that turn many to righteousness as the stars forever and ever" (Daniel 12:3).

For further study: Romans 14:10-12; 1 Corinthians 4:1-5; 2 Corinthians 5:9-10; 1 Thessalonians 2:19-20.

Action assignment: Write down the names of any you believe you have won to Christ. If you feel you are weak in pointing others to Christ, talk to God and ask Him to give you courage. Ask your pastor about a course on winning people to Christ.

COVETOUSNESS VS. CONTENTMENT

The word *covetousness* literally means "love of money," but it can be applied to a love for more of anything. Covetousness is the desire for more, whether we need it or not.

Contentment cannot come from material things, for they can never satisfy the heart. Only God can do that. When we have God, we have all we need. Material things can decay or be stolen, but God will never leave us or forsake us. This promise was made to Joshua when he succeeded Moses and is fulfilled in Jesus Christ, so we may claim this promise for ourselves.

A woman said to evangelist D.L. Moody, "I have found a promise that helps me when I am afraid. It is Psalm 56:3—'What time I am afraid, I will trust in Thee.'"

Mr. Moody replied, "I have a better promise than that! Isaiah 12:2—'I will trust, and not be afraid.'"

Both promises are true; each has its own application. The important thing is that we know Jesus Christ as our Lord and Helper, and that we not put our trust in material things. Contented Christians are people with priorities, and material things are not high on their priority lists.

The Bible commands: "Watch out! Be on your guard against all kinds of greed; a man's life does not consist in the abundance of his possessions" (Luke 12:15, NIV).

For further study: Hebrews 13:6; Psalm 118:6; Deuteronomy 31:7-8; Joshua 1:5, 9; Matthew 28:20; Acts 18:9-10.

Action assignment: Write down five concerns that cause you fear today. Make a deliberate act of placing each fear into God's hand.

FLEE FALSE BELIEFS

The Gnostics believed that the angels and the heavenly bodies influenced people's lives. Paul's warnings to the Colossians about "new moon" and other religious practices determined by the calendar may be related to this Gnostic teaching, although the Jewish people also watched the calendar. One thing is certain: such teachings about demons and angels were not a part of true Christian doctrine. If anything, such teachings were satanic.

The fact that this teaching is not after Christ is sufficient to warn us against horoscopes, astral charts, Ouija boards, and other spiritist practices. The whole zodiac system is contrary to the teaching of the Word of God. The Christian who dabbles in mysticism and the occult is only asking for trouble.

Why follow empty philosophy when we have all fullness in Christ? The fundamental test of any religious teaching is, "Where does it put Jesus Christ—His Person and His Work? Does it rob Him of His fullness? Does it deny either His deity or His humanity? Does it affirm that the believer must have some new experience to supplement this experience with Christ?" If so, that teaching is wrong and dangerous.

Verse for today: "For in Him dwelleth all the fullness of the Godhead bodily. And ye are complete in Him, which is the head of all principality and power" (Colossians 2:9-10).

Also read: Colossians 2:16-18; Ephesians 3:19; Galatians 4:9-11.

Action assignment: Nothing needs to be added to Christ because He already is the very fullness of God. Ask God to show you if any extras have crept into your belief. Be quick to cut away anything that deters from Christ's adequacy.

WHAT HAVE YOU GIVEN?

Peter made it clear that Christ's death was an appointment, not an accident; it was ordained by God before the foundation of the world. From the human perspective, our Lord was cruelly murdered; but from the divine perspective, He laid down His life for sinners. But He was raised from the dead! Now anyone who trusts Him will be saved for eternity.

When you and I meditate on the sacrifice of Christ for us, certainly we should want to obey God and live holy lives for His glory. When only a young lady, Frances Ridley Havergal saw a picture of the crucified Christ with this caption under it: "I did this for thee. What hast thou done for Me?" Quickly she wrote a poem but was dissatisfied with it and threw it into the fireplace. The paper came out unharmed! Later, at her father's suggestion, she published the poem, and today we sing it.

> *I gave My life for thee,*
> *My precious blood I shed;*
> *That thou might ransomed be,*
> *And quickened from the dead.*
> *I gave, I gave, My life for thee,*
> *What hast thou given for Me?*

A good question indeed! I trust you and I can give a good answer to the Lord.

Today's verse: "Ye have not chosen Me, but I have chosen you, and ordained you, that ye should go and bring forth fruit, and that your fruit should remain" (John 15:16).

Additional verses: John 15:10; Ephesians 2:10; Titus 2:14; 1 John 2:3-6.

Action assignment: See how many things you can jot down that you have given to Christ. Have a time of prayer.

THE DIVINE YEARNING

God wants to use us to share the Gospel with both Jews and Gentiles. Jesus Christ wept over Jerusalem and longed to gather His people in His arms! Instead, those arms were stretched out on a cross where He willingly died for Jews and Gentiles alike. God is long-suffering and patient, "not willing that any should perish, but that all should come to repentance" (2 Peter 3:9).

While Israel as a nation has been set aside, individual Jewish people can be saved and are being saved. When Paul ministered to the Jews in Rome while he was a prisoner, he expounded the Scriptures to them and sought to convince them from morning until evening that Jesus is the Messiah. Through Paul, God was stretching out His arms of love to His disobedient people, yearning over them, and asking them to return. God's favor to the Gentiles did not change His love for the Jews. It is the same love we need to show both Jew and Gentile, saved and unsaved.

Verse for today: "The remnant shall return, even the remnant of Jacob, unto the mighty God" (Isaiah 10:21).

More to read: Isaiah 65:2; Acts 28:23; 2 Peter 3:9.

Action assignment: The old spiritual, "He's Got the Whole World in His Hands," reminds us that God's love includes everybody. Imagine the world in your hands for a moment. Would you love all of it or only a few select continents? Would you drop the world like a gigantic hot potato, letting it drift off into the Milky Way?

God wants us to share His Good News with everyone we can. He has a special yearning for the Jews, with whom He made the first covenant, but that does not mean He wants Gentiles to know Him any less. Ask God to enlarge your understanding of the scope of God's love and your role in proclaiming it.

September

Be Renewed:

"And be ye kind one to another ... even as God for Christ's sake hath forgiven you."

Ephesians 4:32

1

A LOVE PRINCIPLE

The world's worst prison is the prison of an unforgiving heart. If we refuse to forgive others, we are only imprisoning ourselves and causing our own torment. Some of the most miserable people I have met in my ministry have been people who would not forgive others. They lived only to imagine ways to punish these people who had wronged them. But they were really only punishing themselves.

Many professing Christians have *received* forgiveness, but they have not really *experienced* forgiveness deep in their hearts. Therefore they are unable to *share* forgiveness with those who have wronged them. If we live only according to justice, always seeking to get what is ours, we will put ourselves into prison. But if we live according to forgiveness, sharing with others what God has shared with us, then we will enjoy freedom and joy. As recorded in Matthew 18:21, Peter asked for a just measuring rod ("How many times shall I forgive my brother?"). Jesus told him to practice forgiveness and forget the measuring rod.

Verse for today: "And be ye kind to one another . . . even as God for Christ's sake hath forgiven you" (Ephesians 4:32).

Also consider: Matthew 18:21-34; Colossians 3:13.

Action assignment: Let's say that someone close to you has treated you unfairly today or recently, and he or she knows it—but has chosen to ignore the incident. You, on the other hand, think about it constantly. If this is so, ask God to guide your thinking so your actions will show true forgiveness. Then write out a prayer to give you tangible proof of your intent.

WHERE DO YOU SIT?

While attending a convention in Washington, D.C. I watched a Senate committee hearing on TV. The late Senator Hubert Humphrey was making a comment: "You must remember that in politics, how you stand depends on where you sit." He was referring, of course, to the political party seating arrangement in the Senate; but I immediately applied it to my position in Christ. How I stand—and walk—depends on where I sit; *and I am seated with Christ in the heavenlies!*

Now, in view of our wonderful identification with Christ, we have the responsibility to "seek those things which are above" (Colossians 3:1). Through Christ's death, burial, resurrection, and ascension, we have been separated from the old life of this world, and we now belong to a new heavenly life.

But how do we "seek those things which are above"? We habitually set our minds—our attention—on things above, not on things on the earth. Our feet must be on earth, but our minds must be in heaven. This is not to suggest that (as D. L. Moody used to say) we become "so heavenly minded that we are no earthly good."

Verse for today: "If ye then be risen with Christ, seek those things which are above, where Christ sitteth on the right hand of God" (Colossians 3:1).

Also read: Colossians 3:2-4; 1 John 4:1-6; Romans 8:30.

Action assignment: For the practical everyday affairs of life, make sure you get your directions from Christ in heaven. Ask Him to teach you to look at earth from heaven's point of view.

3

WE HAVE GOD'S TRUTH

How can mortal man penetrate beyond the grave and find assurance and peace for his own heart? From Old Testament days till the present, mankind has tried to solve the riddle of death and the afterlife. Philosophers have wrestled with the question of immortality. Spiritists have tried to communicate with those who have gone beyond.

In our modern world, scientists have investigated the experiences of people who claim to have died and returned to life again. They have also studied occult phenomena, hoping to find a clue to the mystery of life after death.

Christians need not wonder about death or life after death, for we have a revelation from God in His Word. Why substitute human speculation for divine revelation?

We must keep in mind that God's revelation was *gradual* and *progressive,* and that it climaxed in the coming of Christ "who abolished death, and brought life and immortality to light through the Gospel" (2 Timothy 1:10, NASB). We look to Christ and the New Testament for the complete revelation concerning death. The authority of God's Word gives us the assurance and comfort we need.

Believe God's Word: "We shall not all sleep, but we shall all be changed . . . and the dead shall be raised incorruptible. . . . Then shall be brought to pass the saying that is written, 'Death is swallowed up in victory'" (1 Corinthians 15:51-54).

For further evidence: John 5:24-29; 11:21-27; 1 Corinthians 15:19-22.

Action assignment: See if you can find in your hymnal "I Know That My Redeemer Lives" by Samuel Medley. If you can sing it, sing it; otherwise read it, and thank God for the thoughts it expresses.

NEEDED: LOYALTY AND PURITY

The home is the first place where Christian love should be practiced. A Christian home begins with a Christian marriage in the will of God. This means loyalty and purity. Sex outside of marriage is sinful and destructive; sex within the protective bonds of marriage can be enriching and glorifying to God.

Fornication is committed by unmarried persons and adultery by married persons. But in the New Testament, the term *fornication* can refer to many kinds of sexual sins.

How does God judge fornicators and adulterers? Sometimes they are judged in their own bodies. Certainly they will be judged at the final judgment. Believers who commit these sins may be forgiven, but they will lose rewards in heaven. David was forgiven, but he suffered the consequences of his adultery for years to come.

In these days, when sexual sins are paraded as entertainment, Christians need to take a stand for the purity of the marriage bond. A dedicated Christian home is the nearest thing to heaven on earth, and it starts with a Christian marriage.

Scripture for today: "Love is patient, love is kind. It does not envy, it does not boast, it is not proud. It is not rude, it is not self-seeking, it is not easily angered, it keeps no record of wrongs. Love does not delight in evil but rejoices with the truth. It always protects, always trusts, always hopes, always perseveres" (1 Corinthians 13:4-7, NIV).

Also read: 15:20; Romans 1:24-27; 1 Corinthians 6:15-20; Ephesians 5:5, 31-32; Hebrews 13:4; Revelation 21:8, 22:14-15.

Action assignment: List three things you can do to show love in your home today. Ask God to help you do them.

5

THE RIGHT ATTITUDE

Jesus did not think of Himself; He thought of others. His attitude was that of unselfish concern for others. This is "the mind of Christ," an attitude that says, "I cannot keep my privileges for myself, I must use them for others; and to do this, I will gladly lay them aside and pay whatever price is necessary."

A reporter was interviewing a successful job counselor who had placed hundreds of workers in their vocations quite happily. When asked the secret of his success, the man replied: "If you want to find out what a worker is really like, don't give him responsibilities—give him *privileges*. Most people can handle responsibilities if you pay them enough, but it takes a real leader to handle privileges. A leader will use his privileges to help others and build the organization; a lesser man will use privileges to promote himself." Jesus used His heavenly privileges for the sake of others—for *our* sake.

Jesus said: "Whoever wishes to become great among you shall be your servant, and whoever wishes to be first among you shall be your slave; just as the Son of man did not come to be served, but to serve, and to give His life a ransom for many" (Matthew 20:26-28, NASB).

Also read: Mark 9:35; John 13:4-17; Romans 15:1-3; 2 Corinthians 8:9; Philippians 2:3, 5-8.

Action assignment: List traits that you know or believe Jesus had, traits that you wish to develop more in your life. Ask God to help you be more Christlike.

BE ONLY A "SOJOURNER"

Peter reminds believers that they are only "sojourners" on earth. Life is too short to waste in disobedience and sin. It was when Lot stopped being a sojourner and became a resident in Sodom that he lost his consecration and his testimony. Everything he lived for went up in smoke! Keep reminding yourself that you are a "stranger and pilgrim" in this world.

In view of the fact that the Father lovingly disciplines His children today, and will judge their works in the future, we ought to cultivate an attitude of godly fear. This is not the cringing fear of a slave before a master, but the loving reverence of a child before his father. It is not fear of judgment, but a fear of disappointing Him or sinning against His love. It is "godly fear," a sober reverence for the Father.

Scripture for today: "Dear friends, I urge you, as aliens and strangers in the world, to abstain from sinful desires, which war against your soul. Live such good lives among the pagans that, though they accuse you of doing wrong, they may see your good deeds and glorify God on the day He visits us" (1 Peter 2:11-12, NIV).

Find and read: 1 Peter 4:1-6; 1 John 4:18; 2 Corinthians 7:1.

Action assignment: Write out your definition of *sojourn,* and compare your definition with that of a good dictionary. Decide whether you are a sojourner. Ask the Lord if He would have you make any adjustments in your attitude in this matter.

7

FEAR NOT

In his First Inaugural Address, on March 4, 1933, President Franklin Delano Roosevelt said to a nation in the grip of an economic depression, "The only thing we have to fear is fear itself." Why? Because fear paralyzes you, and fear is contagious and paralyzes others. Fear and faith cannot live together in the same heart. "Why are you fearful, O you of little faith?" (Matt. 8:26) Frightened people discourage others and help bring defeat (Deut. 20:8).

Nehemiah's first step was to post guards at the most conspicuous and vulnerable places on the wall. The enemy could then see that the Jews were prepared to fight. He armed entire families, knowing that they would stand together and encourage one another.

After looking the situation over, Nehemiah encouraged the people not to be afraid but to look to the Lord for help. If we fear the Lord, we need not fear the enemy. Nehemiah's heart was captivated by the "great and terrible" God of Israel (4:14; see 1:5), and he knew that God was strong enough to meet the challenge. He also reminded the people that they were fighting for their nation, their city, and their families. When the enemy learned that Jerusalem was armed and ready, they backed off (4:15). God had frustrated their plot. "The LORD brings the counsel of the nations to nothing; He makes the plans of the peoples of no effect. The counsel of the LORD stands forever, the plans of His heart to all generations" (Ps. 33:10–11). It is good to remind ourselves that the will of God comes from the heart of God and that we need not be afraid.

A promise: "So do not fear, for I am with you; do not be dismayed, for I am your God. I will strengthen you and help you; I will uphold you with my righteous right hand" (Isa. 41:10, NIV).

Read: Nehemiah 3

Action assignment: Memorize Isaiah 41:10. Believe what it says and remind yourself throughout the day that God indeed is with you. To help you remember, write out the verse and read it several times today.

HONEST EVALUATION

"Not as though I had already attained!" This is the statement of a great Christian who never permitted himself to be satisifed with his spiritual attainments. Obviously, the Apostle Paul was satisfied with Jesus Christ, but he was not satisfied with his Christian life. A sanctified dissatisfaction is the first essential to progress in the Christian race.

Harry came out of the manager's office with a look on his face dismal enough to wilt the roses on the secretary's desk.

Later in the day, the secretary talked to her boss about Harry. The boss chuckled. "Harry is one of our best salesmen and I'd hate to lose him. But he has a tendency to rest on his laurels and be satisfied with his performance. If I didn't get him mad at me once a month, he'd never produce!"

Many Christians are self-satisfied because they compare their "running" with that of other Christians, usually those who are not making much progress. Had Paul compared himself with others, he would have been tempted to be proud and perhaps to let up a bit. But Paul did not compare himself with others; he compared himself *with himself* and with *Jesus Christ!* The mature Christian honestly evaluates himself and strives to do better.

From the Bible: "That I may know Him, and the power of His resurrection and the fellowship of His sufferings, being conformed to His death. . . . Not that I have already obtained it, or have already become perfect, but I press on in order that I may lay hold of that for which also I was laid hold of by Christ Jesus" (Philippians 3:10, 12, NASB).

Read: all of Philippians 3.

Action assignment: Compare yourself with *yourself* and with Jesus Christ. Fix your eyes on Jesus as you go through your day.

9

DON'T BE AFRAID

Jesus is with His people no matter where they are. Dr. G. Campbell Morgan told about an experience in his early Christian life that involved this statement. Morgan used to visit several elderly ladies once a week to read the Bible to them. When he came to the end of Matthew's Gospel, Morgan read, "Lo, I am with you always, even unto the end of the world" (28:20). He added, "Isn't that a wonderful promise?" One of the ladies quickly replied, "Young man, that is not a promise—it is a fact!"

There are no conditions for us to meet, or even to believe, *for Jesus Christ is with us.* Paul discovered this to be true when he was seeking to establish a church in the difficult city of Corinth. He won people to Christ and baptized them and taught them the Word. When the going was tough, Paul had a special visit from the Lord: "Be not afraid . . . for I am with thee" (Acts 18:9-10).

The phrase "the end of the world" indicates that our Lord has a plan; He is the Lord of history. As the churches follow His leading and obey His Word, they fulfill His purposes in the world. It will all come to a climax one day; meanwhile, we must all be faithful.

Verse for today: "Go and make disciples of all nations . . . and . . . I will be with you always. . . ." (Matthew 28:19-20, NIV).

Also read: Matthew 18:20; Acts 1:8; 18:1-11.

Action assignment: Is Jesus' presence a constant fact in your life? Test yourself for awareness of this wonderful truth. When you are negative, ask Him for grace to help you in your need. When you are especially glad, thank Him for His grace in your life. Develop a pattern of belief in His constant presence in your daily walk with Him.

GROWTH THROUGH OPPOSITION

"The Bible tells us to love our neighbors, and also to love our enemies; probably because they are generally the same people."

Those words from Gilbert Keith Chesterton were certainly true in Nehemiah's situation. His arrival in Jerusalem was a threat to Sanballat and his associates (Neh. 2:10), who wanted to keep the Jews weak and dependent. A strong Jerusalem would endanger the balance of power in the region, and would also rob Sanballat and his friends of influence and wealth.

When things are going well, get ready for trouble, because the enemy doesn't want to see the work of the Lord make progress. As long as the people in Jerusalem were content with their sad lot, the enemy left them alone; but, when the Jews began to serve the Lord and bring glory to God's name, the enemy became active.

Opposition is not only evidence that God is blessing, but it is also an opportunity for us to grow. The difficulties that came to the work brought out the best in Nehemiah and his people. Satan wanted to use these problems as weapons to destroy the work, but God used them as tools to build His people. "God had one Son without sin," said Charles Spurgeon, "but He never had a son without trial."

If we spend time pondering the enemy's attacks, we will give Satan a foothold from which he can launch another attack even closer to home. The best thing to do is to pray and commit the whole thing to the Lord; and then *get back to your work!* Anything that keep you from doing what God has called you to do will only help the enemy.

God says: "Be on your guard; stand firm in the faith; be men of courage; be strong" (1 Cor. 16:13, NIV)

Read: Nehemiah 2

Action assignment: Identify any opposition you are experiencing. Tell the Lord about it. Commit the whole matter to the Lord. Then go confidently about your tasks for the day.

"NOBODY'S PERFECT!"

The phrase "make you perfect" in Hebrews 13:21 is the translation of one Greek word, *katartidzo*. This word was familiar to the people who received the letter to the Hebrews. Doctors knew it because it meant "to set a broken bone." To fishermen it meant "to mend a broken net." To sailors it meant "to outfit a ship for a voyage." To soldiers it meant "to equip an army for battle."

Our Saviour wants to equip us for life on earth. He wants to set the "broken bones" in our lives tenderly so that we might walk straight and run our life races successfully. He wants to repair the breaks in the nets so that we might catch fish and win souls. He wants to equip us for battle and outfit us so that we will not be battered in the storms of life. In brief, He wants to mature us so that He can work *in* us and *through* us that which pleases Him and accomplishes His will. The tools God uses to mature and equip His children are His Word, prayer, and the fellowship of the local church. He also uses individual believers to equip us. Finally, He uses suffering to perfect His children.

Verse for today: "For it is God who works in you both to will and to do of His good pleasure" (Philippians 2:13).

Also read: Matthew 4:21; 2 Timothy 3:16-17; 1 Thessalonians 3:9-10; Ephesians 4:11-12; Galatians 6:1; 1 Peter 5:10.

Action assignment: Make a difference in your life by turning Hebrews 13:21 into a personal prayer today. Pray along these lines: "Lord, make me perfect in every good work to do Thy will. Work in me that which is well-pleasing in Thy sight. Do it through Jesus Christ and may He receive the glory."

BE DETERMINED

Are we the kind of leaders and followers God wants us to be? Like Nehemiah, do we have a burden in our hearts for the work God has called us to do? (Neh. 2:12). Are we willing to sacrifice to see His will accomplished? Are we patient in gathering facts and in planning our work? Do we enlist the help of others or try to do everything ourselves? Do we motivate people on the basis of the spiritual—what God is doing—or simply on the basis of the personal? Are they following us or the Lord as He leads us?

As followers, do we listen to what our leaders say as they share their burdens? Do we cling to the past or desire to see God do something new? Are we cooperating in any way with the enemy and thus weakening the work? Have we found the job God wants us to complete?

Anyone can go through life as a destroyer; God has called His people to be builders. What an example Nehemiah is to us! Trace his "so" statements and see how God used him: "So I prayed" (2:4); "So I came to Jerusalem" (v. 11); "So they strengthened their hands for this good work" (v. 18); "So built we the wall" (4:6); "So we labored in the work" (v. 21); "So the wall was finished" (6:15).

Were it not for the and determination that came from his faith in a great God, Nehemiah would never have finished the work.

As Dr. V. Raymond Edman used to say, "It is always too soon to quit."

Paul writes: "Therefore, my dear brothers, stand firm. Let nothing move you. Always give yourselves fully to the work of the Lord, because you know that your labor in the Lord is not in vain" (1 Cor. 15:58, NIV).

Read: Nehemiah 6

Action assignment: Is God calling you to build a "wall"? Some task that is difficult? Do any of the questions in the first paragraph of today's reading apply to your situation? Talk to the Lord about it. Ask Him for strength and wisdom. Determine to complete the task.

BE READY FOR REWARD TIME

When the Lord returns, there will be a time of judgment at "the Judgment Seat of Christ." Each of us will give an account of his works, and each will receive the appropriate reward. This is a "family judgment" as the Father deals with His beloved children. The Greek word translated *judgeth* carries the meaning "to judge in order to find something good." God will search into the motives for our ministry; He will examine our hearts. But He assures us that His purpose is to glorify Himself in our lives and ministries, "and then shall every man have praise of God" (1 Corinthians 4:5). What an encouragement!

God will give us many gifts and privileges as we grow in the Christian life; but He will never give us the privilege to disobey and sin. He never pampers His children or indulges them. He is no respecter of persons. He "shows no partiality and accepts no bribes" (Deuteronomy 10:17, NIV). "For God does not show favoritism" (Romans 2:11, NIV). Years of obedience cannot purchase an hour of disobedience. If one of His children disobeys, God must chasten. But when His child obeys and serves Him in love, He notes that and prepares the proper reward.

Today's Scripture: "Wherefore we labor, that, whether present or absent, we may be accepted of Him. For we must all appear before the Judgment Seat of Christ; that everyone may receive the things done in his body, according to that he hath done, whether it be good or bad" (2 Corinthians 5:9-10).

Read: Romans 14:10-12; Hebrews 12:1-13.

Action assignment: Get your hymnal, find the song "Trust and Obey," and read it aloud. Then talk with the Lord.

GOD'S MIGHTY POWER

The Holy Spirit empowered Paul to minister, enabling him to perform mighty signs and wonders. The miracles God gave Paul to do were "signs" that they came from God and revealed Him to others. And they were "wonders" in that they aroused the wonder of the people. But their purpose was always to open the way for the preaching of the Gospel. Miracles were given to authenticate the messenger and the message, but by themselves they could never save the lost.

The Spirit of God also empowered Paul to share the Word in order to "make the Gentiles obedient" (Romans 15:18). It was "by word and deed" that the apostle shared the Good News.

"By word and deed" we today can share the love of God with the lost around us. Changes in conduct and character are just as much miracles of the Holy Spirit as the healing of the sick.

Verse for today: "I will not venture to speak of anything except what Christ has accomplished through me in leading the Gentiles to obey God by what I have said and done—by the power of signs and miracles, through the power of the Spirit" (Romans 15:18-19).

More to consider: Hebrews 2:1-4; Acts 1:8; Psalm 147:5; 2 Corinthians 4:7.

Action assignment: Define the word *power:*_____

_____.

Now think about the awesomeness of God's power. Compare it to the most powerful thing mankind has discovered—atomic power. God's power is still infinitely greater. Praise Him for His power and love to work in you His perfect will. Ask Him to help you share His love "by word and deed" as you go through this day.

15

POWER WITHIN

While flying back to Chicago from upper New York via New York City, we had to stay in our holding pattern over Kennedy Airport for more than an hour. When the stewardess announced that we would be landing an hour late, a man across the aisle shouted, "Bring out the booze!" This was his only resource when things were going against him.

All of nature depends on hidden resources. The great trees send their roots down into the earth to draw up water and minerals. Rivers have their sources in the snow-capped mountains. The most important part of a tree is the part you cannot see, the root system, and the most important part of the Christian's life is the part that only God sees. Unless we draw upon the deep resources of God by faith, we fail against the pressures of life. Paul depended on the power of Christ at work in his life. "I can—through Christ!" was Paul's motto, and it can be our motto too.

"I am ready for anything through the strength of the One who lives within me," is the way J.B. Phillips translates Philippians 4:13. *The Living Bible* puts it this way: "I can do everything God asks me to with the help of Christ who gives me the strength and power." No matter which translation you prefer, they all say the same thing: the Christian has all the power *within* that he needs to be adequate for the demands of life. We need only release this power by faith.

A verse to live by: "I have been crucified with Christ; and it is no longer I who live, but Christ lives in me; and the life which I now live in the flesh I live by faith in the Son of God, who loved me, and delivered Himself up for me" (Galatians 2:20, NASB).

Read: Isaiah 40:29-31; 2 Corinthians 12:19; Ephesians 1:19; Philippians 1:6, 21; 2 Timothy 1:12.

Action assignment: Select a verse in today's reading; memorize it and act upon it!

DEPRESSION: WHO CAN ESCAPE IT?

"You seem to imagine that I have no ups and downs, but just a level and lofty stretch of spiritual attainment with unbroken joy and equanimity. By no means! I am often perfectly wretched and everything appears most murky." So wrote the man called in his day (1864-1923) "the greatest preacher in the English-speaking world," Dr. John Henry Jowett.

Charles Haddon Spurgeon, undoubtedly the greatest preacher England ever produced, once said in a sermon: "I am subject to depressions of spirit so fearful that I hope none of you ever get to such extremes of wretchedness as I go to."

Discouragement is no respecter of persons. It seems to attack the successful far more than the unsuccessful, for the higher we climb, the farther down we can fall. Even the Apostle Paul himself was "pressed out of measure" and "despaired even of life" (2 Corinthians 1:8).

What was Paul's secret of victory when experiencing pressures and trials? His secret was *God*. When you find yourself discouraged and ready to quit, get your attention off yourself and focus it on God. Out of his own difficult experience, Paul fellowshiped with God and found encouragement in His promises.

Remember: "Ye shall not need to fight in this battle: set yourselves, stand ye still, and see the salvation of the Lord . . . fear not, nor be dismayed; tomorrow go out against them: for the Lord will be with you" (2 Chronicles 20:17).

Consider: Psalm 23:1; 34:7; 103:3-4; 2 Corinthians 1:8-11.

Action assignment: Find your hymnal and turn to "It Is Well with My Soul," the song written by H. G. Spafford after his wife wired him that their children had perished in a shipwreck. Sing or even whistle it. Thank God that you can trust Him in all situations of life.

TURN THE OTHER CHEEK

The original Law kept people from forcing the offender to pay a greater price than the offense deserved. It also prevented people from taking personal revenge. Jesus replaced a law with an attitude: Be willing to suffer loss yourself rather than cause another to suffer. Of course, He applied this to *personal insults*, not to groups or nations. The person who retaliates only makes himself and the offender feel worse; the result is a settled war and not peace.

In order to "turn the other cheek," we must stay where we are and not run away. This demands both faith and love. It also means that *we* will hurt, but it is better to be hurt on the outside than to be harmed on the inside. It further means that *we should try to help the sinner*. We are vulnerable, because he may attack us anew; but we are also victorious, because Jesus is on our side, helping us and building our characters.

Psychologists tell us that violence is born of weakness, not strength. It is the strong man who can love and suffer hurt; it is the weak man who thinks only of himself and hurts others to protect himself.

The Bible says: "Do not say, 'I'll pay you back for this wrong!' Wait for the Lord, and He will deliver you" (Proverbs 20:22, NIV).

Read also: Leviticus 24:19-22; Matthew 5:38-42; Romans 12:17-19; 1 Peter 3:9.

Action assignment: Has someone wronged you? Ask God to help you have an attitude of "turning the other cheek" and to respond with love to a past injury or one that may occur today.

CONCERN FOR OTHERS

Some people prefer *not* to know what's going on, because information might bring obligation. "What you don't know can't hurt you," says the old adage; but is it true? In a letter to a Mrs. Foote, Mark Twain wrote, "All you need in this life is ignorance and confidence; then success is sure." But what we don't know *could* hurt us a great deal! There are people in the cemetery who chose not to know the truth. The slogan for the 1987 AIDS publicity campaign was "Don't die of ignorance"; and that slogan can be applied to many areas of life besides health.

Nehemiah asked about Jerusalem and the Jews living there because he had a caring heart. When we truly care about people, we want the facts, no matter how painful they may be. "Practical politics consists in ignoring facts," American historian Henry Adams said; but Aldous Huxley said, "Facts do not cease to exist because they are ignored." Closing our eyes and ears to the truth could be the first step toward tragedy for ourselves as well as for others.

Are we like Nehemiah, anxious to know the truth even about the worst situations? Is our interest born of concern or idle curiosity? When we read missionary prayer letters, the news in religious periodicals, or even our church's ministry reports, do we want the facts, and do the facts burden us? Are we the kind of people who care enough to ask?

Think about it: "Each of you should look not only to your own interests, but also to the interests of others" (Phil. 2:4, NIV).

Read: Nehemiah 1

Action assignment: Do you know someone who is experiencing hardships? Until now you haven't done much more than pray for that person. Talk to God about the matter. Determine to do something for that person. Even a phone call is a starter.

19

DO YOU QUALIFY?

Not every believer is equipped to establish other Christians in the faith. Ideally, every Christian should be mature enough to help others grow in the Lord and learn to stand on their own two feet. Unfortunately, some Christians are like those described in Hebrews 5:11-14. They have gone backward in their spiritual walk and have forgotten the basic truth of the Word. Instead of teaching others, they themselves need to be taught again. They are going through a second childhood spiritually.

What kind of person can help younger believers grow in the Lord? To begin with, *he must be a Christian himself.* We cannot lead another where we have not been ourselves, nor can we share that which we do not possess. He must also be a *true minister.* The Greek word for minister is simply *servant.* And to help establish others, he must not be afraid to work. It is a demanding thing to establish new Christians. They have many problems and often do not grow as fast as we think they should. Teaching them requires love and patience.

Above all, one who disciples others must be a *fellow worker with God,* allowing God to work in and through him.

Don't forget: "For we are laborers together with God: ye are God's husbandry, ye are God's building" (1 Corinthians 3:9).

Consider: 1 Corinthians 4:2; Philippians 2:19-23.

Action assignment: Think of someone you could help grow as a Christian. Consider the details of how you could work with that person. Meditate on the matter for at least a couple of minutes. Talk to God about it.

SUBSTANCE, EVIDENCE, WITNESS

Three words in Hebrews 11:1-3 summarize what true Bible faith is: *substance, evidence,* and *witness.* The word translated *substance* means literally "to stand under, to support." Faith is to a Christian what a foundation is to a house: it gives confidence that he will stand. When a believer has faith, it is God's way of giving him confidence that what is promised will be experienced.

The word *evidence* simply means "conviction." This is the inward conviction from God that what He has promised, He will perform. The presence of God-given faith in one's heart is conviction enough that He will keep His Word.

Witness ("obtained a good report") is an important word in Hebrews 11. The summary in Hebrews 12:1 calls this list of men and women "so great a cloud of witnesses." They are witnesses to us because God witnessed to them. In each example cited, God gave witness to that person's faith. This witness was His divine approval of their lives and ministries.

The writer of Hebrews makes it clear that faith is a very practical thing, in spite of what unbelievers say. Faith enables us to understand what God does. Faith enables us to see what others cannot see and to do what others cannot do! People laughed at these great men and women when they stepped out by faith, but God was with them and enabled them to succeed to His glory.

Remember this: "Now faith is the substance of things hoped for, the evidence of things not seen" (Hebrews 11:1).

Also consider: Hebrews 11:2-40.

Action assignment: Review Hebrews 11 to see what faith enabled these great men and women to accomplish. What would you like God to accomplish in your life before this time tomorrow? Commit today's verse to memory.

BRIDLING THE TONGUE

In selecting the bit and the rudder, the Apostle James presented two items in his epistle that are small of themselves, yet exercise great power, just like the tongue. A small bit enables the rider to control the great horse, and a small rudder enables the pilot to steer the huge ship. The tongue is a small member in the body, and yet it has the power to accomplish great things.

Both the bit and the rudder must overcome contrary forces. The bit must overcome the wild nature of the horse, and the rudder must fight the winds and currents that would drive the ship off its course. The human tongue also must overcome contrary forces. We have an old nature that wants to control us and make us sin. There are circumstances around us that would make us say things we ought not to say. Sin on the inside and pressures on the outside are seeking to get control of the tongue.

This means that both the bit and the rudder must be under the control of a strong hand. The expert horseman keeps the mighty power of his steed under control, and the experienced pilot courageously steers the ship through the storm. When Jesus Christ controls the tongue, then we need not fear saying the wrong things— or even saying the right things in a wrong way!

Verse for today: "Set a watch, O Lord, before my mouth; keep the door of my lips. Incline not my heart to any evil thing" (Psalm 141:3-4.).

Other Scripture: Job 27:4; Psalm 15:1-3; 139:1-4; Proverbs 15:1-2; Colossians 4:6; James 1:19-26.

Action assignment: Ask God to enable you to put your tongue to good use today.

SUSTAINING HOPE

When people are experiencing intense grief and pain, it is easy for them to feel that the future is hopeless and that God has forsaken them. The eminent American psychiatrist Karl Menninger called hope "the major weapon against the suicide impulse." Hopeless people feel that life is not worth living since they have nothing to look forward to but suffering and failure. They conclude that it is better for them to die than to live and be a burden to themselves and to others.

The German philosopher Friedrich Nietzsche called hope "the worst of all evils, because it prolongs the torments of man." But an individual who believes in Jesus Christ shares in a "living hope" that grows more wonderful every day (1 Peter 1:3ff.). Dead hopes fade away because they have no roots, but our "living hope" gets better because it is rooted in the living Christ and His Living Word. The assurance of resurrection and life in glory with Christ is a strong motivation for us to keep going even when the going is tough (1 Cor. 15:58).

Charles L. Allen has written, "When you say a situation or a person is hopeless, you are slamming the door in the face of God."

Today's verse: "Why are you downcast, O my soul? Why so disturbed within me? Put your hope in God, for I will yet praise Him, my Savior and my God" (Ps. 43:5, NIV).

Read: Hebrews 6:11, 18–19

Action assignment: Write out your own definition of hope and what it means to have hope in the Lord. Scan the references to hope in your concordance. Find some of the passages in your Bible and underline those that are especially meaningful to you. Find a song such as "My Hope Is in the Lord" and sing it.

23

IS DOCTRINE DULL?

The successful Christian learns the vocabulary of the Spirit and makes use of it. He knows the meaning of justification, sanctification, adoption, propitiation, election, inspiration, and so forth. In understanding God's vocabulary, we come to understand God's Word and God's will for our lives. If the engineering student can grasp the technical terms of chemistry, physics, or electronics, why should it be difficult for Christians, taught by the Spirit, to grasp the vocabulary of Christian truth?

Yet I hear church members say, "Don't preach doctrine. Just give us heartwarming sermons that will encourage us!" Sermons based on what? If they are not based on doctrine, they will accomplish nothing! "But doctrine is so dull!" people complain. Not if it is presented the way the Bible presents it. Doctrine to me is exciting! What a thrill to be able to study the Bible and let the Spirit teach us "the deep things of God" (1 Corinthians 2:10).

I suggest that you make time every day to read the Word and meditate on it. Follow a regular schedule in your reading and give yourself time to pray, think, and meditate. Let the Spirit of God search the Word and teach you. The study and application of basic Bible doctrine can transform your life.

Scripture to remember: "Jesus therefore answered them, and said, 'My teaching is not Mine, but His who sent Me. If any man is willing to do His will, he shall know of the teaching, whether it is of God, or whether I speak from Myself'" (John 7:16-17, NASB).

Also read: Ephesians 4:14; Colossians 2:4, 8; 1 Timothy 1:3, 7; 2 John 7, 9-11.

Action assignment: Make it a point to strengthen your beliefs. Read a good book on doctrine such as *Know What You Believe* by Paul Little (Victor).

BE PATIENT

Nothing that is given to Christ in faith and love is ever wasted. Job was bankrupt and sick, and all he could give to the Lord was his suffering by faith; *but that is just what God wanted in order to silence the devil.*

When William Whiting Borden died in Egypt in 1913 while on his way to the mission field, some people may have asked, "Why this waste?" But God is still using the story of his brief life to challenge people to give Christ their all.

When John and Betty Stam were martyred in China in 1934, there were some who asked, "Why this waste?" But *The Triumph of John and Betty Stam* by Mrs. Howard Taylor has been a life-changing book since it was published in 1935.

When the five missionaries were martyred in Ecuador at the hands of Auca Indians, some called the event a "tragic waste of manpower." But God thought differently, and the story of these five heroes of faith has been ministering to the church ever since.

Job asked, "Why was I born?" In the light of his losses and his personal suffering, it all seemed such a waste! But God knew what He was doing *then,* and He knows what He is doing *now.*

"You have heard of Job's perseverance and have seen what the Lord finally brought about," wrote James. "The Lord is full of compassion and mercy" (James 5:11, NIV). If you had told that to Job, he might not have believed it; but it was still true.

It was true for him, and it is true for us today.

Believe it!

Just do it: "Be still before the LORD and wait patiently for Him; do not fret when men succeed in their ways, when they carry out their wicked schemes" (Ps. 37:7, NIV).

Read: James 5

Action assignment: You may be going through a difficult experience. Talk to the Lord about it. Ask Him to help you trust Him and be patient.

TRUE WISDOM

What is the Christian's wisdom? Does he look to the philosophies of this world? No! To begin with, Jesus Christ is our wisdom. In Jesus Christ "are hid all the treasures of wisdom and knowledge" (Colossians 2:3). The first step toward true wisdom is the receiving of Jesus Christ as Saviour.

The Word of God is also our wisdom. "Behold, I have taught you statutes and judgments. . . . Keep therefore and do them; for this is your wisdom and your understanding in the sight of the nations" (Deuteronomy 4:5-6). The Scriptures are able to make us "wise unto salvation" (2 Timothy 3:15).

James 1:5 indicates that we find wisdom through believing prayer: "If any of you lack wisdom, let him ask of God." The Holy Spirit of God is "the Spirit of wisdom and revelation" (Ephesians 1:17) and He directs us in the wisest paths as we trust the Word and pray.

The origin of true spiritual wisdom is God. To get your wisdom from any other source is to ask for trouble. There is no need to get the counterfeit wisdom of the world, the wisdom that caters to the flesh and accomplishes the work of the devil. Get your wisdom from God!

A wise man wrote: "The Lord gives wisdom; from His mouth come knowledge and understanding. He stores up sound wisdom for the upright; He is a shield to those who walk in integrity" (Proverbs 2:6-7, NASB).

Consider: Isaiah 30:21; 1 Corinthians 1:24-31; Colossians 3:16.

Action assignment: Determine to keep in touch with Christ, who is your wisdom. If you lack wisdom in any situation today, "ask of God."

STUDY THE BANK BOOK

On January 6, 1822, the wife of a poor German pastor had a son, never dreaming that he would one day achieve world renown and great wealth. When Heinrich Schliemann was seven years old, a picture of ancient Troy in flames captured his imagination. Contrary to what many people believed, Heinrich argued that Homer's great poems, *The Iliad* and *The Odyssey,* were based on historic facts and he set out to prove it. In 1873, he uncovered the ancient site of Troy, along with some fabulous treasure which he smuggled out of the country—much to the anger of the Turkish government. Schliemann became a famous, wealthy man because he dared to believe an ancient record and act upon his faith.

You were "born rich" when you trusted Christ. But this is not enough, for you must grow in your understanding of your riches if you are going to use them to the glory of God. Too many Christians have never carefully studied "the Bank Book" to find out the vast spiritual wealth that God has put in their account through Jesus Christ. Don't be a Christian who is only casually acquainted with "the Bank Book."

Remember this: "He has given us His very great and precious promises, so that through them you may participate in the divine nature and escape the corruption in the world caused by evil desires" (2 Peter 1:4, NIV).

Consider also: Psalm 119:16, 18, 24; Romans 15:4.

Action assignment: Make it a point, beginning today, to read the entire Epistle of Ephesians. Underline the many gems you dig out and discover for yourself how rich you really are!

RESISTING THE TEMPTER

God's Word is one of the best tools for resisting temptation. When Jesus was tempted by Satan, He used the Word of God to defeat him. Paul admonished believers to take "the sword of the Spirit, which is the Word of God" (Ephesians 6:17) in their battle against Satan and his demonic assistants.

The Bible is able to establish us because it is inspired of God. It is not simply a book of religious ideas or good moral advice; it is the very Word of God. It is "profitable for doctrine, for reproof, for correction, for instruction in righteousness" (2 Timothy 3:16). It has been well said that *doctrine* tells us what is right, *reproof* tells us what is not right, *correction* tells how to get right, and *instruction* tells us how to stay right.

Know this: "We wrestle not against flesh and blood, but against principalities, against powers, against the rulers of the darkness of this world, against spiritual wickedness in high places. . . . Take . . . the sword of the Spirit, which is the Word of God" (Ephesians 6:12, 17).

For further study: Matthew 4:1-11; 2 Timothy 3:16.

Action assignment: Commit Ephesians 6:12, 17 to memory (see above) and talk to God, asking Him to enable you to grasp more fully the message of this passage and its relationship to you.

LOOK AHEAD

Throughout the Epistle to the Hebrews, the writer emphasized the importance of the *future hope*. His readers were prone to *look back* and want to *go back*, but he encouraged them to follow Christ's example and *look ahead* by faith. The heroes of faith named in Hebrews 11 lived for the future, and this enabled them to endure. Like Peter, when we get our eyes of faith off the Saviour, we start to sink!

Since Christ is the "author and finisher of our faith," trusting Him releases His power in our lives. I could try to follow the example of some great athlete for years and still be a failure. But if, in my younger days, that athlete could have entered into my life and shared his know-how and ability with me, that would have made me a winner. Christ is both the exemplar *and the enabler!* As we see Him in the Word, and yield to His Spirit, He increases our faith and enables us to run the race.

Scripture says: "Looking for that blessed hope, and the glorious appearing of the great God and our Saviour Jesus Christ" (Titus 2:13).

Also consider: Hebrews 11:10, 14-16, 24-27; 12:2; Philippians 4:13; Revelation 4:11.

Action assignment: Decide to focus your eyes on Christ Jesus for the challenges you will face today, and for the uncertainties of life in the future. Thank Him that His power is released as you trust Him.

A WALKING MIRACLE

The church is a miracle. No amount of skill, talents, or programs can make the church what it ought to be. Only God can do that. If each believer is depending on the grace of God, walking in the love of God, and participating in the fellowship of the Spirit, not walking in the flesh, then he will be part of the answer and not part of the problem. He will be a *living* benediction—to God and to others!

Our God is the "God of love and peace" (2 Corinthians 13:11). Can the outside world tell that from the way we live and the way we conduct the business of our churches? "Behold how they love one another!" was what the lost world said about the early church, but it has been a long time since the church has earned that kind of commendation.

Verse for today: "Not by might nor by power, but by My Spirit, says the Lord Almighty" (Zechariah 4:6, NIV).

Consider: Matthew 16:13-18; John 3:5-8; Romans 1:8-12; Colossians 1:25-29.

Action assignment: Do you believe that the Holy Spirit can do things through you that are beyond your comprehension? Write down one truth of the Christian faith that you do not understand. Affirm that truth sincerely. Now think about someone you do not understand or have a hard time "figuring out." Go out of your way today to get in touch with that person. Pray for wisdom in knowing how to better understand and hence love that person.

UNCONDITIONAL SURRENDER

The word *submit* is a military term that means "get into your proper rank." When a buck private acts like the general, there is going to be trouble! Unconditional surrender is the only way to complete victory. If there is any area of the life kept back from God, there will always be battles. This explains why uncommitted Christians cannot live with themselves or with other people.

"Neither give place to the devil," cautions Paul in Ephesians 4:27. Satan needs a foothold in our lives if he is going to fight against God; and *we give him that foothold.* The way to resist the devil is to submit to God.

After King David committed adultery with Bathsheba and killed her husband, he hid his sins for almost a year. There was war between him and God, and David had declared it. When he finally submitted to God, David experienced peace and joy. Submission is an act of the will; it is saying, "Not my will but Thine be done."

From the Book: "If you love Me, you will keep My commandments" (John 14:15, NASB).

Read: Psalms 32 and 51; Mark 14:32-36; 1 Peter 1:14.

Action assignment: Ask God to show you any area of your life that is not yielded to Him. Tell Him you want Him to be Lord of *all* today and every day.

October

Be Renewed:

"God . . . hath begotten us . . . unto a lively hope by the resurrection of Jesus Christ from the dead, to an inheritance incorruptible, and undefiled, and that fadeth not away, reserved in heaven for you."

1 Peter 1:3-4

1

LIVING IN THE FUTURE TENSE

Christians live in the future tense; their present actions and decisions are governed by the knowledge that they have a living, resurrected Saviour whom they will someday see. Just as an engaged couple makes all their plans in the light of that future wedding, so Christians should live with the expectation of seeing Jesus Christ.

"Gird up the loins of your mind," Peter urges. This simply means, "Pull your thoughts together! Have a disciplined mind!" The image is that of a robed man, tucking his skirts under the belt, so he can be free to run. When you center your thoughts on the return of Christ, and live accordingly, you escape the many worldly things that would encumber your mind and hinder your spiritual progress. Peter may have borrowed the idea from the Passover supper. The Jews were supposed to eat the Passover meal in haste, ready to move.

Outlook determines outcome; attitude determines action. A Christian who is looking for the glory of God has a greater motivation for present obedience than a Christian who ignores the Lord's return.

Remember this: "God . . . hath begotten us . . . unto a lively hope by the resurrection of Jesus Christ from the dead, to an inheritance incorruptible, and undefiled, and that fadeth not away, reserved in heaven for you" (1 Peter 1:3-4).

Read: Titus 2:11-15.

Action assignment: Look up the word *hope* in a good dictionary. Meditate on the idea of a *living hope* in relationship to today's reading. Thank God for this living hope.

THE BODY PRINCIPLE

What is true Christian dedication? For one thing, it means giving God your body. Before we trusted Christ we used our bodies for sinful pleasures and purposes, but now that we belong to Him we want to use our bodies for His glory. The Christian's body is God's temple because the Spirit of God dwells within him. It is our privilege to glorify Christ in our body and magnify Christ in our body.

Just as Jesus Christ had to take upon Himself a body in order to accomplish God's will on earth, so we must yield our bodies to Christ that He might continue God's work through us. We must yield the members of the body as "instruments of righteousness" (Romans 6:13) for the Holy Spirit to use in the doing of God's work. The Old Testament sacrifices were dead sacrifices, but we are to be living ones.

Verse for today: "Therefore, I urge you, brothers, in view of God's mercy, to offer your bodies as living sacrifices, holy and pleasing to God—which is your spiritual worship" (Romans 12:1, NIV).

Also read: 1 Corinthians 6:19-20; Romans 6:13; 8:9; Philippians 1:20-21; Hebrews 10:22.

Action assignment: Mentally list the aspects of your body for which you are thankful and those which somehow are less than pleasing to you. Do you realize that God accepts you just as you are and wants you to give Him both what you consider your "assets" and "deficits"?

Imagine worshiping God without a body. Hard, isn't it? Now thank Him for your body and yield every aspect of your self to Him afresh. See how this act of true worship affects your day today.

3

WHEN TESTING COMES

In times of severe testing, our first question must not be, "*How* can I get out of this?" but "*What* can I get out of this?" Job's wife thought she had the problem solved; but if Job had followed her counsel, it would have only made things worse. Faith is living without scheming. It is obeying God in spite of feelings, circumstances, or consequences, knowing that He is working out His perfect plan in His way and in His time.

The two things Job would not give up were his faith in God and his integrity, and that's what his wife wanted him to do. Even if God did permit evil to come into his life, Job would not rebel against God by taking matters into his own hands. Job had never read *The Letters of Samuel Rutherford*, but he was following the counsel of that godly Scottish pastor who suffered greatly: "It is faith's work to claim and challenge loving-kindness out of all the roughest strokes of God." Job was going to trust God—and even argue with God!—and not waste his sufferings or his opportunity to receive what God had for him.

When life is difficult, it's easy to give up; but giving up is the worst thing we can do. A professor of history said, "If Columbus had turned back, nobody would have blamed him—but nobody would have remembered him either." If you want to be memorable, sometimes you have to be miserable.

In the end, Job's wife was reconciled to her husband and to the Lord, and God gave her another family (Job 42:13). We don't know how much she learned from her sufferings; but we can assume it was a growing experience for her.

Today's verse: "Consider it pure joy, my brothers, whenever you face trials of many kinds, because you know that the testing of your faith develops perseverance" (James 1:2–3, NIV).

Read: Job 1

Action assignment: Look up songs about trials in your hymnal. Read several and let their messages soak in. Sing one that is especially meaningful to you.

YOU CAN WIN!

What does Job's story mean to believers today? It means that some of the trials of life are caused directly by satanic opposition. God permits Satan to try His children, but He always limits the extent of the enemy's power. When you find yourself in the fire, remember that God keeps His gracious hand on the thermostat!

Satan wants us to get impatient with God, for an impatient Christian is a powerful weapon in the devil's hands. Moses' impatience robbed him of a trip to the Holy Land; Abraham's impatience led to the birth of Ishmael, the enemy of the Jews; and Peter's impatience almost made him a murderer. When Satan attacks us, it is easy for us to get impatient and run ahead of God and lose God's blessing as a result.

When you find yourself in the furnace, go to the throne of grace and receive from the Lord all the grace you need to endure. Remind yourself that the Lord has a gracious purpose in all of this suffering, and that He will work out His purposes in His time and for His glory. You are not a robot caught in the jaws of fate. You are a loving child of God, privileged to be a part of a wonderful plan. There is a difference!

Believe this: "The Lord will deliver me from every evil deed, and will bring me safely to His heavenly kingdom; to Him be the glory forever and ever. Amen" (2 Timothy 4:18, NASB).

Also read: Job 1:12; 2:6; 23:10; 2 Corinthians 12:7-9; Hebrews 4:14-16.

Action assignment: If you are hurting, make a special point to turn from negative thinking to the positive truth of 2 Timothy 4:18.

RUNNING THE RACE

It makes no difference how loudly our friends applaud if God is displeased with us. "Everything is uncovered and laid bare before the eyes of Him to whom we must give account" (Heb. 4:13, NIV), so it's futile to try to hide. According to 1 John 1:5–10, once we start lying to others (v. 6), we'll soon start lying to ourselves (v. 8); and the result will be trying to lie to God (v. 10). This leads to a gradual deterioration of character that brings collapse and shame. We seek to live a holy life, not to be recognized as "holy people," but to please a holy God. We live before Him openly and sincerely, hiding nothing, fearing nothing.

For several years, I've had a plaque on the wall of my study containing this quotation from A. W. Tozer: "To know God is at once the easiest and the most difficult thing in the world."

Knowing God and becoming more like Him is the easiest thing in the world because God is for us and gives us all the help we want as we seek to attain the goal. But it's the hardest thing because almost everything within us and around us fights against us, and we have to exercise a holy determination to run the race and keep our eyes on the Lord (Heb. 12:1–3).

But it can be done; otherwise, God would never have said eight times in His Word, "Be holy, for I am holy!"

Consider: "Therefore, since we are surrounded by such a great cloud of witnesses, let us throw off everything that hinders and the sin that so easily entangles, and let us run with perseverance the race marked out for us. Let us fix our eyes on Jesus, the author and perfecter of our faith, who for the joy set before Him endured the cross, scorning its shame, and sat down at the right hand of the throne of God" (Heb. 12:1–2, NIV).

Read: Hebrews 12

Action assignment: What in your life is fighting you to keep you from being more Christlike and knowing God better? What can you do about it? Talk it over with God. Determine to run a better race.

OBEY AND BELIEVE

True Bible faith is confident obedience to God's Word in spite of circumstances and consequences. Read that sentence again and let it soak into your mind and heart.

This faith operates quite simply. God speaks and we hear His Word. We trust His Word and act on it no matter what the circumstances are or what the consequences may be. The circumstances may be impossible and the consequences frightening and unknown; but we obey God's Word just the same and believe Him to do what is right and what is best.

The unsaved world does not understand true Bible faith, probably because it sees so little faith in action in the church today. The cynical editor H.L. Mencken defined faith as "illogical belief in the occurrence of the impossible." The world fails to realize that faith is only as good as its object, and the object of our faith is God. Faith is not some "feeling" that we manufacture. It is our total response to what God has revealed in His Word.

Scripture for today: "He [Abraham] staggered not at the promise of God through unbelief; but was strong in faith, giving glory to God; and being fully persuaded that, what He had promised, He was able also to perform" (Romans 4:20-21).

For additional study: Proverbs 3:5-6; Psalm 91; Isaiah 41:10; Luke 18:27.

Action assignment: Fix your thoughts again on that first sentence. Talk to God about the impossible circumstances in your life—and the difference faith can make.

7

MARRIAGE: COMMITMENT FOR LIFE

It is God's will that the marriage union be permanent, a lifetime commitment. There is no place in Christian marriage for a "trial marriage," nor is there any room for the "escape-hatch" attitude: "If the marriage doesn't work, we can always get a divorce."

For this reason, marriage must be built on something sturdier than good looks, money, romantic excitement, and social acceptance. There must be Christian commitment, character, and maturity. There must be a willingness to grow, to learn from each other, to forgive and forget, to minister to one another. The kind of love Paul described in 1 Corinthians 13 is what is needed to cement two lives together.

God has put "walls" around marriage, not to make it a prison, but to make it a safe fortress. The person who considers marriage a prison should not get married. When two people are lovingly and joyfully committed to each other—and to their Lord—the experience of marriage is one of enrichment and enlargement. They grow together and discover the richness of serving the Lord as a team in their home and church.

Scripture to remember: "For this cause a man shall leave his father and mother, and the two shall become one flesh; consequently they are no longer two, but one flesh. What therefore God has joined together, let no man separate" (Mark 10:7-9, NASB).

Also read: Mark 10:2-12; Luke 16:18; Romans 7:1-3.

Action assignment: Ask God to help you toward a greater grasp of the biblical view of marriage and not let your philosophy be tainted by the modern, worldly view.

WHEN THE GOING IS TOUGH

The word *afflicted* means "suffering in difficult circumstances."
The phrase *in trouble* is a good translation. The Apostle Paul
used this word to describe the circumstances he was in as he suffered for the Gospel's sake (2 Timothy 2:9). As God's people going
through life, we must often endure difficulties that are not the results of sin or the chastening of God.

What should we do when we find ourselves in such trying circumstances? We must not grumble and criticize the saints who
are having an easier time of it, nor should we blame the Lord.
We should pray, asking God for the wisdom we need to understand the situation and use it to His glory.

Prayer can remove affliction, if that is God's will. But prayer
can also give us the grace we need to endure troubles and use
them to accomplish God's perfect will. *God can transform troubles into triumphs.* "He giveth more grace" (James 4:6). Paul
prayed that God might change his circumstances, but instead God
gave Paul the grace he needed to turn his weakness into strength.
Our Lord prayed in Gethsemane that the cup might be removed,
and it was not; yet the Father gave Him the strength He needed
to go to the cross and die for our sins.

From the Book: "I sought the Lord, and He answered me, and
delivered me from all my fears" (Psalm 34:4, NASB).

Also: 2 Corinthians 12:7-10; James 1:5; 5:9; Hebrews 5:8-9; 1 Peter
1:6-7.

Action assignment: If you have trials, ask God to show you if
your difficulties are a result of sin or if they are solely from God.
Any sin, of course, should be confessed to God.

GRACE AT WORK

What is grace? It is God's provision for our every need when we need it. Someone has made an acrostic of the word *grace:* God's Riches Available at Christ's Expense.

There is never a shortage of grace. God is sufficient for our spiritual ministries as well as for our material and physical needs. If God's grace is sufficient to save us, surely it is sufficient to keep us and strengthen us in our times of suffering. Paul claimed God's promise and drew upon the grace that was offered to him, thus turning seeming tragedy into triumph. No matter how we look at it, God is adequate for every need that we have.

But God does not give us His grace simply that we might "endure" our sufferings. Even unconverted people can manifest great endurance. God's grace should enable us to *rise above* our circumstances and feelings and cause our afflictions to work *for us* in accomplishing positive good. As with Paul, our suffering need not be a tyrant that controls us, but a servant that works for us.

Verse for today: "Let us then approach the throne of grace with confidence, so that we may receive mercy and find grace to help us in our time of need" (Hebrews 4:16, NIV).

Further reading: John 1:16; Romans 5:20; 2 Corinthians 3:4-6; 8:7; 9:8; 12:9; James 4:6; 1 Peter 5:10; 2 Peter 3:18.

Action assignment: How has God's grace been sufficient in your life? In ministering to others? In meeting your material and physical needs? Ask God to help you be a channel of His grace to others.

CAN OTHERS SEE JESUS IN YOU?

Trials are controlled by God. They do not last forever; they are "for a season." When God permits His children to go through the furnace, He keeps His eye on the clock and His hand on the thermostat. If we rebel, He may have to reset the clock; but if we submit, He will not permit us to suffer one minute too long. The important thing is that we learn the lesson He wants to teach us and that we bring glory to Him alone.

Peter illustrated this truth by referring to the goldsmith. No goldsmith would deliberately waste the precious ore. He would put it into the smelting furnace long enough to remove the cheap impurities; then he would pour it out and make from it a beautiful article of value. It has been said that the eastern goldsmith kept the metal in the furnace until he could see his face reflected in it. So our Lord keeps us in the furnace of suffering until we reflect the glory and beauty of Jesus Christ.

Verse for today: "But the God of all grace, who hath called us unto His eternal glory by Christ Jesus, after that ye have suffered a while, make you perfect, stablish, strengthen, settle you" (1 Peter 5:10).

Read: Romans 8:17; 2 Corinthians 1:7.

Action assignment: In an encyclopedia look up the listing entitled "Refining" and consider the processes mentioned to get a better grasp of this thought. Talk with God about refining as it may apply to you.

11

THEY SHALL BEHOLD HIM

The accounts of Paul's conversion tell very little that parallels our salvation experience today. Certainly none of us has seen Christ in glory or actually heard Him speak from heaven. We are neither blinded by the light of heaven nor thrown to the ground. In what way, then, is Paul's conversion "a pattern"?

It is a picture of how the nation of Israel will be saved when Jesus Christ returns to establish his kingdom on earth. The nation Israel will see Him as He returns, recognize him as the Messiah, repent, and receive Him. It will be an experience similar to that of Saul of Tarsus when he was on his way to Damascus to persecute Christians.

Verse for today: "Look, He is coming with the clouds, and every eye will see Him, even those who pierced Him; and all the peoples of the earth will mourn because of Him. So shall it be! Amen" (Revelation 1:7, NIV).

More to read: 1 Corinthians 15:8; 1 Timothy 1:16; Zechariah 12:10; 14:4; Acts 1:11; 9.

Action assignment: Recall your own conversion to Christ. Was it an instantaneous event similar to Paul's, or was yours a gradual one? List the clearly unmistakable signs of your conversion:___

_____

_____.

Now reflect upon the Second Coming of Christ that will take place in a flash. Praise God for His grace in giving you the opportunity to turn to Him now and pray for those who are yet to turn to Him.

NATURE DETERMINES APPETITE

Yes, nature determines *appetite.* The pig wants slop but the sheep desires green pastures. Nature also determines *behavior.* An eagle flies because it has an eagle's nature, and a dolphin swims because that is the nature of the dolphin. Nature determines *environment:* squirrels climb trees, moles burrow underground, and trout swim in the water. Nature also determines *association:* lions travel in prides, sheep in flocks, and fish in schools.

If nature determines appetite, and we have God's nature within, then we ought to have an appetite for that which is pure and holy. Our behavior ought to be like that of the Father, and we ought to live in the kind of "spiritual environment" that is suited to our nature. We ought to associate with that which is true to our nature.

Because we possess this divine nature, we have "completely escaped" the defilement and decay in this present evil world. If we feed the new nature the nourishment of the Word, then we will have little interest in the garbage of the world. But if we "make provision for the flesh" (Romans 13:14), our sinful nature will lust after the "old sins" and we will disobey God. Godly living is the result of cultivating the new nature within.

The Bible commands: "Let us ... lay aside the deeds of darkness and put on the armor of light. Let us behave properly as in the day, not in carousing and drunkenness, not in sexual promiscuity and sensuality, not in strife and jealousy. But put on the Lord Jesus Christ, and make no provision for the flesh in regard to its lusts" (Romans 13:12-14, NASB).

Also: 2 Corinthians 6:14-18; 7:1; 2 Peter 1:3-11.

Action assignment: Take inventory. How have you spent the last twenty-four hours? Any "garbage" intake? Have you given God opportunity to speak quietly to you through His Word? Think about it. Talk to God about it.

13

TREASURES IN HEAVEN

Materialism will enslave the heart, the mind, and the will. We can become shackled by the material things of life, but we ought to be liberated and controlled by the Spirit of God.

If the heart loves material things and puts earthly gain above heavenly investments, the result can only be a tragic loss. The treasures of earth may be used for God. But if we gather material things for ourselves, we will lose them; *and we will lose our hearts with them.* Instead of spiritual enrichment, we will experience impoverishment.

What does it mean to lay up treasures in heaven? It means to use *all we have* for the glory of God. It means to "hang loose" when it comes to the material things of life. It also means measuring life by the true riches of the kingdom and not by the false riches of this world.

Today's Scripture: "Do not wear yourself out to get rich; have the wisdom to show restraint. Cast but a glance at riches, and they are gone, for they will surely sprout wings and fly off to the sky like an eagle" (Proverbs 23:4-5, NIV).

Also read: Matthew 6:19-24; 19:16-24; 1 Timothy 6:6-11; Luke 9:25.

Action assignment: Are you enslaved to a material thing? Substitute in its place a "treasure in heaven." Do something of eternal value today. Ask God to direct you.

A GREAT NEED: PRAYER SUPPORT

The Word of God and prayer should go together. The Prophet Samuel told the people of Israel, "God forbid that I should sin against the Lord in ceasing to pray for you: but I will teach you the good and the right way" (1 Samuel 12:23). Peter said, "But we [the apostles] will give ourselves continually to prayer, and to the ministry of the Word" (Acts 6:4). Paul had this same emphasis: "And now, brethren, I commend you to God, and to the Word of His grace, which is able to build you up" (Acts 20:32).

Jesus prayed for His disciples, just as Paul prayed for the Thessalonican Christians, that their faith would not fail. I ministered for several weeks in Kenya and Zaire, and when I arrived home, I was more convinced than ever that the greatest need of missionaries and national churches is *prayer*. We must also pray for young Christians here at home. It is not enough to teach them Bible truth; we must also support them in our prayers.

A reminder: "If My people, which are called by My name, shall humble themselves, and pray, and seek My face, and turn from their wicked ways; then will I hear from heaven, and will forgive their sin, and will heal their land" (2 Chronicles 7:14).

For further thought: Luke 22:31-32; 1 Corinthians 14:15; Ephesians 6:18; Hebrews 4:16; James 5:16.

Action assignment: Act on Hebrews 4:16 and talk to God about the needs of at least two of God's workers at home or abroad and one young Christian.

15

WALK BY FAITH

The believer who lives by faith will "go on unto perfection" (Hebrews 6:1). But the believer who lives by sight will "draw back unto perdition" (Hebrews 10:39). The Greek word translated "perdition" is used about twenty times in the New Testament and is translated by different words: "perish" (Acts 8:20), "die" (Acts 25:16), "destruction" (Romans 9:22), and "waste" (Matthew 26:8). The word *can* mean eternal judgment, but it need not in *every* instance. I personally believe that "waste" is the best translation for this word in Hebrews 10:39. A believer who does not walk by faith goes back into the old ways and wastes his life.

"The saving of the soul" is the opposite of "waste." To walk by faith means to obey God's Word and live for Jesus Christ. We lose our lives for His sake—but we save them! People who turn their backs on God's will (like Israel), spend years "wandering in the wilderness" of waste.

But we can be confident! As we walk by faith, our great High Priest will guide us and perfect us!

Verse for today: "For we walk by faith, not by sight" (2 Corinthians 5:7).

Consider: Matthew 16:25-27; Numbers 14:1-35; Psalm 31:3.

Action assignment: Go back over today's reading and underline two important truths. How well are you doing? Determine how you can put these truths to work before this day is over.

THIS MIND REALLY WORKS!

What a tragedy it would be to go through life and not be a blessing to anyone! Epaphroditus was a blessing to Paul. Epaphroditus stood with Paul in his prison experience and did not permit even his own sickness to hinder his service. What times he and Paul must have had together! But Epaphroditus was also a blessing to his own church. Paul admonishes the church to honor Epaphroditus because of his sacrifice and service. (Christ gets the glory, but there is nothing wrong with the servant receiving honor.) Epaphroditus sacrificed himself with no thought of reward, and Paul encouraged the church to hold him in honor to the glory of God.

He was a blessing to Paul and to his own church, and he is also a blessing *to us today!* He proves to us that the joyful life is the life of sacrifice and service and that the submissive mind really does work. He and Timothy together encourage us to submit ourselves to the Lord, and to one another, in the Spirit of Christ. Christ is the Pattern we follow. Paul shows us the power; and Timothy and Epaphroditus are the proof that this mind really works.

Will you permit the Spirit to reproduce "the mind of Christ" in you?

Remember this: "Let this mind be in you, which was also in Christ Jesus: who . . . made Himself of no reputation, and took upon Him the form of a servant" (Philippians 2:5-7).

Also read: Philippians 2:5-12, 25-30; 4:12-19; 1 Thessalonians 5:12-13.

Action assignment: Think of being a person like Epaphroditus as you go through your day. Make it a point to be a faithful Christian servant.

17

THE HERD INSTINCT

One of the ministries of our risen Lord is that of perfecting His people. He uses the Word of God in the fellowship of the local church. As Christians pray for one another and personally assist one another, the exalted Lord ministers to His church and makes us fit for ministry.

Someone has said, "There are no Lone Rangers in the Christian faith." That's because balanced Christian growth and ministry are impossible in isolation. Someone has said that you can no more raise one Christian than you can raise one bee. Christians belong to each other and need each other. A baby must grow up in a loving family if it is to be balanced and normal.

People who emphasize the "individual Christian" as apart from his place in a local assembly are wandering into very dangerous territory. We are sheep, and we must flock together. We are members of the same body and have been called to minister to one another, as well as to the world.

Verse for today: "If you have any encouragement from being united with Christ, if any comfort from His love, if any fellowship with the Spirit, if any tenderness and compassion, then make my joy complete by being like-minded, having the same love, being one in spirit and purpose" (Philippians 2:1-2, NIV).

Consider: Hebrews 13:20-21; Romans 12:4-5; 1 Corinthians 12:14-20; Ephesians 1:22-23; 4:11-15; Galatians 6:1.

Action assignment: Think of the rich diversity of Christians worshiping all around the world. Think about your own congregation or fellowship group. What talents do these people have? Have you discovered your own talents? Ask God how you can share them with the body of believers you know.

USING FREEDOM

As Christians, we *do* have freedom. This freedom was purchased for us by Jesus Christ, so it is very precious. Freedom comes from knowledge: "And ye shall know the truth, and the truth shall make you free" (John 8:32). The more we understand about the atom, for example, the more freedom we have to use it wisely. But knowledge must be balanced by love; otherwise, it will tear down instead of build up.

The strong Christian knows that he has this freedom, but he also knows that freedom involves responsibility. I have the freedom, for example, to take my car out of the garage and drive it on the highway; *but I must drive it responsibly.* I am not free to drive at any speed on my street; nor am I free to ignore the traffic signs along the way.

There are several "tests" we may apply to our own decisions and activities. "All things are lawful," but—

- Will they lead to freedom or slavery?
- Will they make me a stumbling block or a stepping stone?
- Will they build me up or tear me down?
- Will they only please me, or will they glorify Christ?
- Will they help to win the lost to Christ or turn them away?

The way we use our freedom and relate to others indicates whether we are mature in Christ. Strong and weak Christians need to work together in love to edify one another and glorify Jesus Christ.

Verse to remember: "If therefore the Son shall make you free, you shall be free indeed" (John 8:36, NASB).

Also: 1 Corinthians 6:12; 8:13; 10:23-33.

Action assignment: Thank God for your freedom in Christ and assure Him that you want to use your freedom in ways He would approve.

19

POWER IN THE BLOOD

According to Leon Morris in his book *Apostolic Preaching of the Cross* (Eerdmans), the word "*blood*" is used 460 times in the Bible, 362 of them in the Old Testament. In Leviticus 17, you find the word "blood" thirteen times; you also find in this chapter the key text in biblical theology on the significance of the blood in salvation: "For the life of the flesh is in the blood, and I have given it to you upon the altar to make atonement for your souls; for it is the blood that makes atonement for the soul" (v. 11).

Long before medical science discovered the significance of the circulation of the blood in the human body and its importance for life, Scripture told us that the blood was the life. When a sacrifice was offered and its blood was shed, it meant the giving of a life for the life of another. The innocent victim died in the place of the guilty sinner. Throughout Scripture, it's the blood that makes the atonement.

Believers today need to appreciate the importance of the "precious" blood of Christ (1 Peter 1:19). Among other things, through His blood, we are justified (Rom. 5:9), redeemed (Eph. 1:7), washed (Rev. 1:5), sanctified (Heb. 13:12), brought near (Eph. 2:13), and cleansed (1 John 1:7). The church was purchased by the blood of Christ and therefore is very precious to God (Acts 20:28).

It's a fact: "For you know that it was not with perishable things such as silver or gold that you were redeemed from the empty way of life handed down to you from your forefathers, but with the precious blood of Christ, a lamb without blemish or defect" (1 Peter 1:18–19, NIV).

Read: Leviticus 17

Action assignment: Write out several verses pertaining to blood in sacrifice that are meaningful to you. List them under various headings, such as: washed, sanctified, cleansed, kept, sustained. Concentrate on the meaning of these verses for you, personally, as the day progresses. Memorize one or two verses for useful future reference in witnessing to others.

INTO ALL THE WORLD

Trusting Christ is a matter not only of believing, but also of obeying. Part of obeying includes heeding Christ's Great Commission. In addition, God "commandeth all men everywhere to repent" (Acts 17:30).

We must never minimize the missionary outreach of the church. Lost souls around the world cannot be saved unless they call upon the Lord Jesus Christ. But they cannot call unless they believe. Faith comes by hearing, so they must hear the message.

How will they hear? A messenger must go to them with the message. But this means that God must call the messenger and the messenger must be sent. What a privilege it is to be one of His messengers and have beautiful feet!

Verse for today: "Then Jesus came to them and said, 'All authority in heaven and on earth has been given to me. Therefore go and make disciples of all nations, baptizing them in the name of the Father and of the Son and of the Holy Spirit" (Matthew 28:18-19, NIV).

More to read: Romans 10:15; Philippians 1:15-18; Psalm 40:9.

Action assignment: List how many missionary groups or missionaries you have supported through prayer, money, letters, and other means. With Bible translators going full speed ahead, it is conceivable that around the year 2000 everyone will have the Bible in his or her own tongue. Still, missionaries will be needed to present the Gospel. What can you do to advance the missionary outreach of the Body of Christ? List three ways.

SEEING SIN IN YOURSELF

Christians are obligated to help each other grow in grace. When we do not judge ourselves, we not only hurt ourselves, but we also hurt those to whom we could minister. The Pharisees judged and criticized *others* to make themselves look good. But Christians should judge *themselves* so that they can help others look good. There is a difference!

Let's look at our Lord's illustration of this point (Matthew 7:3-5). Jesus chose the symbol of the eye because this is one of the most sensitive areas of the human body. The picture of a man with a two-by-four stuck in his eye, trying to remove a speck of dust from another man's eye, is ridiculous indeed! If we do not honestly face up to our own sins and confess them, we blind ourselves to ourselves; then we cannot see clearly enough to help others. The Pharisees saw the sins of other people, but they would not look at their own sins.

The Bible commands: "Therefore judge nothing before the time, until the Lord come, who both will bring to light the hidden things of darkness, and will make manifest the counsels of the hearts: and then shall every man have praise of God" (1 Corinthians 4:5).

Also consider: Matthew 7:3-5; Luke 18:9-14; Romans 14:10-13.

Action assignment: Are you blinded by a "plank" in your eye? It could be that the sin you see in a brother is actually in your own life, not his. Confess it to God today.

JESUS, OUR PROVIDER

Jesus provides all that we need. He is our burnt offering, and we must yield ourselves wholly to Him. He is our meal offering, the seed crushed and put through the fire, that we might have the bread of life; and we must feed upon Him. He is our drink offering, who poured Himself out in sacrifice and service, and we must pour ourselves out for Him and for others. He is our fellowship offering, making life a joyful feast instead of a painful famine. He is our sin offering and our guilt offering, for He bore our sins on His body (1 Peter 2:24) and paid the full price for our sins (1:18–19).

The nation of Israel had to offer six different kinds of sacrifices in order to have a right relationship with God, but Jesus Christ "offered one sacrifice for sins forever" (Heb. 10:12) and took care of our sin problem completely.

Do *you* believe that Jesus Christ died for all you sins and paid your full debt? Can you say with Mary, "My soul magnifies the Lord, and my spirit has rejoiced in God my Savior" (Luke 1:46–47)? If not, then trust Him today; if you have trusted Him, share the good news with others.

"Your faith has saved you," Jesus said to a repentant sinner. "Go in peace" (Luke 7:50).

What wonderful words to hear!

Be thankful: "He Himself bore our sins in His body on the tree, so that we might die to sins and live for righteousness; by His wounds you have been healed" (1 Peter 2:24, NIV).

Read: Leviticus 6

Action assignment: As suggested in today's reading, make it a point to share the Good News with someone today, by a personal note, a phone call, or in conversation. Memorize some Scripture that you can pass along to a needy soul. God's Word is powerful and will not return void (Isa. 55:11).

23

CHRISTIANS ARE BORN FOR GLORY

Because of the death and resurrection of Jesus Christ, believers have been "begotten again" to a living hope, and that hope includes the glory of God. But what do we mean by "the glory of God"?

The glory of God means the sum of all that God is and does. "Glory" is not a separate attribute or characteristic of God, such as His holiness, wisdom, or mercy. Everything He is and does is characterized by glory. He is glorious in wisdom and power, so that everything He thinks and does is marked by glory. He reveals His glory in Creation, in His dealings with the people of Israel, and especially in His plan of salvation for lost sinners.

When we were born for the first time, we were not born for glory. Whatever feeble glory man has will eventually fade and disappear; but the glory of the Lord is eternal. The works of man done for the glory of God will last and be rewarded. But the selfish human achievements of sinners will one day vanish to be seen no more. One reason that we have encyclopedias is so that we can learn about the famous people who are now forgotten!

Meditate on: "For all flesh is as grass, and all the glory of man as the flower of grass" (1 Peter 1:24). "And the world passeth away, and the lust thereof: but he that doeth the will of God abideth forever" (1 John 2:17).

Read: Psalm 19.

Action assignment: Write in your own words how you would explain "the glory of God" to someone. Talk with God about your desire to bring Him glory and honor through your life.

THE REAL McCOY

In one of the churches I pastored, a teenager seemed to be the center of every problem in the youth group. He was a gifted musician and a member of the church, but nevertheless a problem. One summer when he went to our church youth camp, the youth leaders and church officers and I agreed to pray for him daily. At one of the meetings, he got up and announced that he had been saved that week! His Christian profession up to that time had been counterfeit. He experienced a dramatic change in his life, and today he is serving the Lord faithfully.

No doubt many of the problems in our churches are caused by people who profess salvation, but who have never truly repented and trusted Jesus Christ. Paul called such people *reprobate* (2 Corinthians 13:5), which means "counterfeit, discredited after a test." He later emphasized the fact that it is important for a person to know for sure that he is saved and going to heaven.

Verse for today: "Examine yourselves, whether ye be in the faith; prove your own selves. Know ye not your own selves, how that Jesus Christ is in you, except ye be reprobates?" (2 Corinthians 13:5)

Consider: Psalm 19:12-13; 2 Corinthians 13:6-7; 1 Timothy 3:1-9; Titus 1:15-16; James 2:14-26; 1 John 5:11-13, 18.

Action assignment: Do you know someone who claims he or she is a Christian, yet whose actions consistently disprove the claim? Pray for that individual today and at least three times a week from now on. Ask God to give you a heart of love for that person. Go out of your way, if possible, to extend Christian concern and love to that person "for whom Christ died."

If you cannot think of someone who fits the criterion, then pray for yourself, your loved ones, and your church. Ask God to help you to live genuinely Christian lives in thought, word, and deed.

A MILE IN MY SHOES

An old Indian saying goes something like this: "Don't criticize me until you've walked a mile in my moccasins." Because of sin, that's sometimes a hard thing to do.

Sin makes people selfish. Sin can blind us to the hurts of others. Sin can harden our hearts and make us judgmental instead of sympathetic. Remember when King David was confronted with a story of a rich man's sin? He had no sympathy for him, even though David himself was a worse sinner (2 Samuel 12).

You would think that one sinner would have compassion for another sinner, but this is not always the case. No, it is the spiritually minded person with a clean heart who sympathizes with a sinner and seeks to help him. Because we are so sinful, we have a hard time helping other sinners; but because Jesus is perfect, He is able to meet our needs when we sin.

Verse for today: "Rejoice with those who rejoice; mourn with those who mourn" (Romans 12:15, NIV).

More reading: Galatians 6:1-2; 1 Peter 3:8; Zechariah 7:9.

Action assignment: Whom have you criticized recently or in the past? Were your criticisms really fair? Were they more judgmental than sympathetic? Is there anything you can do now to truly help that person or those persons? Ask God to help you follow Christ's example more faithfully from now on.

THREE PRAYER REQUESTS

In ministering to the Thessalonians, the Apostle Paul prayed for three specific requests that serve to show us how we ought to pray for others (1 Thessalonians 3:10-13).

First, he prayed *that their faith might mature* (v.10). The faith of Christians never reaches perfection; there is always need for adjustment and growth. Faith that cannot be tested cannot be trusted. God tries our faith, not to destroy it, but to develop it.

Second, Paul prayed *that their love might abound* (v.12). When I counsel young couples in preparation for marriage, I often ask the man: "If your wife became paralyzed three weeks after you were married, do you love her enough to stay with her and care for her?" True love deepens in times of difficulty; shallow romance disappears when difficulties appear.

But true Christian love is shown not only to believers, but also "toward all men" (v. 12). We love one another, but we also love the lost and our enemies. Abounding love must not be bound. It must be free to expand and touch all people.

Paul's third request was for *holiness of life* (v. 13). The expected return of Jesus Christ should motivate the believer to live a holy life.

Paul's prayers for his friends were not careless or occasional. He prayed "night and day." True prayer is hard work.

Verse for today: "Epaphras . . . is always wrestling in prayer for you, that you may stand firm in all the will of God, mature and fully assured" (Colossians 4:12, NIV).

Other Scripture: Luke 18:1-7; 22:44; Romans 8:26; Ephesians 6:18.

Action assignment: Try to pray fervently for five minutes.

27

TRIALS DEVELOP PATIENCE

The Lord has chosen to develop patience and character in our lives through trials. Endurance cannot be attained by reading a book (even this one), listening to a sermon, or even praying a prayer. We must go through the difficulties of life, trust God, and obey Him. The result will be patience and character. Knowing this, we can face trials joyfully. We know what trials will do in us and for us, and we know that the end result will bring glory to God.

This fact explains why studying the Bible helps us grow in patience. As we read about Abraham, Joseph, Moses, David, and even our Lord, we realize that God has a purpose in trials. God fulfills His purposes as we trust Him. There is no substitute for an understanding mind. Satan can defeat the ignorant believer, but he cannot overcome the Christian who knows his Bible and understands the purposes of God.

Verse for today: "The trial of your faith, being much more precious than of gold that perisheth, though it be tried with fire, might be found unto praise and honor and glory at the appearing of Jesus Christ" (1 Peter 1:7).

Also read: Romans 5:3-4; 8:28; 15:4; 2 Corinthians 4:17; John 18:1-11; James 1:3-4; Revelation 14:12.

Action assignment: Faith is always tested. God *tests* us to bring out the best; Satan *tempts* us to bring out the worst. The testing of our faith proves that we are truly born again. Today think about temptations and trials. Is the Bible your guide book? Do you understand the purposes of God? If perplexities overwhelm you, a good Bible study or correspondence course may be what you need. The Christian who knows his Bible will bring glory to God, because he knows the purposes of God, and trusts His promises, and overcomes trials to develop patience and character.

CONFIDENCE IN GOD

We must keep in mind that our enemies (the flesh and blood variety) are tools of the real enemy, Satan. "For our struggle is not against flesh and blood, but against the rulers, against the powers, against the world forces of this darkness, against the spiritual forces of wickedness in the heavenly places" (Ephesians 6:12, NASB).

God's people have enemies. The nation of Israel was often attacked by enemies; the prophets aroused the opposition of unbelievers; even the early church experienced attack from religious people. Our Lord came with a message of peace, but sometimes the result is war. The believer who avoids persecution is either hiding his light or compromising the truth. When fear grips the heart, it also paralyzes the mind and body. David ("a man after God's own heart") saw his foes as wild beasts, stalking him in order to eat him up. But he was not afraid, for his confidence was in God.

Verse for today: "The Lord is my light and my salvation; whom shall I fear? The Lord is the strength of my life; of whom shall I be afraid?" (Psalm 27:1)

Also read: Matthew 5:43-48; 10:32-39; Psalm 27:2-3; Ephesians 6:10-20.

Action assignment: Recognizing that fear is a tool of Satan, determine to make confidence in God a priority in your life. Using Ephesians 6:10-20, write down Paul's formula for being strong in the Lord. He used the tools of warfare as symbols for our spiritual battle. Truth, righteousness, peace, faith, salvation, and the Word of God are the Christian's tools to defeat Satan's attacks.

REAL LIVING

Sir Walter Scott wrote:

> "Oh, what a tangled web we weave
> When first we practice to deceive!"

The life that is real cannot be built on things that are deceptive. Before we can walk in the light, we must know and accept ourselves and yield ourselves to God. It is foolish to try to deceive others because God already knows what we really are!

The life that is real also has no love for sin. Instead of trying to cover sin, a true believer confesses sin and tries to conquer it by walking in the light of God's Word. He is careful to match his walk and his talk.

All this helps to explain why walking in the light makes life so much easier and happier. When you walk in the light, you live to please only one Person—God. If we live to please ourselves and God, we are trying to serve two masters, and this never works. If we live to please people, we will always be in trouble because no two will agree and we will find ourselves caught in the middle.

Walking in the light—living to please God—simplifies our goals, unifies our lives, and gives us a true sense of peace and poise.

Verse for today: "Finally, brothers, we instructed you how to live in order to please God, as in fact you are living. Now we ask you and urge you in the Lord Jesus to do this more and more" (1 Thessalonians 4:1, NIV).

Also consider: John 8:29; Proverbs 16:7; 1 Thessalonians 2:4.

Action assignment: On a scale from 1 to 10, rate how much you are trying to please God and yourself in everything you do. Remember that in truly pleasing God, you end up pleasing yourself. Ask God to help you identify those areas over which you have tended to write "Keep out"; be ruthlessly honest as you begin turning those areas over to Him. List one area today and write down what you can do to make it pleasing to God.

"I BITED HER!"

All of us have lost our joy because of people: what they are, what they say, and what they do. But we have to live and work with people; we cannot isolate ourselves and still live to glorify Christ. We are the light of the world and the salt of the earth. And we should not let the light grow dim and the salt become bitter because of other people.

A mother and her little son got on an elevator to go to the doctor's office. At the second floor a group of people got on, among them a rather large woman. As the elevator sped upward, the quiet was broken by a scream from the lips of the plump passenger. She turned to the mother and said, "Your son just bit me!"

The mother was horrified, but the little boy had an explanation: "She sitted in my face and I bited her!"

What took place on that elevator is taking place all over the world: people and nations bite each other because they get sat on or crowded.

But the Christian with the submissive mind does not expect others to serve him; he serves others. He considers the good of others to be more important than his own plans and desires.

Scripture to obey: "For whosoever exalteth himself shall be abased; and he that humbleth himself shall be exalted" (Luke 14:11).

For further study: Read all of Philippians 2 and note the submissive mind in relation to Jesus, Paul, Timothy, and Ephaphroditus.

Action assignment: Ask God to enable you to have a truly submissive mind in your daily relationships.

ON THE GLORY ROAD

Did God enjoy watching a tyrant like Pharaoh? No, He endured it. The fact that God was long-suffering indicates that He gave Pharaoh opportunities to be saved.

God prepares men for glory, but sinners prepare themselves for judgment. In Moses and Israel God revealed the riches of His mercy; in Pharaoh and Egypt He revealed His power and wrath. Since neither deserved any mercy, God cannot be charged with injustice.

Ultimately, of course, God's purpose was to form His church from both Jews and Gentiles. Believers today are, by God's grace, "vessels of mercy" which He is preparing for glory. Doesn't it feel good to be on the glory road?

Verse for today: "Dear friends, now we are children of God, and what we will be has not yet been made known. But we know that when He appears, we shall be like Him, for we shall see Him as He is" (1 John 3:2, NIV).

Take time to read: Romans 8:28-30; 9:22-24; 2 Peter 3:9; Exodus 3:7; 7:6-13; 8:8-15; 1 Peter 5:1; Genesis 3.

Action assignment: From the very beginning, God has allowed us to choose between good and evil. Our choices are very important.

C.S. Lewis said that we are becoming now what we will be in eternity—something beautiful and full of glory, or something hideous and full of darkness. Write down the names of three living Christians whose character seems to you most "prepared for glory." Next to each name, write down at least one trait that person has which seems valuable.

Now, use one of these Christian examples to guide some of your own actions today. Also, write a short note to that person, expressing your appreciation to God for him or her and mentioning the inspiration his or her life has given you.

November

Be Renewed:

"Walk worthy of the vocation wherewith ye are called, with all lowliness and meekness, with longsuffering, forbearing one another in love."

Ephesians 4:1-2

1

GLORIFYING GOD

No amount of good works or religious efforts can make a sinner holy. Only the blood of Jesus Christ can cleanse us from our sins (1 John 1:7). And only the risen, glorified Savior can intercede for us at the throne of God as our Advocate (1 John 2:1) and high priest (Heb. 8:1; Rom. 8:34). What the Old Testament Jews saw only in shadows, believers today see in the bright light of Jesus Christ.

Just as the nation of Israel had to beware of that which was unclean and defiling, so must believers today "cleanse [themselves] from all filthiness of the flesh and spirit, perfecting holiness in the fear of God" (2 Cor. 7:1). God wants us to be a "holy priesthood" and a "holy nation" so that we will advertise His virtues and glorify His name (1 Peter 2:5, 9).

On Sunday morning, January 24, 1861, Charles Spurgeon closed his sermon at the Metropolitan Tabernacle with these words:

"An unholy church! It is of no use to the world, and of no esteem among men. Oh, it is an abomination, hell's laughter, heaven's abhorrence. And the larger the church, the more influential, the worst nuisance does it become, when it becomes dead and unholy. The worst evils which have ever come upon the world, have been brought upon her by an unholy church."

Eight times in His Word, the Lord says, "Be holy, for I am holy!" Are we listening?

Remember this: "But you are a chosen people, a royal priesthood, a holy nation, a people belonging to God, that you may declare the praises of Him who called you out of darkness into His wonderful light" (1 Peter 2:5–9, NIV).

Read: Ephesians 5; 1 John 2:1–17

Action assignment: Think of some ways in which you can advertise God's virtues and glorify His name as you pursue your daily chores. Concentrate on your speech. Is your voice well-seasoned with grace? Does it depict patience and love? Small mannerisms often reveal one's innermost thoughts. Determine that they will honor your Lord.

WHEN TRUTH BECOMES ALIVE

In Bible times, a scribe's work was to examine the Law and discover its teachings. Remember that the scribes began as a very noble group. They devoted themselves to the protection and preservation of the Law. But sad to say, the scribes degenerated into an unspiritual clique and were more interested in protecting dead tradition than teaching living truth. Jesus accused them of putting the people under spiritual bondage, not liberty. They so revered the past that they ignored God's lessons in the present. Instead of opening doors for sinners to be saved, they closed them. They became blind leaders of the blind. Why? Because they had not become disciples.

Every scribe should become a disciple, a person who follows the Lord and puts His truth into practice. We *learn* the truth to *live* the truth. The truth becomes alive to us when we live it, and in the process we learn more truth! A desperate need exists today for a balance between theory and practice, learning and living, the schoolroom and the marketplace. Jesus taught His disciples by precept *and by practice*. There was a balance between objective truth and subjective experience. It is not enough to be hearers of the Word—we must be *doers* if we are going to grow and glorify God.

Remember this: "Do not merely listen to the word, and so deceive yourselves. Do what it says" (James 1:22, NIV).

Other Scripture: Matthew 5:3-12; Luke 11:28, 46-52; Romans 6:22-23; James 1:22-27.

Action assignment: If you have been redeemed and are a member of God's family, live today by your Father's Rule Book.

3

THE DISCIPLINED LIFE

Paul was fond of athletic images and used them often in his letters. The Corinthians would have been familiar with the Greek Olympic Games as well as their own local Isthmian Games. Knowing this, Paul used a metaphor very close to their experience.

An athlete must be disciplined if he is to win the prize. Discipline means giving up the good and the better for the best. The athlete must watch his diet as well as his hours. He must smile and say "No, thank you" when people offer him fattening desserts or invite him to late-night parties. There is nothing wrong with food or fun, but if they interfere with your highest goals, then they are hindrances and not helps.

The Christian does not run the race in order to get to heaven. He is in the race because he has been saved through faith in Jesus Christ. Only Greek citizens were allowed to participate in the games, and they had to obey the rules both in their training and in their performing. Any contestant found breaking the training rules was automatically disqualified.

In order to give up his rights and have the joy of winning lost souls, Paul had to discipline himself. Authority (rights) must be balanced by discipline. If we want to serve the Lord and win His reward and approval, we must pay the price.

Scripture to remember: "Do you not know that those who run in a race all run, but only one receives the prize? Run in such a way that you may win. . . . I buffet my body and make it my slave, lest possibly, after I have preached to others, I myself should be disqualified" (1 Corinthians 9:24, 27, NASB).

Also consider: Philippians 3:7-14; 2 Timothy 2.

Action assignment: Talk to God about how your personal race is going and confirm that you want to win His reward and approval.

BE HOLY

God is "glorious in holiness" (Exod. 15:11), and His glory dwelt in the holy of holies in both the tabernacle (Exod. 40:34–38) and the temple (1 Kings 8:10). The presence of the cloud of glory and the pillar of fire reminded Israel that Jehovah was a holy God and "a consuming fire" (Deut. 4:24; Heb. 12:29). In fact, the very structure of the tabernacle declared the holiness of God: the fence around the tent, the brazen altar where the blood was shed, the laver where the priests washed their hands and feet, and the veil that kept everybody but the high priest out of the holy of holies.

The whole sacrificial system declared to Israel that "the wages of sin is death" (Rom. 6:23) and "the soul who sins shall die" (Ezek. 18:4). God hates sin, but because He loves sinners and wants to forgive them, He provides a substitute to die in the sinner's place. All of this is a picture of the promised Savior who laid down His life for the sins of the world.

You could never call any of the heathen deities "holy." But "Holy One of Israel" is one of the repeated names of Jehovah in Scripture. It's used thirty times in Isaiah alone.

In declaration and demonstration, Jehovah made it clear to the people of Israel that He is a holy God, righteous in all His works and just in all His judgments.

Verse for Today: "Who among the gods is like You, O LORD? Who is like You majestic in holiness, awesome in glory, working wonders?" (Exod. 15:11, NIV).

Read: 1 Peter 2

Action assignment: Share your worship time blessings with a friend, reminding yourself that He who is holy is willing to dwell with "him who is of a contrite and humble spirit." That is grace beyond human comprehension! List on paper some personal benefits from your wonderfully benevolent Lord and Savior. Or write a definition of "holy."

5

THE SCHOOL OF PRAYER

No Christian rises any higher than his praying. Everything we are and everything we do for the Lord depends on prayer. Most of us would rather work than pray. But we know that without prayer our work is useless. What a difference it would make in our personal lives, our homes, our churches, and our world if Christians really learned to pray—*and prayed!*

If you had the privilege of asking the Lord for one specific blessing, would you ask, "Teach me to pray"? Someone may ask, "Lord, teach me how to make money!" or, "Lord, teach me how to preach." But "Teach me to pray" is the wisest request, because every other blessing in the Christian life depends in one way or another on our ability to pray.

The most important part of our lives is the part that only God sees. The hidden life of prayer is the secret of an open life of victory. The School of Prayer has four steps, and each step emphasizes a particular lesson about prayer. First, we must pray, and then pray in the will of God. We must pray as children coming to a father. And we must pray for the best blessings of the Holy Spirit.

Jesus tells you: "Ask and it will be given to you; seek and you will find; knock and the door will be opened to you. For everyone who asks receives; he who seeks finds; and to him who knocks, the door will be opened" (Matthew 7:7-8, NIV).

Other Scripture: Luke 11:1-13; Philippians 4:6; 1 Thessalonians 5:17-18.

Action assignment: If you're used to praying briefly, see if you can extend your time. Pray aloud if you have privacy.

SILVER SERVICE

How do you value your service to God? The way you look at it helps to determine how you will fulfill it. If you look upon serving Christ as a burden or even a punishment from God instead of a sterling privilege, you will be a drudge and do only what is required of you.

As a minister of Jesus Christ, Paul was overwhelmed by the grace and mercy of God. His positive attitude toward the ministry *kept him from being a quitter.* In spite of his great gifts and vast experience, Paul was still subject to human frailties. But how could he lose heart when he was involved in such a wonderful ministry? With the divine calling came the divine enabling; he knew that God would see him through.

A discouraged Methodist preacher wrote to the great Scottish preacher, Alexander Whyte, to ask his counsel. Should he leave the ministry? "Never think of giving up preaching!" Whyte wrote to him. "The angels around the throne envy you your great work!" That was the kind of reply Paul would have written, the one all of us need to ponder whenever we feel our work is in vain.

Verse for today: "Therefore, my dear brothers, stand firm. Let nothing move you. Always give yourselves fully to the work of the Lord, because you know that your labor in the Lord is not in vain" (1 Corinthians 15:58, NIV).

Also read: Psalm 31:24; Philippians 2:12-18; 2 Thessalonians 2:13-17.

Action assignment: Do you ever feel discouraged as a witness for Christ? When? Think of some things you have to be thankful for as you share your faith, such as the freedom to worship or having your own Bible. Next time you are tempted to feel discouraged, ask God to renew in you the vision of His calling. In fact, why not do it right now?

7

OUR WORKS SHALL FOLLOW US

The Judgment Seat of Christ is where Christians will have their works judged by the Lord. It has nothing to do with our sins, since Christ has paid for them and they can be held against us no more.

The word for "judgment seat" in the Greek is *bema,* meaning the place where the judges stood at the athletic games. If during the games they saw an athlete break the rules, they immediately disqualified him. At the end of the contests, the judges gave out the rewards.

Paul gives us another picture of the judgment seat of Christ when he compares our ministries with the building of a temple. If we build with cheap materials, the fire will burn them up. If we use precious, lasting materials, our works will last and we will receive a reward. If they are burned up, we lose the reward, but we are still saved "yet so as by fire."

Verse for today: "According to the grace of God which is given unto me, as a wise master builder, I have laid the foundation, and another buildeth thereon. But let every man take heed how he buildeth thereupon" (1 Corinthians 3:10).

Also consider: 1 Corinthians 3:11-15; 6:19-20; 9:24-27; 2 Corinthians 9:6; Matthew 16:27; 2 John 8; Revelation 22:12.

Action assignment: Did you ever participate in a sports event and find yourself unprepared? Or have you ever started a building or handcraft project and realized you lacked the skill or adequate materials to get the job done? How did you feel at the time?

You may have been able to keep your failure a secret. When Christ returns, none of us will have that luxury—the books will be open. Ask the Lord to help you keep a strict account of your life so that you will not be "disqualified" at the Judgment Seat of Christ.

HOW TO COMMUNICATE IN MARRIAGE

It is amazing that two married people can live together and not really know each other! Ignorance is dangerous in any area of life, but it is especially dangerous in marriage. A Christian husband needs to know his wife's moods, feelings, needs, fears, and hopes. He needs to "listen with his heart" and share meaningful communication with her. There must be in the home such a protective atmosphere of love and submission that the husband and wife can disagree and still be happy together.

It has well been said that love without truth is hypocrisy, and truth without love is brutality. We need both truth and love if we are to grow in our understanding of one another. How can a husband show consideration for his wife if he does not understand her needs or problems? To say, "I never knew you felt that way!" is to confess that, at some point, one mate excommunicated the other. When either mate is afraid to be open and honest about a matter, then you are building walls and not bridges.

Verse for today: "But speaking the truth in love, [we] may grow up into Him [Christ] in all things" (Ephesians 4:15).

Also read: 1 Peter 3:7; Ecclesiastes 9:9; 1 Corinthians 7:3; Colossians 3:19.

Action assignment: List in order of importance, as you see it, ten things a husband can do to show he loves his wife—or vice versa. If you are married, ask God to help you show more love to your spouse. If not, pray for a married person who needs to show more love to his or her spouse.

9

TIME TO PRAISE!

If you had lived during the Thirty Years' War, could you have praised God? This war occurred from 1618-48 and was the last of the great religious wars of Europe, a conflict that began between Protestants and Roman Catholics. But before it was over it spread from Germany, where it began, over most of Europe—and became a general struggle for territory and political power.

During the horrors of the Thirty Years' War, Pastor Martin Rinkart faithfully served the people in Eilenburg, Saxony. He conducted as many as 40 funerals a day, a total of over 4,000 during his ministry. Yet out of this devastating experience, he wrote a "table grace" for his children which today we use as a hymn of thanksgiving:

> *Now thank we all our God,*
> *With heart and hands and voices,*
> *Who wondrous things hath done,*
> *In whom His world rejoices!*

The Apostle Paul learned that praise is an important factor in achieving victory when all around was dark and the future unknown. He learned that "praise changes things" just as much as "prayer changes things."

Praise God because He is the Father of our Lord Jesus Christ! Praise Him because He is the Father of mercies! Praise Him because He is the God of all comfort!

Today's verse: "It is a good thing to give thanks unto the Lord, and to sing praises unto Thy name, O most High; to show forth Thy loving kindness in the morning, and Thy faithfulness every night" (Psalms 92:1-2).

Reflect on: 1 Corinthians 15:57; 2 Corinthians 1:3; Ephesians 1:3; 1 Peter 1:3.

Action assignment: List five of the greatest blessings you can think of, and thank God for them.

A MATURE WITNESS

We encourage others by our walk and our witness. We also encourage others by the way we go through testing. I like the way the *New Berkley Version* translates Psalm 71:20-21: "Thou, who hast made me experience troubles great and sore, wilt revive me again and wilt bring me up again from the depths of the earth. Thou wilt add to my stature, and comfort me again."

The longer we walk with God, the more clearly we see His ways and understand His heart. A mature saint knows that the Judge of all the earth will do right. There are no mistakes in His plans. God is in control of all testing; He will revive us where we feel dead, resurrect us when we feel low, and renew and enlarge us in our spiritual life.

The lesson is clear: Occupy yourself with the Lord, and He will take care of your enemies. Fill your day with praise to the Lord, and that praise will defeat your foes. Along with your praise, pray to Him for help; and be sure to give witness to those around you. This is a combination that is unbeatable! What you are going to be, you are becoming right now. The seed you are sowing now will give the harvest in later years. The Lord will return; so we must prepare for the future. The best way to meet the Lord is by faithfully doing His will each day. Then you will always be ready!

Verse for today: "For thou, O God, hast proved us: Thou hast tried us, as silver is tried" (Psalm 66:10).

Also read: John 16:33; Acts 14:22; Romans 5:3; 8:35; 12:12; 1 Thessalonians 3:4-5; 1 Peter 1:7; 4:12-13.

Action assignment: The word *testing* has a negative connotation. But with God, testing can become positive. What test are you facing today? Ask God to help you trust Him for the results of this test. Think about your witness to others. Can their faith in God be encouraged by your attitude toward this testing? If so, thank God that you can rejoice in the privilege of being a role model for others.

11

THE WORD MADE FLESH

Jesus Christ is the Incarnate Word. He was not a phantom or a spirit when He ministered on earth, nor was His body a mere illusion. John and the other disciples had personal experience that convinced them of the reality of the body of Jesus (1 John 1:1-2). Even though the Apostle John's emphasis in his Gospel is on the deity of Christ, he makes it clear that the Son of God came *in the flesh* and was subject to the sinless infirmities of human nature.

In his Gospel, John points out that Jesus was weary (4:6) and thirsty (4:7). He groaned within (11:33) and openly wept (11:35). On the cross, He bled (19:34) and died (19:30). After His resurrection, He proved to Thomas and the other disciples that He still had a real body (20:24-29), albeit a glorified one.

How was the "Word made flesh"? By the miracle of the Virgin Birth. Christ took upon Himself sinless human nature and identified with us in every aspect of life from birth to death. "The Word" was not an abstract concept of philosophy, but a real person who could be seen, touched, and heard. Christianity is Christ, and Christ is God.

Scripture for today: "That which was from the beginning, which we have heard, which we have seen with our eyes, which we have looked at and our hands have touched—this we proclaim concerning the Word of life. The life appeared; we have seen it and testify to it, and we proclaim to you the eternal life, which was with the Father and has appeared to us" (1 John 1:1-2, NIV).

Also: Read the Scripture listed in today's reading for deeper understanding.

Action assignment: Thank God that the Word became flesh so that you could pass from death to life and become a member of God's royal family.

BE COMFORTED

Throughout his book, Isaiah presents us with alternatives: Trust the Lord and live, or rebel against the Lord and die. He explains the grace and mercy of God and offers His forgiveness. He also explains the holiness and wrath of God and warns of His judgment. He promises glory for those who will believe and judgment for those who scoff. He explains the foolishness of trusting man's wisdom and the world's resources.

The prophet calls the professing people of God back to spiritual reality. He warns against hypocrisy and empty worship. He pleads for faith, obedience, a heart that delights in God, and a life that glorifies God.

"'There is no peace,' saith the LORD, 'unto the wicked'" (Isa. 48:22; 57:21); for in order to have peace, you must have righteousness (Isa. 32:17). The only way to have righteousness is through faith in Jesus Christ (Rom. 3:19–31).

Isaiah's message is "Be comforted by the Lord!" See Isaiah 12:1; 40:1–2; 49:13; 51:3, 19; 52:9; 54:11; 57:18; 61:2; 66:13. *But God cannot comfort rebels!* If we are sinning against God and comfortable about it, something is radically wrong. That false comfort will lead to false confidence, and that will lead to the chastening hand of God.

"Seek ye the LORD while He may be found" (55:6).

"Though your sins are like scarlet, they shall be as white as snow" (1:18).

Isaiah declared: "In that day you will say: 'O LORD, I will praise You; though You were angry with me, Your anger is turned away, and You comfort me'" (Isa. 12:1).

Read: Isaiah 12

Action assignment: Look up and read all of the Scripture mentioned in today's reading. Ask God to show you any rebelliousness that may be in your heart and determine to follow God wholeheartedly.

FACE ANGER HONESTLY

I have read that one out of every thirty-five deaths in Chicago is a murder, and that most of these murders are "crimes of passion" caused by anger among friends or relatives. Jesus did not say that anger leads to murder; He said that anger *is* murder.

There is a holy anger against sin, but Jesus talked about an unholy anger against people (Matthew 5:21-26). Anger is such a foolish thing. It makes us destroyers instead of builders. It robs us of freedom and makes us prisoners. To hate someone is to commit murder in our hearts.

This does not mean that we should go ahead and murder someone we hate, since we have already sinned inwardly. Obviously, sinful feelings are not excuses for sinful deeds. Sinful anger robs us of fellowship with God as well as with our brothers, but it does not put us into jail as murderers. But more than one person has become a murderer because he failed to control sinful anger.

Sinful anger must be faced honestly and must be confessed to God as sin. We must go to our brother and get the matter settled, and we must do it quickly. The longer we wait, the worse the bondage becomes! We put ourselves into a terrible prison when we refuse to be reconciled. It has well been said that the person who refuses to forgive his brother destroys the very bridge over which he himself must walk.

The Bible says: "Refrain from anger and turn from wrath; do not fret—it leads only to evil" (Psalm 37:8, NIV).

Also read: Matthew 5:21-26; James 1:19-20; Ephesians 4:26, 31.

Action assignment: Are you harboring sinful anger against someone? Prayerfully consider the counsel in Matthew 18:15-20 and settle the matter.

OUR OBLIGATION TO THE SPIRIT

It is not enough for us to have the Spirit; the Spirit must have us! Only then can He share with us the abundant, victorious life that can be ours in Christ. We have no obligation to the flesh, because the flesh has only brought trouble into our lives. We do have an obligation to the Holy Spirit, for it is the Spirit who convicted us, revealed Christ to us, and imparted eternal life to us when we trusted Christ. Because He is "the Spirit of Life," He can empower us to obey Christ, and He can enable us to be more like Christ.

But He is also the Spirit of death. He can enable us to "put to death" (mortify) the sinful deeds of the body. As we yield the members of our bodies to the Spirit, He applies to us and in us the death and resurrection of Christ. He puts to death the things of the flesh, and He reproduces the things of the Spirit.

Does the Spirit have you?

Scripture to remember: "Walk in the Spirit, and ye shall not fulfill the lust of the flesh" (Galatians 5:16).

Other Scripture: Romans 6:12-17; 8:1-17; Ephesians 1:12-14.

Action assignment: Commit yourself to the Holy Spirit and make a point of talking to Him frequently during the next several hours.

SUBMISSION: GOD COMMANDS IT

Younger believers should submit to older believers, not only out of respect for their age, but generally speaking also out of respect for their spiritual maturity. But this is not to suggest that older church members should "run the church" and never listen to the younger members! Too often there is a generational war in the church, with older people resisting change and younger people resisting the older people!

The solution is twofold: (1) all believers, young and old, should submit to each other; (2) all should submit to God. "Be clothed with humility" (1 Peter 5:5) is the answer to the problem. Just as Jesus laid aside His outer garments and put on a towel to become a servant, so each of us should have a servant's attitude and minister to each other. Humility is not demeaning ourselves and thinking poorly of ourselves. It is simply not thinking of ourselves at all!

We can never be submissive to each other until we are first submissive to God. It takes grace to submit to another believer, but God can give that grace *if* we humble ourselves before Him.

Remember this: "Ye younger, submit yourselves unto the elder. Yea, all of you be subject one to another, and be clothed with humility: for God resisteth the proud, and giveth grace to the humble" (1 Peter 5:5).

Other Scripture: Philippians 2:1-11; Ephesians 5:21; James 4:6.

Action assignment: Put your imagination to work. Think of at least two ways that you could or should submit to another Christian, whether older or younger. Ask God to give you a better grasp of this matter of submission.

BLESSED ARE THE PLODDERS

If we trust ourselves, we will faint and fall; but if we wait on the Lord by faith, we will receive strength for the journey. The word "wait" does not suggest that we sit around and do nothing. It means "to hope," to look to God for all that we need (Isa. 26:3; 30:15). This involves meditating on His character and His promises, praying, and seeking to glorify Him.

The word "renew" means "to exchange," as taking off old clothes and putting on new. We exchange our weakness for His power (2 Cor. 12:1–10). As we wait before Him, God enables us to soar when there is a crisis, to run when the challenges are many, and to walk faithfully in the day-by-day demands of life. It is much harder to walk in the ordinary pressures of life than to fly like the eagle in a time of crisis.

The journey of a thousand miles begins with one step. The greatest heroes of faith are not always those who seem to be soaring; often it is the ones who are patiently plodding. As we wait on the Lord, He enables us not only to fly higher and fun faster, but also to walk longer. Blessed are the plodders, for they eventually arrive at their destination!

Today's verse: "But he said to me, 'My grace is sufficient for you, for my power is made perfect in weakness.' Therefore I will boast all the more gladly about my weaknesses, so that Christ's power may rest on me" (2 Cor. 12:9, NIV).

Read: Isaiah 40

Action assignment: Are you a reluctant follower? Step out today in faith as you obediently serve Christ by clinging to some meaningful promise from God's Word. Write it out and look at it if your faith falters. Concentrate on God's constant concern for your welfare, remembering that He promises never to forsake you. Remember, God may choose what you go through today, but you choose how you go through it. God delights in giving the garment of praise for the spirit of heaviness (Isa. 61:3).

17

THE FAITH LOOK

How is a person born from above? How is he or she saved from eternal perishing? By believing on Jesus Christ; by looking to Him by faith.

On January 6, 1850, a snowstorm almost crippled the city of Colchester, England, and a teenage boy was unable to get to the church he usually attended. So he made his way to a nearby Primitive Methodist chapel, where an ill-prepared layman was substituting for the absent preacher. His text was Isaiah 45:22— "Look unto Me, and be ye saved, all the ends of the earth." For many months this young teenager had been miserable and under deep conviction, but though he had been reared in church (both his father and grandfather were preachers), he did not have the assurance of salvation.

The unprepared substitute minister did not have much to say, so he kept repeating the text! "A man need not go to college to learn to look," he shouted. "Anyone can look—a child can look!" About that time, he saw the visitor sitting to one side, and he pointed at him and said, "Young man, you look very miserable. Young man, look to Jesus Christ!"

The young man did look by faith, and that was how the great preacher Charles Haddon Spurgeon was converted.

Verse to remember: "I am not ashamed; for I know whom I have believed and I am convinced that He is able to guard what I have entrusted to Him until that day" (2 Timothy 1:12, NASB).

Also: Romans 1:16; John 3:1-20; 1 Corinthians 1:18; 1 Thessalonians 5:9; 1 Timothy 2:3-4; 2 Timothy 1:9.

Action assignment: Thank God that you can know you have eternal life, and that becoming a member of God's forever family is not complicated.

"TRY THE UPLOOK"

For young Isaiah, the outlook was bleak, but the uplook was glorious! God was still on the throne and reigning as the Sovereign of the universe! From heaven's point of view, "the whole earth" was "full of His glory" (Isa. 6:3; see Num. 14:21–22; Ps. 72:18–19). When your world tumbles in, it is good to look at things from heaven's point of view.

The sight of a holy God, and the sound of the holy hymn of worship, brought great conviction to Isaiah's heart; and he confessed that he was a sinner. Unclean lips are caused by an unclean heart (Matt. 12:34–35). Isaiah cried out to be cleansed inwardly (Ps. 51:10), and God met his need. If this scene had been on earth, the coals would have come from the brazen altar where sacrificial blood had been shed, or perhaps from the censer of the high priest on the Day of Atonement (Lev. 16:12). Isaiah's cleansing came by blood and fire, and it was verified by the word of the Lord (Isa. 6:7).

Before we can minister to others, we must permit God to minister to us. Before we pronounce "woe" upon others, we must sincerely say, "Woe is me!" Isaiah's conviction led to confession, and confession led to cleansing (1 John 1:9). Like Isaiah, many of the great heroes of faith saw themselves as sinners and humbled themselves before God: Abraham (Gen. 18:27), Jacob (Gen. 32:10), Job (Job 40:1–5), David (2 Sam. 7:18), Paul (1 Tim. 1:15), and Peter (Luke 5:8–11).

Today's verse: "And they were calling to one another: 'Holy, holy, holy is the LORD Almighty; the whole earth is full of his glory'" (Isa. 6:3, NIV).

Read: Isaiah 6

Action assignment: Make up a motto using the following quotation and place it in a place where you will see it often, perhaps on your refrigerator or your bathroom mirror: "If you would be miserable look to self; if you would be perplexed, look to others; but if you would be happy, look to Jesus!"

WHEN THE BOOKS WILL BE BALANCED

I once heard Dr. W.A. Criswell tell about the faithful missionary couple who returned to the United States on the same ship that brought Teddy Roosevelt home from a safari in Africa. Many reporters and photographers were on the dock, waiting to see Roosevelt and interview him and take pictures; but nobody was on hand to welcome home the veteran missionaries who had spent their lives serving Christ in Africa.

That evening, in their modest hotel room, the couple reviewed their arrival in New York City. The husband was somewhat bitter.

"It isn't fair," he said to his wife. "Mr. Roosevelt comes home from a hunting trip, and the whole country is out to meet him. We get home after years of service, and nobody is there to greet us."

But his wife had the right answer: "Honey, we aren't home yet."

In my own travels, I have seen situations in local churches that have broken my heart. I have seen congregations show little or no appreciation to faithful pastors who were laboring sacrificially to see the church grow. Some of these men were underpaid and overworked, yet the churches seemed to have no love for them. But their successors were treated like kings! Perhaps you are being overlooked for your faithfulness. Certainly at the Judgment Seat of Christ, the books will be balanced.

From God's Word: "He that is faithful in that which is least is faithful also in much" (Luke 16:10).

Consider: Proverbs 28:20; Matthew 24:45-47; Revelation 2:10.

Action assignment: In your hymnal, find "What if It Were Today?" Give special attention to the third stanza. Thank God for His faithfulness to you, and ask Him to help you be faithful to Him and to others throughout this day.

WHERE IS GOD?

Because we are human, it is natural for us to think mainly of ourselves when we are going through difficult times. We must constantly remind ourselves to walk by faith and to see God in the picture. After all, God is in control of this universe! "Yet the Lord will command His loving kindness in the daytime, and in the night His song shall be with me, and my prayer unto the God of my life" (Psalm 42:8). God is in command! We can pray to Him and He will give us a song, even in the night. The living God is the "God of my life," and we must daily look to Him.

The most important thing about any difficult experience is not *that* we get out of it, but *what* we get out of it. If we are truly thirsting after God, and not just His help and deliverance, then the experience that could tear us down will actually build us up. Instead of complaining, we will be praying and praising God. Life will not be a mirror in which we see only ourselves; it will be a window through which we see God.

Verse for today: "God is our refuge and strength, a very present help in trouble" (Psalm 46:1).

Also read: Job 35:10; Psalms 27:5; 37:39; 42; 43.

Action assignment: Reflect on your attitude toward difficulty. Can you see that God is in control? Zero in on your worst trial. Confess that you know God is in control and ask Him to show Himself to you in a new and wonderful way—even if you don't get out of your trouble today. Then read and claim the promise of 1 Corinthians 10:13.

21

CAN YOU FORGIVE AND FORGET?

What does it mean that God remembers our sins and iniquities no more? Does it mean that our all-knowing God can actually *forget* what we have done? If God forgot anything, He would cease to be God! The phrase "remember no more" means "hold against us no more." God recalls what we have done, but He does not hold it against us. He deals with us on the basis of grace and mercy, not law and merit. Once sin has been forgiven, it is never brought before us again. The matter is settled eternally.

As a pastor, I have often heard counselees say, "Well, I can forgive—but I cannot forget!"

"Of course you can't forget," I usually reply. "The more you try to put this thing out of your mind, the more you will remember it. But that isn't what it means to forget." Then I go on to explain that "to forget" means "not to hold it against the person who has wronged us." We may remember what others have done, but we treat them *as though they never did it.*

How is this possible? It is possible because of the Cross, for there God treated His Son *as though He had done it!* Our experience of forgiveness from God makes it possible for us to forgive others.

God declares: "I will forgive their wickedness and will remember their sins no more" (Hebrews 8:12, NIV).

Also read: Hebrews 10:16-17; Psalm 103:12; Isaiah 1:18; 43:25; 56:6-7.

Action assignment: If someone has wronged you and you have not forgiven him or her, write on a piece of paper what that person did to you. In prayer talk to God about it and then tear the paper into shreds as a symbol of forgetting and forgiving.

PLEASING GOD

Everybody lives to please somebody. Many people live to please themselves. They have no sensitivity to the needs of others. "The soul of a journey," wrote William Hazlitt, "is liberty, perfect liberty, to think, feel, and do just as one pleases." That advice may work for a vacation, but it could never work in the everyday affairs of life. Christians cannot go through life pleasing only themselves.

Pleasing God means much more than simply doing God's will. It is possible to obey God and yet not please Him. Jonah is a case in point. He obeyed God and did what he was commanded, but his heart was not in it. God blessed His Word, but He could not bless His servant. So Jonah sat outside the city of Nineveh angry with everybody, including the Lord!

How do we know what pleases God? How do we know what pleases an earthly father? By listening to him and living with him. As we read the Word, and as we fellowship in worship and service, we get to know the heart of God; and this opens us up to the will of God.

Remember: "Rid yourselves of all malice and deceit, hypocrisy, envy, and slander of every kind. You are a chosen people, a royal priesthood, a holy nation, a people belonging to God, that you may declare the praises of Him who called you out of darkness into His wonderful light. Dear friends, I urge you . . . to abstain from sinful desires, which war against your soul. Live such good lives among the pagans that . . . they may see your good deeds and glorify God" (1 Peter 2:1, 9, 11-12, NIV).

Reach for your Bible: Romans 15:1; Galatians 1:10; John 3:20; Ephesians 6:6; Hebrews 11:5.

Action assignment: Open your hymnal to "Trust and Obey" and sing it as loudly as you dare. Determine to do one special thing today that will please God and ask Him to help you do it.

A WONDERFUL RELATIONSHIP

In John 3, the Apostle John emphasizes a personal relationship with Jesus Christ. It is a *living relationship* that begins with the new birth, the birth from above. When we receive Jesus Christ into our lives, we share His very life and become children in the family of God.

It is also a *loving relationship*, for He is the Bridegroom and we are part of the bride. Like John the Baptist, we desire that Jesus Christ increase as we decrease. He must receive all the honor and glory.

It is a *learning relationship*, for He is the faithful witness who shares God's truth with us. What a delight it is to receive His Word, meditate on it, and make it a part of our very lives.

But we must never forget the cost of these blessings. For us to be born into God's family, Jesus Christ had to die. For us to enter into the loving relationship of salvation, He had to endure the hatred and condemnation of men. He had to be lifted up on the cross so that we might experience forgiveness and eternal life.

May we never take this for granted!

Verse for today: "He must increase, but I must decrease" (John 3:30).

Additional Scripture: John 3:17-18; 1 John 1:1-7; Romans 8:1-4, 11, 13-16, 23, 26-27.

Action assignment: Determine how in the day ahead you can honor Christ and live out John 3:30.

ONLY FEAR THE LORD

The person who fears God alone need never fear any person or group of people. The fear of God is the fear that cancels fear.

God cares for His own. It did not cost much to purchase sparrows in the market. Yet the Father knows when a sparrow falls to the ground, *and the Father is there.* If God cares for sparrows in such a marvelous way, will He not also care for His own who are serving Him? He certainly will! To God, we are of greater value than many sparrows.

God is concerned about all of the details of our lives. Even the hairs of our heads are numbered—not "counted" in a total, but numbered individually! God sees the sparrow fall to the ground, and God sees when a hair falls from the head of one of His children. When He protects His own, He protects them down to the individual hairs. There is no need for us to fear when God is exercising such wonderful care over us.

The Bible says: "Only fear the Lord, and serve Him in truth with all your heart: for consider how great things He hath done for you" (1 Samuel 12:24).

Also read: Psalms 31:19; 34:7-11; 103:11-17.

Action assignment: Take a few moments to consider the great things the Lord has done for you. Thank Him for these evidences in your life of His worthiness to be feared.

BE THANKFUL (17 WERE NOT!)

Just a short drive from my former home is the campus of North-western University in Evanston, Illinois. Years ago, the school had a life-saving squad that assisted passengers on the Lake Michigan boats. On September 8, 1860, a passenger boat, the *Lady Elgin,* floundered near Evanston, and a ministerial student, Edward Spencer, personally rescued seventeen persons. The exertion of that day permanently damaged his health and he was unable to train for the ministry. When he died some years later, it was noted that not one of the seventeen persons he had saved ever came to thank him.

Some people are appreciative by nature, but some are not; and it is these latter people who especially need God's power to express thanksgiving. We should remember that every good gift comes from God and that He is (as the theologians put it) "the Source, Support, and End of all things." The very breath in our mouths is the free gift of God.

Thankfulness is the opposite of selfishness. The selfish person says, "I *deserve* what comes to me! Other people *ought* to make me happy!" But the mature Christian realizes that life is a gift from God, and that the blessings of life come only from His bountiful hand.

Scripture for today: "Let the peace of Christ rule your hearts. . . . And be thankful. Let the word of Christ dwell in you richly as you teach and admonish one another with all wisdom, and as you sing psalms, hymns, and spiritual songs with grati-tude in your hearts" (Colossians 3:15-16, NIV).

Also read: Colossians 1:3, 12; 2:7; 4:2; James 1:17.

Action assignment: Let the Scripture for today rule your life. Don't wait for Thanksgiving Day. Cultivate a truly thankful spirit! Ask God to help you.

SUFFERING MEANS FELLOWSHIP WITH CHRIST

It is an honor and a privilege to suffer *with* Christ and be treated by the world the way it treated Him. "The fellowship of His sufferings" is a gift from God. Not every believer grows to the point where God can trust him with this kind of experience, so we ought to rejoice when the privilege comes to us. "And they [the apostles] departed from the presence of the council, rejoicing that they were counted worthy to suffer shame for His name" (Acts 5:41).

Christ is with us in the furnace of persecution. When the three Hebrew children were cast into the fiery furnace, they discovered they were not alone. The Lord was with Paul in all of his trials, and He promises to be with us "to the end of the age" (Matthew 28:20, NASB).

Paul wrote: "That I may know Him, and the power of His resurrection, and the fellowship of His sufferings, being made conformable unto His death" (Philippians 3:10).

Also read: Philippians 1:29; Isaiah 41:10; Daniel 3:23-25; 2 Timothy 4:9-18.

Action assignment: Memorize today's verse and talk to God about its meaning to you.

27

BLESSINGS ARE WINDOWS

The material blessings of life come from God. The person who looks at himself and forgets God when blessings are abundant is only revealing his pride. David responded to God's blessings by saying, "Who are I, O Lord God, and what is my house, that Thou hast brought me this far?" (2 Samuel 7:18, NASB)

The material blessings of life are either a *mirror* in which we see ourselves, or a *window* through which we see God. The proud, selfish person thinks he deserves all these blessings and thinks only of himself. The person who knows that all blessings come from God looks away from himself to the Lord who gives so richly. For that matter, we ought to see the hand of God in a piece of bread as much as in a field of grain. Jesus saw His Father's goodness in the beautiful lily and the lowly sparrows.

It is all a matter of the heart. Jesus said, "For where your treasure is, there will your heart be also" (Matthew 6:21). The eyes see what the heart loves. If we love God and put His will first in our lives, then whatever material blessings we receive will only draw us closer to Him. Wealth will be our servant, not our master, and we will invest in things eternal.

Remember this: "Instruct those who are rich in this present world not to be conceited or to fix their hope on the uncertainty of riches, but on God, who richly supplies us with all things to enjoy" (1 Timothy 6:17, NASB).

Also read: Genesis 1:31; John 1:16; 2 Corinthians 3:5; James 1:17.

Action assignment: Read or sing "Now Thank We All Our God" or some other hymn related to thanking God for His goodness. Name things that are yours from His hand, and forthrightly thank Him.

IN CHRIST WE TRUST

We need to decide what kind of righteousness we are seeking, whether we are depending on good works and character, or trusting Christ alone for salvation. God does not save people on the basis of birth or behavior. He saves them "by grace, through faith" (Ephesians 2:8-9).

It is not a question of whether or not we are among God's elect. That is a mystery known only to God. He offers us His salvation by faith. The offer is made to "whosoever will" (Revelation 22:17). After we have trusted Christ, we have the witness and evidence that we are among His elect. But first we must trust Him and receive by faith His righteousness which alone can guarantee heaven.

How fitting that American coinage has the inscription "In God We Trust." May it ever be so—for the nation and ourselves.

Verse for today: "In Thee, O Lord, do I put my trust: let me never be put to confusion" (Psalm 71:1).

Also read: Ephesians 1:4-14; 2:8-9; Revelation 22:17; 1 Thessalonians 1; Psalm 56:4.

Action assignment: We often judge people on the basis of their appearance, behavior, speech, or cultural background. Have you ever thanked God that that is not the way He operates? Salvation is free to those who receive it. Ask God to help you trust in Him with more awareness of His grace and acceptance.

JESUS IS A TEETOTALER

Wine was the normal drink of the people in New Testament days, but we must not use Jesus' miracle of turning water into wine as an argument for the use of alcoholic beverages today. A man given to drink once said to me, "After all, Jesus turned water into wine!" My reply was, "If you use Jesus as your example for drinking, why don't you follow His example in everything else?" Then I read Luke 22:18 to him. This verse clearly implies that, in heaven today, Jesus is a teetotaler!

Sincere Christians today will want to consider certain Scripture (see below) before concluding that the use of alcoholic beverages is a wise thing today. I am reminded of the story of a drunken coal miner who was converted and became a vocal witness for Christ. One of his friends tried to trap him by asking, "Do you believe that Jesus turned water into wine?"

"I certainly do!" the believer replied. "In my home, He has turned wine into furniture, decent clothes, and food for my children!"

Finally, it is worth noting that the Jews always diluted the wine with water, usually to the proportion of three parts water to one part wine. While the Bible does not command total abstinence, it certainly magnifies it and definitely warns against drunkenness.

Verse for today: "Take care lest this liberty of yours somehow become a stumbling block to the weak. . . . Therefore, if food causes my brother to stumble, I will never eat meat again, that I might not cause my brother to stumble" (1 Corinthians 8:9, 13, NASB).

Also: Read 1 Corinthians 8; 10:23, 31.

Action assignment: If you are in any way facing the question of the use of alcoholic beverages, take time now to think the matter through. Pray about it.

LIVING MANNA

When Jesus called Himself "the Living Bread," He was not claiming to be exactly like manna. He was claiming to be even greater! The manna only sustained life for the Jews, but Jesus gives life to the whole world. The Jews ate the daily manna and eventually died; but when you receive Jesus Christ within, you live forever. When God gave the manna, He gave only a gift; but when Jesus came, He gave Himself. There was no cost to God in sending the manna each day, but He gave His Son at great cost. The Jews had to eat the manna every day, but the sinner who trusts Christ once is given eternal life.

It is not difficult to see in the manna a picture of our Lord Jesus Christ. The manna was a mysterious thing to the Jews; in fact, the word *manna* means "What is it?" Jesus was a mystery to those who saw Him. The manna came at night from heaven, and Jesus came to this earth when sinners were in moral and spiritual darkness. The manna was small (His humility), round (His eternality), and white (His purity). It was sweet to the taste (compare Psalm 34:8), and it met the needs of the people adequately.

The manna was given to a rebellious people; it was the gracious gift of God. All they had to do was stoop and pick it up. If they failed to pick it up, they walked on it. The Lord is not far from any sinner. All the sinner has to do is humble himself and take the gift that God offers.

Verse for meditation: "Jesus said unto them, 'I am the Bread of Life; he that cometh to Me shall never hunger; and he that believeth on Me shall never thirst'" (John 6:35).

Also consider: Exodus 16; John 6:25-59.

Action assignment: Thank God for the Living Bread and consider how you can give this Bread to some spiritually hungry person.

December

Be Renewed:

"But now being made free from sin, and become servants to God, ye have your fruit unto holiness, and the end everlasting life."

Romans 6:22

TRUE HUMILITY

Submission to God and others is an act of faith. There is danger in submitting to others; they might take advantage of us. But we can trust God. His mighty hand that directs our lives can also direct the lives of others.

God never exalts anyone until that person is ready for it. First the Cross, then the crown; first the suffering, then the glory. Moses was under God's hand for forty years before God sent him to deliver the Jews from Egypt. Joseph was under God's hand for at least thirteen years before God lifted him to the throne. It was pride—a desire to be like God—that stirred Eve to take the forbidden fruit. The only antidote to pride is the grace of God, and we receive that grace whenever we yield ourselves to God. The evidence of that grace is that we yield to one another.

Verse for today: "For whosoever exalteth himself shall be abased; and he that humbleth himself shall be exalted" (Luke 14:11).

Also read: Proverbs 6:16-17; 8:13; Philippians 2:1-11; 1 Peter 5:5-6; 1 John 2:16.

Action assignment: Pride can be very subtle. After all, we have rights, don't we? Are you ever on the defensive? Watch today for defensiveness in your attitudes. Then give these defenses to God. Write them down to help you become more aware of subtle pride. God wants to give you the grace to be humble and submissive to Himself and others.

MAKING A DIFFERENCE

A fruitful life is a happy life. It was in a context of teaching about fruitfulness that Jesus said to His disciples, "These things have I spoken unto you, that My joy might remain in you, and that your joy might be full" (John 15:11). For what kind of spiritual fruit is our Lord looking? Souls that we win to Christ, holy lives, our generous gifts to His work, the "fruit of the Spirit"— Christian character, and good works. Even the songs of praise that come from our lips are fruit for His glory.

Why is a fruitful life a happy life? Because a fruitful Christian is experiencing God's power in his life and fulfilling his greatest potential. Furthermore, he is serving others, and this is a constant source of joy. The more faithful he is to the Lord, the more blessing (and trials) he experiences; but this prepares him to be even more useful to the Lord.

Verse for today: "But now being made free from sin, and become servants to God, ye have your fruit unto holiness, and the end everlasting life" (Romans 6:22).

Also read: Romans 1:13; 15:28; Galatians 5:22-23; Colossians 1:10; Hebrews 13:15.

Action assignment: In Jesus Christ, happiness is fruitfulness— your life making a difference in the world as you labor in God's harvest. Aim to be more fruitful for God's glory. Make up a "new spiritual goals" list from today's study. Then pray about each goal and follow the Holy Spirit's guidance in at least one specific action. For example, visit a new family in your church or neighborhood; witness to a coworker about your joy in the Lord; pray for wisdom in knowing how to serve others.

3

OUR FORGIVING GOD

As you study Isaiah and discover God's prophetic plan for the nations of the world, don't miss his emphasis on *the personal message of God's forgiveness.* "Though your sins are like scarlet, they shall are as white as snow; though they are red like crimson, they shall be as wool" (1:18). "I have blotted out, like a thick cloud, your transgressions, and, like a cloud, your sins" (44:22). "I, even I, am He, who blots out your transgressions for My own sake; and I will not remember your sins" (43:25).

How can "the Holy One of Israel," a just and righteous God, forgive our sins and remember them no more?

"But [Jesus] was wounded for our transgressions, He was bruised for our iniquities; the chastisement for our peace was upon Him, and by His stripes we are healed" (53:5).

It was on the basis of this truth that Peter declared, "To [Jesus] all the prophets witness that, through His name, whoever believes in Him shall receive remission of sins" (Acts 10:43).

"Who has believed our report?" Isaiah asks us (Isa. 53:1).

"If you will not believe, surely you shall not be established," he warns us (7:9).If you have never believed on the Lord Jesus Christ and received Him into your life, then do so now. "Look to Me, and be saved, all you ends of the earth! For I am God, and there is no other" (45:22).

"Nor is there salvation in any other, for there is no other name under heaven given among men by which we must be saved" (Acts 4:12).

God says: "I, even I, am He who blots out your transgressions, for My own sake, and remembers your sins no more" (Isa. 43:25, NIV).

Read: Isaiah 53

Action assignment: Reflect on the time when you received Christ as your personal Lord and Savior. Give Him special thanks for some of the ensuing blessings which have accrued to you since that time. Sing a song of praise to the Lord. Remind yourself of some Scripture verses pertaining to salvation.

"MORE THAN CONQUERORS!"

God does not shelter us from the difficulties of life, because we need them for our spiritual growth. In Romans 8:28 God assures us that the difficulties of life are working *for* us and not *against* us. God permits trials to come that we might use them for our good and His glory. We endure trials for His sake, and since we do, do you think that He will desert us? Of course not! Instead, He is closer to us when we go through the difficulties of life.

Furthermore, He gives us the power to conquer. We are "more than conquerors," literally, "we are superconquerors" through Jesus Christ! He gives us victory and more victory! We need not fear life or death, things present or things to come, because Jesus Christ loves us and gives us the victory. This is not a promise with conditions attached: "If you do this, God will do that." This security in Christ is an established fact, and we claim it for ourselves because we are in Christ. Nothing can separate you from His love! Believe it—and rejoice in it!

Scripture for meditation: "In all these things we are more than conquerors through Him who loved us. For I am persuaded, that neither death, nor life . . . nor powers, nor things present, nor things to come, nor height, nor depth, nor any other creature, shall be able to separate us from the love of God, which is in Christ Jesus our Lord" (Romans 8:37-39).

Also: Romans 8:28-36; Hebrews 4:15-16.

Action assignment: Thank God for His great love and for the fact that *nothing* can separate you from his love. Ask Him to enable you to be "more than a conqueror" in the day ahead.

5

AN OBLIGATION TO ISRAEL

Paul warned the Gentiles that they were obligated to Israel, and therefore they dared not boast of their new spiritual position. The Gentiles entered into God's plan because of faith, and not because of anything good they had done. Paul was discussing the Gentiles collectively, and not the individual experience of one believer or another.

It is worth noting that, according to Bible prophecy, the professing Gentile church will be "cut off" because of apostasy. First Timothy 4 and 2 Timothy 3, along with 2 Thessalonians 2, indicate that the professing church in the last days will depart from the faith. *There is no hope for the apostate church, but there is hope for apostate Israel!* Why? Because of roots of the olive tree. God will keep His promises to the patriarchs, but God will break off the Gentiles because of their unbelief.

No matter how far Israel may stray from the truth of God, the roots are still good. God is still the "God of Abraham, and the God of Isaac, and the God of Jacob." He will keep His promises to these patriarchs. This means that the olive tree will flourish again when Jesus Christ returns to set up His kingdom on earth!

Paul's great concern: "Brethren, my heart's desire and prayer to God for Israel is, that they might be saved" (Romans 10:1).

Other Scripture: Romans 9:1-5; 11.

Action assignment: Make a point to understand the meaning of Yom Kippur, the Jewish Day of Atonement, ten days after the Jewish New Year, Rosh Hashanah (usually in September). Pray for the nation Israel, and for any individual Jewish person you may know.

HOW REAL IS YOUR WORSHIP?

The rebellious people of Isaiah's day were also a religious people. They attended the temple services and brought a multitude of sacrifices to the Lord but their hearts were far from God, and their worship was hypocritical. Sacrifices alone can never please God; for along with the outward observance, God wants inward obedience (1 Sam. 15:22), a broken heart (Ps. 51:17), and a godly walk (Mic. 6:6–8). Judah's worship of Jehovah was iniquity, not piety; and God was sick of it! Instead of lifting up "holy hands" in prayer (1 Tim. 2:8), their hands were stained with blood because of their many sins (Isa. 59:3; Ezek. 7:23; and see Acts 20:26).

But before passing judgment on worshipers in a bygone era, perhaps we should confess the sins of the "worshiping church" today. According to researcher George Barna, 93 percent of the households in the United States contain a Bible and more than 60 percent of the people surveyed claim to be religious; but we would never know this from the way people act. One Protestant church exists for every 550 adults in America, but does all this "religion" make much of a difference in our sinful society? At least 62 percent of the people Barna surveyed said that the church is not relevant to today's world. Could it be that, like the worshipers in the ancient Jewish temple, we are only going through the motions?

Verse for Today: "Samuel replied: 'Does the LORD delight in burnt offerings and sacrifices as much as in obeying the voice of the Lord? To obey is better than sacrifice, and to heed is better than the fat of rams' "(1 Sam. 15:22, NIV).

Read: Isaiah 1

Action assignment: Write out your personal definition of worship. Think about it prayerfully.

The psalmist asks that praise and thanks be given to God on an instrument of ten strings (Ps. 92:3). Could that possibly refer to a believer's two ears, two eyes, two hands, two feet, a mouth, and a heart? The Bible records a rich supply of verses pertaining to these various members. How "musical" are you today in worship?

7

THE ONLY "REAL WORLD"

Dr. A.W. Tozer used to remind us that the invisible world described in the Bible is the only "real world." If we would only see the visible world the way God wants us to see it, we would never be attracted by anything it has to offer. The great men and women of faith mentioned in Hebrews 11 achieved what they did because they "saw the invisible."

The things of this world seem so real because we can see and feel them; but they are all temporal and destined to pass away. Only the eternal things of the spiritual life will last. We must not press this truth into extremes and think that "material" and "spiritual" oppose each other; when we use the material in God's will, He transforms it into the spiritual, and this becomes part of our treasure in heaven. We value the material because it can be used to promote the spiritual, and not for what it is in itself.

How can you look at things that are invisible? By faith, when you read the Word of God. We have never seen Christ or heaven, yet we know they are real because the Word of God tells us so.

From the Word: "Now faith is the substance of things hoped for, the evidence of things not seen" (Hebrews 11:1).

Dig for more: 1 John 2:15-17; Hebrews 11:6, 10, 13-14, 27; 2 Corinthians 4:18.

Action assignment: Think of three things the Bible tells you about that you can see only by faith. Thank God for the reality of the invisible world.

A TRUE DISCIPLER

Epaphras is an example of a New Testament person who not only won people to Christ, but taught them the Word and helped them to grow. He also prayed that they might become mature in Christ. When danger threatened the members of the church, Epaphras went to Rome to get counsel from Paul. He loved his people and wanted to protect them from false doctrines that would destroy the fellowship and hinder their spiritual development.

We who disciple other believers must be careful not to get in the way. We are not to make disciples *for ourselves,* but for Jesus Christ. We must relate people to Him so that they love and obey Him. Epaphras faithfully taught his people and related them to Christ, but the false teachers came in and tried to "draw away disciples." Human nature has the tendency to want to follow men instead of God—to want "something new" instead of the basic foundational truths of the Gospel.

Verse for today: "We, who with unveiled faces all reflect the Lord's glory, are being transformed into His likeness with ever-increasing glory, which comes from the Lord, who is the Spirit" (2 Corinthians 3:18, NIV).

See also: Colossians 1:1-13; 4:12-13; Acts 20:28-30.

Action assignment: List the qualities that you believe made Epaphras the kind of person he was. Ask God to make you more like him. Begin reading a good book on discipling, such as Walter A. Henrichsen's *Disciples Are Made—Not Born* (Victor).

9

SUFFERING CAN GLORIFY GOD

God's pattern for life is that suffering must come before glory. This was true of our Savior (Luke 24:26; 1 Peter 1:11) and it is true of His people (1 Peter 4:13; 5:10). When we suffer in the will of God and depend on His grace, that suffering has a maturing and purifying effect on our lives. Sadly, we have too many leaders today who proudly display their medals, but they can't show you any scars. Our Lord's Calvary wounds are now glorified in heaven, eternal reminders that suffering and glory go together in the purposes of God.

Of itself, suffering doesn't make people better. Sometimes it makes them bitter. But when suffering is mixed with faith and God's grace, then it becomes a wonderful tool for building godly character (2 Cor. 12:1–10). If suffering alone gave people wisdom and character, then our world would be a far better place, because everybody suffers in one way or another. When we accept our suffering as a gift from God and use it for His glory, then it can work in us and for us to accomplish the will of God.

Your desire? "I want to know Christ and the power of His resurrection and the fellowship of sharing in His sufferings, becoming like Him in His death" (Phil. 3:10, NIV).

Read: 2 Corinthians 12:1–10

Action assignment: Before adversity overtakes you, prepare yourself by reading some of God's special promises, such as 1 Kings 8:56, Psalm 73:26, Lamentations 3:6 and 3:26, Psalm 18:28–29 and 73:26, 28. and 1 Peter 5:7. Someone has said, "I can struggle wildly and make my predicament worse, or I can wait for God's guidance." Determine to wait for God's guidance if you face adversity.

GOD ORDERS PURITY

Paul gave the believers at Thessalonica the commandments of God regarding personal purity. The word *commandments* is a military term. It refers to orders handed down from superior officers. We are soldiers in God's army, and we must obey orders. Paul reminded these new believers that sexual immorality does not please God. God created sex, and He has the authority to govern its use. From the beginning He established marriage as a sacred union between one man and one woman. God created sex both for the continuance of the race and for the pleasure of the marriage partners. God's commandments concerning sex are not for the purpose of robbing people of joy, but rather of protecting them that they might not lose their joy. "Thou shalt not commit adultery" (Exodus 20:14) builds a wall around marriage that makes the relationship not a prison, but a safe and beautiful garden.

We never have to seek to know the will of God in this matter; He has told us clearly. "Abstain from fornication" is His commandment, and no amount of liberal theology or modern philosophy can alter it. God's purpose is *our sanctification,* that we might live separated lives in purity of mind and body.

Be advised: "No one serving as a soldier gets involved in civilian affairs—he wants to please his commanding officer" (2 Timothy 2:4, NIV).

For further study: 1 Corinthians 6:9-10; Galatians 5:19-21; 1 Thessalonians 4:3; Hebrews 13:4.

Action assignment: In your own words, write down how you believe God wants you to live to be pure in your own life. Talk to God about temptations you may have had and tell Him how you want to live.

ATTITUDES FOR TODAY

The Beatitudes of Matthew 5 describe the attitudes that ought to be in our lives today. Four attitudes are described in the Matthew passage.

Our attitude toward ourselves (5:3). To be poor in spirit means to be humble, the opposite of the world's attitudes of self-praise.

Our attitude toward our sins (5:4-6). We should not only mourn over sin and despise it, but we should also meekly submit to God.

Our attitude toward the Lord (5:7-9). We experience God's mercy when we trust Christ, and he gives us a clean heart and peace within. But having received His mercy, we then *share* His mercy with others. We become peacemakers in a troubled world.

Our attitude toward the world (5:10-16). It is not easy to be a dedicated Christian. Our society is not a friend to God nor to God's people. Whether we like it or not, there is a *conflict* between us and the world. Why? Because we are different from the world and we have different attitudes.

The Beatitudes represent an outlook radically different from that of the world. The world praises pride, not humility. The world endorses sin, especially if you "get away with it." The world is at war with God, while God is seeking to reconcile His enemies and make them His children. We must expect to be persecuted *if* we are living as God wants us to live.

Today's Scripture: "Ye are the light of the world. A city that is set on a hill cannot be hid. . . . Let your light so shine before men, that they may see your good works, and glorify your Father which is in heaven" (Matthew 5:14, 16).

Read also: Matthew 5:1-16.

Action assignment: Take a sheet of paper and write four sentences completing these phrases: "My attitude toward myself (my sins, the Lord, the world) should be . . ." Ask God to build these attitudes in you.

I *WILL* DO THY WILL!

Christian living is a matter of the will, not the feelings. I often hear believers say, "I don't feel like reading the Bible." Or, "I don't feel like attending prayer meeting." Children operate on the basis of feeling, but adults operate on the basis of will. They act because it is right, no mater how they feel. This explains why immature Christians easily fall into temptation: they let their feelings make the decisions. The more you exercise your will in saying a decisive *no* to temptation, the more God will take control of your life.

Disobedience gives birth to death, not life. It may take years for the sin to mature, but when it does, the result will be death. If we will only believe God's Word and see this final tragedy, it will encourage us not to yield to temptation. God has erected this barrier because He loves us.

Verse for today: "But whoso looketh into the perfect law of liberty, and continueth therein, he being not a forgetful hearer, but a doer of the word, this man shall be blessed in his deed" (James 1:25).

Also read: Philippians 2:13; Ezekiel 18:23; James 1:13-15; Romans 7:24-25; Matthew 26:39, 42.

Action assignment: If Christ had said, "I don't feel like dying on the cross," we would still be in our sins. But He chose to do the will of His Father. You can choose to follow His example of obedience. Try to determine the areas of your life that are controlled solely by your feelings. Make a list of the feelings-controlled areas in your life so you can stay alert to the dangers. Then pray seriously for God's will to become your will.

13

AN ANCHOR THAT HOLDS

The hope of heaven is also an encouragement in times of suffering. As believers, we have our share of suffering; but in the midst of trials, we can rejoice "with joy unspeakable and full of glory" (1 Peter 1:8). When unbelievers suffer, they get discouraged and they want to give up. But when Christians suffer, their faith can become stronger and their love can deepen because their hope shines brighter.

How do we know that we have this hope? The promise is given in "the word of the truth of the Gospel" (Colossians 1:5). We believers do not have to "work up" a good feeling of hope. God's unchanging Word assures us that our hope is secure in Christ. In fact, this hope is compared in Hebrews to an anchor that can never break or drift.

Scripture to remember: "We have this hope as an anchor for the soul, firm and secure. It enters the inner sanctuary behind the curtain, where Jesus, who went before us, has entered on our behalf. He has become a high priest forever" (Hebrews 6:19-20, NIV).

Also meditate on: Ephesians 3:12; 2 Timothy 1:12; Hebrews 6:11.

Action assignment: Sing or read "My Anchor Holds" in your hymnal. Go out today believing that Christ, your anchor, will hold you safe and sure no matter how the winds of life may blow.

GOD PROVIDES A NEW NATURE

The New Covenant is *wholly* of God's grace; no sinner can become a part of this New Covenant without faith in Jesus Christ. Grace and faith go together just as the Law and works go together. The Law says, "The man that doeth them [the things written in the Law] shall live in them" (Galatians 3:12). But grace says, "The work is done—believe and live!"

The Law of Moses could *declare* God's holy standard, but it would never *provide* the power needed for obedience. Sinful people need a new heart and a new disposition within; this is just what the New Covenant provides.

The Law was external; God's demands were written on tablets of stone. But the New Covenant makes it possible for God's Word to be written on human minds and hearts. God's grace makes possible an internal transformation that makes a surrendered believer more and more like Jesus Christ.

From the Word: "You yourselves are our letter, written on our hearts, known and read by everybody. You show that you are a letter from Christ, the result of our ministry, written not with ink but with the Spirit of the Living God, not on tablets of stone but on tablets of human hearts" (2 Corinthians 3:2-3, NIV).

Also think on: Hebrews 8:7-13; Ezekiel 36:26-27.

Action assignment: List on paper traits of an unsaved person; then list the traits that God gives a Christian. Thank Him for the new nature He provides.

15

A HOLY WALK

A church member criticized her pastor because he was preaching against sin in the lives of Christians. "After all," she said, "sin in the life of a believer is different from sin in the lives of unsaved people."

"Yes," replied the pastor. "*It is worse.*"

While it is true that the Christian is not under condemnation, he is not free from the harvest of sorrow that comes when we sow to the flesh. When King David committed adultery he tried to cover his sin, but God chastened him severely. When David confessed his sins, God forgave him; *but God could not change the consequences.* David reaped what he sowed, and it was a painful experience for him.

"But I am one of God's elect!" a Christian may argue. "I belong to Him, and He can never cast me out." Election is not an excuse for sin—it is an encouragement for holiness. The privilege of election also involves responsibilities of obedience.

A holy walk involves a right relationship with God the Father (who called us), God the Son (who died for us), and God the Spirit (who lives in us). It is the presence of the Holy Spirit that makes your body the temple of God. Furthermore, it is by walking in the Spirit that you gain victory over the lust of the flesh. To despise God's commandments is to invite the judgment of God and to grieve His Spirit.

Your call: "But as He which hath called you is holy, so be ye holy" (1 Peter 1:15).

Dig deeper: Colossians 3:23-25; John 5:24; Romans 8:1; Galatians 6:7-8; 1 Thessalonians 4:7; 1 Corinthians 6:19-20; Galatians 5:16-25.

Action assignment: Read Psalm 51 and list the things David felt he had lost and wanted back as a result of his sin. Talk with God about any sin He may see in your life.

EXERCISE WAITING

The ability to calm your soul and wait before God is one of the most difficult things in the Christian life. Our old nature is restless. The world around us is frantically in a hurry. Even some of our Christian friends might suggest that we are "backslidden" because we are not running to every seminar, listening to every visiting speaker, and attending every religious meeting. Years ago, Dr. A.W. Tozer suggested that the church might experience revival if we would cancel all our meetings and just gather for prayer and worship.

God can help us conquer fear if we will learn to worship, walk, and wait; the most difficult of these is to wait. A restless heart usually leads to a reckless life. All religious activity is not necessarily ministry. Instead of building us up, it might be tearing us down.

Verse for today: "My soul, wait thou only upon God; for my expectation is from Him. He only is my rock and my salvation: He is my defense; I shall not be moved" (Psalm 62:5-6).

Also read: Jeremiah 14:22; Psalm 25:5; 27:14; 39:7-8; 104:27-28; 145:15-16; Habakkuk 2:3; Acts 1:4; Galatians 5:5.

Action assignment: The secret of waiting is in the heart. The successful general plans his strategy and knows exactly when to attack. As you wait before the Lord in worship and walk with Him daily, He puts strength into your heart. Keep a notebook and plan your strategy for "waiting on the Lord."

"SORRY, BUT WE DIED!"

Years ago I heard a story about two sisters who enjoyed attending dances and wild parties. Then they were converted and found new life in Christ. They received an invitation to a party and sent the RSVP in these words: "We regret that we cannot attend because we recently died."

The fullest explanation of this wonderful truth is found in Romans 6–8. Christ not only died *for* us (substitution), but we died *with* Him (identification). This means that we can have victory over the old sin nature that wants to control us. "How shall we, that are dead to sin, live any longer therein?" (Romans 6:2)

Christ is our life. Eternal life is not some heavenly substance that God imparts when we, as sinners, trust the Saviour. Eternal life is Jesus Christ Himself. "He that hath the Son hath life; and he that hath not the Son of God hath not life" (1 John 5:12). We are both dead and alive at the same time—dead to sin and alive to Christ.

Someone has said, "Life is what you are alive to." A child may come alive when you talk about a baseball game or an ice-cream cone. A teenager may come alive when you mention cars or dates. Paul wrote, "For to me to live is Christ" (Philippians 1:21). Christ was Paul's life, and he was alive to anything that related to Christ. So should it be with every believer.

Scripture for today: "Set your minds on things above, not on earthly things. For you died, and your life is now hidden with Christ in God" (Colossians 3:2-3, NIV).

Also read: Romans 6–8.

Action assignment: Take time to examine your life—and your lifestyle. List things that you should say good-bye to: "Sorry, I can't—I'm dead." Ask God to enable you today to live according to Colossians 3:1-3.

BE A DOER

Obedience to God's will is the test of true faith in Christ. The test is not words—saying "Lord, Lord," and failing to obey His commands. How easy it is to learn a religious vocabulary, even memorize Bible verses and religious songs, yet not obey God's will. When a person is truly born again, he has the spirit of God living within; the Spirit enables him to know and do the Father's will. God's love in his heart motivates him to obey God and serve others.

Words are not a substitute for obedience, and neither are religious works. Preaching, casting out demons, and performing miracles can be divinely inspired, but they give no assurance of salvation. It is likely that even Judas participated in some or all of these activities, and yet he was not a true believer. In the last days, Satan will use "lying wonders" to deceive people.

We are to *hear* God's words and *do* them. We must not stop with only hearing (or studying) His words. Our hearing must result in doing.

Today's Scripture: "Do not merely listen to the Word, and so deceive yourselves. Do what it says" (James 1:22, NIV).

Also read: Luke 6:46-49; 11:28; Mark 3:35.

Action assignment: Concentrate today on being a doer. Make your life evidence of God's Word in action. Mentally list several things you want to do today that would please God.

A GRIPPING MESSAGE

Paul's Epistle to the Romans is still transforming people, just as it transformed Martin Luther and John Wesley. The one Scripture above all others that brought Luther out of mere religion into the joy of salvation by grace, through faith, was Romans 1:17: "The just shall live by faith." The Protestant Reformation and the Wesleyan Revival were the fruit of this wonderful letter written by Paul from Corinth about the year A.D. 56. The letter was carried to the Christians at Rome by one of the deaconesses of the church at Cenchrea, Sister Phebe (Romans 16:1).

Imagine! You and I can read and study the same inspired letter that brought life and power to Luther and Wesley! And the same Holy Spirit who taught them can teach us! You and I can experience revival in our hearts, homes, and churches if the message of this letter grips us as it has gripped men of faith in centuries past.

God's Word says: "But God be thanked, that you were the servants of sin, but you have obeyed from the heart that form of doctrine which was delivered you. Being then made free from sin, you became the servants of righteousness" (Romans 6:17-18).

Read: Romans 1–5; 6:4-11; 9.

Action assignment: Reflect on today's verse. Then think of six changes—transformations—Christ has made in your life since you believed.

A NOBLE CALLING

Paul saw himself as a priest at the altar, offering up to God the Gentiles he had won to Christ. They were a "spiritual sacrifice" to the glory of God. Even his preaching of the Gospel was a "priestly duty." This insight into ministry certainly adds dignity and responsibility to our service. It was important that the priests offer God only the best.

Paul was the minister of Jesus Christ; he preached "The Gospel of God," serving in the power of the Holy Spirit, who sanctified his ministry. What a privilege, and yet what a responsibility to be the servant of the Triune God, winning the lost to Jesus Christ!

Soul-winning is a priestly ministry, a sacred obligation. Thus we must serve the Lord with dedication and devotion, just as the priest in the temple did.

Verse for today: "You also, like living stones, are being built into a spiritual house to be a holy priesthood, offering spiritual sacrifices acceptable to God through Jesus Christ" (1 Peter 2:5, NIV).

Read: 1 Peter 2:9; Malachi 1:6-14; James 5:20; Proverbs 11:30.

Action assignment: As a Christian you have the privilege of coming directly to God, as did the high priest of ancient Israel. Have you ever thanked Him for this opportunity? Have you recognized the responsibility that goes along with the privilege— sharing the Good News of salvation with others? If not, what keeps you from doing so? Take time now and ask God to give you the heart of a soul-winner.

HOW GOD CAN WORK THROUGH YOU

The same resurrection power that saved you and took you out of the graveyard of sin can daily help you live for Christ and glorify Him. At great expense to Himself, God worked for us on the Cross. Today, on the basis of that price paid at Calvary, He is working in us to conform us to Christ. God cannot work *in* us unless He has first worked *for* us, and we have trusted His Son. He also cannot work *through* us unless He works *in* us. This is why it is important for you to spend time daily in the Word and in prayer, and to yield to Christ during times of suffering. For it is through the Word, prayer, and suffering that God works in you.

The Bible shows many examples of this principle. During forty years in the desert, Moses experienced God's working in his life, a working that prepared him for forty more years of magnificent service. Joseph suffered for thirteen years before God put him on the throne of Egypt, second to Pharaoh. David was anointed king when he was a youth, but he did not gain the throne until he had suffered many years as an exile. Even the Apostle Paul spent three years in Arabia after his conversion, no doubt experiencing God's deeper work to prepare him for his ministry. God makes it a point to work *in* us before He works *through* us.

Today's verse: "We are His workmanship, created in Christ Jesus unto good works, which God hath before ordained that we should walk in them" (Ephesians 2:10).

Also read: 2 Corinthians 5:17-21; Romans 8:29; Philippians 2:13; Hebrews 13:20-21; 1 Thessalonians 2:13; Ephesians 3:20-21.

Action assignment: Determine before God to take time to meditate and understand the Word of God and let it cleanse and nourish you. As you pray, thank God that you belong to Him and tell Him how you want to be a person through whom He can work.

OUR FAITHFUL CREATOR

Why did Peter refer to God as a "faithful Creator" (1 Peter 4:19) rather than a "faithful Judge" or even a "faithful Saviour"? Because God the Creator meets the needs of His people. It is the Creator who provides food and clothing to persecuted Christians, and who protects them in times of danger. When the early church was persecuted, they met together for prayer and addressed the Lord as the "God, which hast made heaven, and earth, and the sea, and all that in them is" (Acts 4:24). They prayed to the Creator!

Our heavenly Father is "Lord of heaven and earth" (Matthew 11:25). With that kind of Father, we have no need to worry! He is the *faithful* Creator, and His faithfulness will not fail.

Before God pours out His wrath upon this evil world, a "fiery trial" will come to God's church, to unite and purify it, that it might be a strong witness to the lost. There is nothing for us to fear if we are suffering in the will of God. Our faithful Father-Creator will see us through victoriously!

From the Word: "Let them that suffer according to the will of God commit the keeping of their souls to Him in well doing, as unto a faithful creator" (1 Peter 4:19).

Other Scripture: Jeremiah 32:17; Lamentations 3:22-23; Amos 4:13; 5:8; Acts 17:24-26; Matthew 6:24-34.

Action assignment: Name ten things God has made. Meditate on His great power and ability to care for you; commit yourself to Him "as unto a faithful Creator."

23

WINNING THE RACE

The word *castaway* is a technical word familiar to those who knew the Greek Olympic games. Paul used the term to say he did not want to be "disapproved" or "disqualified" as a servant of God. At the Greek games, there was a herald who announced the rules of the contest, the names of the contestants, and the names and cities of the winners. He would also announce the names of any contestants who were disqualified.

Paul saw himself as both a "herald" and a "runner." He was concerned lest he get so busy trying to help others in the race that he ignore himself and find himself disqualified. Again, it was not a matter of losing personal salvation. (The disqualified Greek athlete did not lose his citizenship, only his opportunity to win a prize.) The whole emphasis is on *rewards*, and Paul did not want to lose his reward.

Only one runner could win the olive-wreath crown in the Greek games, but every believer can win an incorruptible crown when he stands before the Judgment Seat of Christ. This crown is given to those who discipline themselves for the sake of serving Christ and winning lost souls. They keep their bodies under control and keep their eyes on the goal.

There is something to be said for disciplined eating, exercising, and resting, and a Spirit-directed balanced life. We smugly congratulate ourselves if we do not smoke or use alcohol, but what about our overeating and overweight? And many Christians cannot discipline their time so as to have a consistent devotional life.

Paul had one great goal in life: to glorify the Lord by winning the lost and building up the saints. He sacrificed immediate gains for eternal rewards, immediate pleasures for eternal joys.

Scripture for today: "Let us . . . lay aside every encumbrance, and the sin which so easily entangles us, and let us run with endurance the race that is set before us, fixing our eyes on Jesus" (Hebrews 12:1-2, NASB).

Other Scripture: 1 Corinthians 9:24-27; Hebrews 10:35-36.

Action assignment: Consider how the race is going for you. Is there an area in which you need more self-discipline? Pray about it.

A SERVANT APPROVED

When Verdi produced his first opera in Florence, the composer stood by himself in the shadows and kept his eye on the face of one man in the audience—the great Rossini. It mattered not to Verdi whether the people in the hall were cheering him or jeering him; all he wanted was a smile of approval from the master musician. So it was with the Apostle Paul. He knew what it was to suffer for the Gospel, but the approval or disapproval of men did not move him. "Therefore also we have as our ambition . . . to be pleasing to Him" (2 Corinthians 5:9, NASB). Paul wanted the approval of Christ.

The servant of God is constantly tempted to compromise in order to attract and please people. When D.L. Moody was preaching in England, a worker came to him on the platform and told him that a very important nobleman had come into the hall. "May the meeting be a blessing to him!" was Moody's reply, and he preached just as before, without trying to impress anybody.

From the Word: "We request and exhort you in the Lord Jesus, that, as you received from us instruction as to how you ought to walk and please God (just as you actually do walk), that you may excel still more" (1 Thessalonians 4:1, NASB).

Also: Colossians 1:10; John 8:28-29; 1 John 3:18-22.

Action assignment: Perhaps it's time to take a bit of an inventory. On a sheet of paper, list a few things you do that you believe please the Lord. Then list anything you sense does not please the Lord. Ask Him to help you concentrate on things that really please Him and to eliminate things that displease Him.

GOD REVEALS HIMSELF AT CHRISTMAS

If you were God, how would *you* go about revealing yourself to earth's people? How could you tell them about and give them the kind of life you wanted them to enjoy?

God has revealed Himself in creation, but creation alone could never tell us the story of God's love. God has also revealed Himself much more fully in His Word, the Bible. But God's final and most complete revelation is in His Son, Jesus Christ—God incarnate. He is the great gift of Christmas.

Because Jesus is God's revelation of Himself, He has a very special name: "The Word of Life" (1 John 1:1).

Why does Jesus Christ have this name? Because He is to us what our words are to others. Our words reveal to others just what we think and how we feel. Christ reveals to us the mind and heart of God. He is the living means of communication between God and men. To know Jesus Christ is to know God!

Jesus said: "He that hath seen Me hath seen the Father" (John 14:9).

Also read: John 1:1-14; John 7:28-29; 1 Timothy 2:5.

Action assignment: Ask God to give you a sense of Christ's actual presence in your life. Consciously take Him wherever you go today, being mindful of His holiness. Let Him transform your life.

TIME FOR AN APPOINTMENT!

Many believers have such a comfortable situation here on earth that they rarely think about going to heaven and meeting the Lord. They forget that they must one day stand at the Judgment Seat of Christ. It helps to hold us up and builds us up when we recall that Jesus is coming again.

If you have never trusted Him, then your future is judgment. You needn't be ignorant, for God's Word gives you the truth. You needn't be unprepared, for today you can trust Christ and be born again. Why should you live for the cheap, sinful experiences of the world when you can enjoy the riches of salvation in Christ?

If you are not saved, then you have an appointment with judgment. And it may come sooner than you expect, for it is "appointed unto men once to die, but after this the judgment" (Hebrews 9:27). Why not make an "appointment" with Christ, meet Him personally, and trust Him to save you?

God declares: "For whosoever shall call upon the name of the Lord shall be saved" (Romans 10:13).

Additional verses: Romans 3:21-28; 5:1; Galatians 2:16; 1 John 5:11; Revelation 22:17.

Action assignment: If this message applies to you, trust Christ now. If you know Christ as your Saviour and Lord, commit all or most of these Scriptures to memory and share them with an unsaved friend.

27

FACING TEMPTATION

Our Lord's experience of temptation prepared Him to be our sympathetic High Priest. It is important to note that Jesus faced the enemy *as man,* not as the Son of God. He said, "Man shall not live by bread alone" (Matthew 4:4). We must not think that Jesus used His divine powers to overcome the enemy, because that is just what the enemy wanted Him to do! Jesus used the spiritual resources that are available to us today: the power of the Holy Spirit of God and the power of the Word of God. Jesus had nothing in His nature that would give Satan a foothold, but His temptations were real just the same. Temptation involves *the will,* and Jesus came to do the Father's will.

After Christ had defeated Satan, He was ready to begin His ministry. No man has a right to call others to obey who has not obeyed himself. Our Lord proved Himself to be the perfect King whose sovereignty is worthy of our respect and obedience.

Today's Scripture: "Because He himself suffered when He was tempted, He is able to help those who are being tempted" (Hebrews 2:18, NIV).

Also consider: Matthew 4:1-11; Hebrews 4:15-16.

Action assignment: Ask God to show you an area of your life in which you often fall into sin. Then call on the Holy Spirit, read the Word, and talk to Jesus, the Mediator, in claiming victory over that temptation.

GOD WILL REMEMBER ISRAEL

Has God abandoned His kingdom program for Israel? Of course not! Israel is merely set aside until the time comes for God's plans for Israel to be fulfilled.

Today the saved Gentiles provoke Israel "to jealousy" because of the spiritual riches they have in Christ. Israel today is spiritually bankrupt, while Christians have "all spiritual blessings" in Christ. (But if an unsaved Jewish person visited the average church service, would he be provoked *to jealousy* and wish he had what we have—or would he just be provoked?)

There is a future for Israel. Today Israel is fallen spiritually, but when Christ returns, the nation will rise again. Today, Israel is cast away from God, but one day when Christ establishes His kingdom on earth, Israel shall be received again. God will never break His covenant with His people, and he has promised to restore them.

God says: "Israel has experienced a hardening in part until the full number of the Gentiles has come in. And so all Israel will be saved, as it is written: 'The deliverer will come from Zion; he will turn godlessness away from Jacob. And this is My covenant with them when I take away their sins" (Romans 11:25-27, NIV).

Other Scripture: Jeremiah 31:31-34; Romans 10.

Action assignment: Ask God to help you get a clear understanding of God's dealing with the nation Israel and to give you opportunity to tell a Jewish person about Christ, the Messiah.

THE BLESSINGS OF ADOPTION

The Holy Spirit is called "the Spirit of adoption." The word *adoption* in the New Testament means "being placed as an adult son." We come into God's family by birth. But the instant we are born into the family, God adopts us and gives us the position of an adult son. A baby cannot walk, speak, make decisions, or draw on the family wealth. But the believer can do all of these the instant he is born again.

He can walk and be "led of the Spirit." The verb here means "willingly led." We yield to the Spirit, and He guides us by His Word day by day. We are not under bondage of Law and afraid to act; we have the liberty of the Spirit and are free to follow Christ. The believer can also speak; "We cry, Abba, Father" (Romans 8:15). Would it not be amazing if a newborn baby looked up and greeted his father? First, the Spirit in us says, "Abba, Father" (Galatians 4:6); then we say it to God. *Abba* means "papa"—a term of endearment.

Verse for today: "For ye have not received the spirit of bondage again to fear; but ye have received the Spirit of adoption, whereby we cry, 'Abba, Father'" (Romans 8:15).

Also: Romans 8:14-17; Galatians 4:6; Hebrews 2:10-15.

Action assignment: List on a piece of paper what it means to you to be adopted into God's family. Go over the list as you thank God for these blessings.

WHY AM I SUFFERING?

Not all suffering is a "fiery trial" from the Lord. If a professed Christian breaks the law and gets into trouble or becomes a meddler in other people's lives, then he *ought* to suffer! The fact that we are Christians is not a guarantee that we escape the normal consequences of our misdeeds. We may not be guilty of murder (though anger can be the same as murder in the heart), but what about stealing, or meddling?

When Abraham, David, Peter, and other Bible "greats" disobeyed God, they suffered for it. Who are we that we should escape? Let's be sure we are suffering because we are Christians and not because we are lawbreakers.

From the Bible: "Let none of you suffer as a murderer, or as a thief, or as an evildoer, or as a busybody in other men's matters. Yet if any man suffer as a Christian, let him not be ashamed; but let him glorify God on this behalf" (1 Peter 4:15-16).

For further study: Romans 8:17-26; 2 Corinthians 4:11-18.

Action assignment: Sing or read the song, "What a Fellowship, What a Joy Divine." Or sing another song of your choice that expresses joy. If you are suffering, ask God to show you why.

31

FAITH LOOKS TO THE FUTURE

Faith looks to the future, for that is where the greatest rewards are found. The people listed in Hebrews 11 had God's witness to their faith that one day they would be rewarded. One day all of us who know Christ will share that heavenly city which true saints look for by faith.

We should give thanks for these saints of old. They were faithful during difficult times, yet *we* received the blessings. They saw some of these blessings afar off, but we enjoy them today through Jesus Christ. If the saints of old had not trusted God and obeyed His will, Israel might have perished and the Messiah might not have been born. Faith is possible to all kinds of believers in all kinds of situations. It grows as we listen to His Word and fellowship in worship and prayer.

Scripture says: "And without faith it is impossible to please God" (Hebrews 11:6, NIV).

Look up: Hebrews 11:13; John 8:56; Romans 10:17.

Action assignment: Note *how* faith grows. Make a deliberate effort today to use these tangible means to increase your faith.

GUIDE TO SOURCE BOOKS

Books from which daily readings were taken are listed below. The capital letters preceding the title appear as codes in the source list, along with numerals indicating the pages from which readings were taken. For example, A/26 = *Be Loyal*, page 26.

Source Books

A—*Be Loyal* (Matthew)

B—*Be Alive* (John 1–12)

C—*Be Right* (Romans)

D—*Be Wise* (1 Corinthians)

E—*Be Encouraged* (2 Corinthians)

F—*Be Free* (Galatians)

G—*Be Rich* (Ephesians)

H—*Be Joyful* (Philippians)

I—*Be Complete* (Colossians)

J.—*Be Ready* (1 & 2 Thessalonians)

K—*Be Faithful* (1 & 2 Timothy, Titus)

L—*Be Confident* (Hebrews)

M—*Be Mature* (James)

N—*Be Hopeful* (1 Peter)

O—*Be Alert* (2 Peter, 2 & 3 John, Jude)

P—*Be Real* (1 John)

Q—*Be Victorious* (Revelation)

R—*Meet Yourself in the Psalms*

S—*Windows on the Parables*

T—*Be Obedient* (Abraham)

U—*Be Holy* (Leviticus)

V—*Be Strong* (Joshua)

W—*Be Available* (Judges)

X—*Be Committed* (Ruth & Esther)

Y—*Be Determined* (Nehemiah)

Z—*Be Patient* (Job)

AA—*Be Skillful* (Proverbs)

BB—*Be Satisfied* (Ecclesiastes)

CC—*Be Comforted* (Isaiah)

DD—*Be Decisive* (Jeremiah)

EE—*Be Amazed* (Minor Prophets)

FF—*Be Concerned* (Minor Prophets)

GG—*Be Heroic* (Minor Prophets

Source List

JANUARY 1 GG/22–23; **2** AA/41; **3** E/134–135 **4** I/57–58; **5** L/26–27; **6** R/15, 17; **7** Z/109; **8** M/66–67; **9** A/47–48; **10** K/85; **11** C/137–138; **12** F/30–31; **13** P/46–47; **14** G/17–24; **15** N/119–120; **16** M/72–73; **17** E/97–99; **18** R/135; **19** Z/65; **20** O/j69; **21**

R/49–50; **22** F/17–18; **23** A/42–44; **24** M/70–71; **25** BB/89–90; **26** K/85–86; **27** P/22; **28** G/13; **29** N/101–102; **30** O/140–141; **31** E/87–88.

FEBRUARY 1 R/41–42; **2** BB/130, 334; **3** F/54; **4** J/126–127; **5** K/60; **6** A/45–46; **7** M/60–61; **8** BB/16; **9** O/86–88; **10** BB/34–35; **11** BB/20; **12** FF/77; **13** G/7, 11; **14** L/61–62; **15** F/18–19; **16** J/99–100; **17** E/85; **18** A/95; **19** O/141–142; **20** C/143; **21** F/148–149; **22** P/19; **23** K/92; **24** A/45; **25** J/102–103; **26** E/53; **27** N/116; **28** L/41; **29** O/100.

MARCH 1 S/88–89; **2** F/72–73; **3** C/29; **4** K/129–130; **5** C/141; **6** FF/59; **7** L/55; **8** FF/43–46; **9** N/107–108; **10** F/117; **11** E/61–63; **12** P/34–35; **13** T/105–106; **14** G/24; **15** T/22–25; **16** O/105–106; **17** A/96–97; **18** K/28; **19** C/69–70; **20** M/67–69; **21** P/38–39; **22** R/17–19; **23** T/20; **24** C/103–104; **25** E/19; **26** P/42–43; **27** T/16; **28** F/143–144; **29** J/155, 158; **30** E/80; **31** A/114–115.

APRIL 1 T/13; **2** Z/155; **3** K/28–29; **4** X/41–42; **5** J/125; **6** DD/59; **7** L/145–146; **8** E/43–44; **9** C/68; **10** N/140–141; **11** DD/51–52; **12** G/25; **13** A/209; **14** C/73, 78; **15** R/12–13; **16** P/41–42; **17** G/45; **18** N/110–111; **19** K/56; **20** E/77–78; **21** F/125–126; **22** C/139; **23** M/52–53; **24** J/130; **25** R/92–93; **26** A/50; **27** E/135–136; **28** Q/54; **29** M/40–43; **30** P/16–18.

MAY 1 L/56; **2** N/112–114; **3** A/38; **4** E/49–50; **5** R/94–95; **6** C/140; **7** M/31–32; **8** J/129; **9** A/38; **10** AA/34–35; **11** L/134–135; **12** X/104; **13** X/70; **14** L/104–105; **15** Q/44; **16** N/58–59; **17** L/136; **18** J/77–78; **19** R/114–115; **20** L/128–129; **21** P/43; **22** C/155–156; **23** X/40–41; **24** M/37; **25** L/144; **26** J/78–79; **27** N/53; **28** L/138–139; **29** J/80; **30** L/48–49; **31** N/95.

JUNE 1 J/50–51; **2** I/40; **3** C/26; **4** L/15; **5** N/85; **6** J/51–52; **7** I/40–41; **8** L/44; **9** X/31; **10** I/37; **11** R/102–104; **12** J/50; **13** J/202; **14** J/76; **15** N/79; **16** I/35; **17** L/31; **18** X/18–19; **19** V/105; **20** I/30; **21** L/106; **22** A/75; **23** R/116; **24** V/51, 55; **25** I/24; **26** L/108; **27** C/153–155; **28** I/47; **29** H/90; **30** N/70.

JULY 1 J/32–33; **2** H/84; **3** J/44–45; **4** FF/145, 148; **5** L/138; **6** V/23–26; **7** H/52; **8** J/48–50; **9** L/96–97; **10** C/138–139; **11** N/72; **12** H/34–35; **13** E/113–114; **14** W/32–33 **15** L/140–141; **16** H/21–22; **17** N/63; **18** C/170; **19** L/42–43; **20** P/47–48; **21**

H/20–21; **22** Q/136; **23** N/80; **24** E/84–85; **25** H/17–18; **26**
EE/164–65; **27** Q/57; **28** EE/109–10; **29** H/13, 16; **30** L/135–136;
31 A/80.

AUGUST 1 C/158–159; **2** S/126; **3** J/19–20; **4** EE/93; **5** N/71; **6**
EE/78; **7** L/114; **8** N/44–45; **9** EE/15, 21; **10** L/113; **11** J/24, 26; **12**
S/55, 65; **13** Y/101–102; **14** C/9–10; **15** I/70–71; **16** N/43–44; **17**
E/111; **18** C/143–144; **19** Y/64; **20** P/39–40; **21** J/53–54; **22**
C/152–153; **23** A/110; **24** C/159–160; **25** A/129–130; **26** B/152; **27**
J/55–56; **28** L/148–149; **29** I/77; **30** N/41; **31** C/121–122.

SEPTEMBER 1 A;/131; **2** I/101; **3** J/84–85; **4** L/147; **5** H/60; **6**
N/38; **7** Y/56–57; **8** H/105–106; **9** A/215–216; **10** Y/49, 53; **11**
L/155–156; **12** Y/35–36; **13** N/37–38; **14** C/168–169; **15**
H/137–138; **16** E/11–13; **17** A/39; **18** Y/15–16; **19** J/61–62; **20**
L/121–122; **21** M/91; **22** Z/54–55; **23** D/36–37; **24** Z/42–43; **25**
M/107; **26** G/29; **27** J/63–64; **28** L/137; **29** E/152–153; **30**
M/125–126.

OCTOBER 1 N/32; **2** C/137; **3** Z/20–21; **4** M/161–162; **5**
V/155–56; **6** L/120–121; **7** D/84; **8** M/166; **9** E/139–140; **10**
N/24–25; **11** C/125; **12** O/13; **13** A/46; **14** J/65–66; **15** L/119; **16**
H/87; **17** E/150; **18** D/96–97; **19** W/77–78, 80; **20** C/118–119; **21**
A/50; **22** V/29–30; **23** N/19; **24** E/148–149; **25** L/53; **26** J/66–67;
27 M/125–126; **28** R/112–113; **29** P/45–46; **30** H/16, 19–20; **31**
C/106–107.

NOVEMBER 1 W/17–18; **2** S/17; **3** D/107; **4** W/12–13; **5** S/;67,
76–77; **6** E/47; **7** C/155; **8** N/74; **9** E/13–14; **10** R/97–99; **11** B/11;
12 CC/164; **13** A/37–38; **14** C/90–91; **15** N/135; **16** CC/111–112;
17 B/39–40; **18** CC/28–29; **19** E/126; **20** R/69; **21** L/90–91, 94; **22**
J/72–73; **23** B/44–45; **24** A/70; **25** I/43; **26** N/115; **27** S/116, 124;
28 C/109; **29** B/28; **30** B/79–80.

DECEMBER 1 N/136; **2** R/52; **3** CC/18; **4** C/97; **5** C/130–131; **6**
CC/21–22; **7** E/54; **8** I/26; **9** V/159; **10** J/73–74; **11** A/33–34; **12**
M/39; **13** I/30–31; **14** L/92–93; **15** J/75–76; **16** R/119; **17** I/99–100;
18 A/54; **19** C/7–8; **20** C/167–168; **21** G/47–48; **22** N/122; **23**
D/107–108; **24** F/20; **25** P/12; **26** J/106; **27** A/26, 28–29; **28**
C/128–129; **29** C/91; **30** N/118–119; **31** L/131–132.

Warren W. Wiersbe is Distinguished Professor of Preaching at Grand Rapids Baptist Seminary and has pastored churches in Indiana, Kentucky, and Illinois (Chicago's historic Moody Church). He is the author of more than one hundred books, including *God Isn't in a Hurry, The Bumps Are What You Climb On,* and *The Bible Exposition Commentary* (2 vols.).